# EXILE ON MAIN STREET

**Books by Robert Greenfield**

*STP: A Journey Through America With
The Rolling Stones*

*The Spiritual Supermarket*

*Haymon's Crowd (novel)*

*Temple (novel)*

*Bill Graham Presents: My Life Inside Rock
and Out* (with Bill Graham)

*Dark Star: An Oral Biography of Jerry Garcia*

*Timothy Leary: A Biography*

# EXILE ON MAIN STREET

## A Season in Hell with the Rolling Stones

Robert Greenfield

**Da Capo Press**
A Member of the Perseus Books Group

Copyright © 2006 by Robert Greenfield

Photographs by Michael Cooper/Raj Pren Collection

Designed by Jill Shaffer
Set in 10.5 point Sabon by Eclipse Publishing Services

Cataloging-in-Publication data for this book is available from the Library of Congress

First Da Capo Press edition 2006
ISBN-10 0-306-81433-1
ISBN-13 978-0-306-81433-4

Published by Da Capo Press
A Member of the Perseus Books Group
www.dacapopress.com

Da Capo Press books are available at special discounts for bulk purchases in the U.S. by corporations, institutions, and other organizations. For more information, please contact the Special Markets Department at the Perseus Books Group, 11 Cambridge Center, Cambridge, MA 02142, or call (800) 255-1514 or (617) 252-5298, or e-mail special.markets@perseusbooks.com.

2 3 4 5 6 7 8 9 — 10 09 08 07 06

**For Brian Cookman,**
who was my great friend in London
when I so badly needed one

"Once, if my memory serves me well, my life was a banquet where every heart revealed itself, where every wine flowed."

ARTHUR RIMBAUD,
*Une Saison en Enfer*

"I think it was just a bunch of stoned musicians cooped up in a basement, trying to make a record."

MICK TAYLOR, then of
the Rolling Stones

"It was a shell out of which all sorts of amazing, amazing behavior happened. People became themselves. You couldn't lie there. The vibes were just too strong. You'd be found out in a second."

TOMMY WEBER, house guest
at Villa Nellcote

# Table of Contents

# EXILE ON MAIN STREET

**Keith Richards** with flowers in a café in the harbor, Villefranche, July 1971

# Prologue

## The Time

**By any standard** you might name, the period which began on September 18, 1970, when Jimi Hendrix died in London from drug-related causes followed less than three weeks later by the death of Janis Joplin from an overdose of heroin in a seedy Hollywood motel which in turn was followed nine months later by the death of Jim Morrison from a heroin overdose in a bathtub in Paris has to rank as the single worst period in the history of rock. In the short space of ten months, a true if somewhat foreshortened *annis horribilis* if ever there was one, three of the greatest individual talents ever to grace a rock 'n' roll stage ended their lives with drugs before their twenty-eighth birthdays. That rock itself did not die seems even now like a miracle, minor though it well may be.

To be sure, the war in Vietnam was still dragging on and Nixon's crew of creeps and crooks and swindlers were just beginning to hit their evil stride in the White House, and the National Guard had opened fire on college students protesting the war at

Kent State—four dead in O-hi-o—but it was more than that. It was in the water you drank and the air you breathed. It was the nature of the time, and there was nowhere you could go and nothing you could do to escape it.

The youth of America, the baby boomers, the spawn of the greatest generation the world had ever known, were in open revolt against their elders. Politically and culturally, the nation was split in two and there was no denying that the Rolling Stones were right in the thick of it. Which did not mean that they understood what was going on around them better than anyone else. More than anything, to be young then was to be utterly confused. About everything.

Marianne Faithfull, whose choir girl looks had made her the face of the early sixties before she became the love of Michael Philip Jagger's life, could now be found smacked out of her head, sitting on a wall in St. Anne's Yard in Soho. Yet even she could feel what was going on around her. "Terrible bits of news kept coming through the haze," she would write twenty years later in her autobiography, *Faithfull*, still the best book ever about the Stones. "It was like hearing reports from a distant battlefield. Hendrix. Jim Morrison. Janis Joplin. Sharon Tate. Charles Manson. Kent State. I seemed twitchily in synch with a disintegrating world. We were entering an era of disillusionment, self-destruction, and tragedy. . . . The days of mind-opening drugs were over. The world had tilted. A major change in key had taken place. It was a Mahler symphony whirling madly out of control."

Something that had once been very much alive was in fact now dying. To be replaced by what, no one seemed to know. As always, you could blame it on the Stones. Two years earlier, Brian Jones, who always liked to refer to himself as "the undisputed leader of the Rolling Stones," had become the first great rock star of his era to die—by drowning under mysterious circumstances in his own swimming pool. At four in the morning at a free concert at the Altamont Motor Speedway in northern California in December of that same year, the Stones performed before a cordon of Hell's Angels who murdered a seventeen-year-old black man named Meredith Hunter. The media quickly dubbed the event the official end of a counterculture which by their own reckoning had begun just three-and-a-half months before at Woodstock. Some sort of seismic shift in basic reality was taking place. But very few people knew how to deal with it.

For the chosen few at the very top of the pyramid of rock, the preferred means of coping with this malaise was heroin. In 1966, Cream had become the first great English rock band to rocket to counterculture stardom in America. Two years later, they played their farewell concert at the Royal Albert Hall in London. Although they no longer performed together, lead guitarist Eric Clapton, bass player Jack Bruce, and drummer Ginger Baker were now all using. In time, half of Ginger Baker's Air Force, his current band, would be dead from drugs. Yet no one seemed to get the message. Rehab as we now know it did not yet exist. The only real form of intervention was death.

Not that anyone particularly wanted to die. Not really. Which did not mean they also expected to live to a ripe old age. "Who says you've got to live three score and ten years?" Keith Richards asked one day as he squinted into the sun at Villa Nellcote. "There's only one source of information I know that says that and even that doesn't say everybody's got to make it. Everybody can't make seventy."

In a world no one under the age of thirty had made, where everything seemed so fucked up as to be far beyond repair, numbing yourself to the pain of just having to wake up every morning to begin yet another hopeless day seemed to make eminent sense. Take it from someone who was there. It was just not that great a time to be alive.

## The Place

**Welcome to Villa Nellcote.** You do know how to get there, right? From Nice, take either the Grand Corniche, the twisting, turning high road built by Napoleon to follow the ancient Roman route along the jagged coast of the French Riviera, or the Moyenne Corniche, the twisting, turning middle road from which Princess Grace of Monaco plunged to her death in 1982, or more conveniently, the always crowded Basse Corniche, which runs at sea level right beside the sparkling blue Mediterranean.

At the turnoff for St. Jean Cap Ferrat, make a sharp right toward the water and then another sharp right on to what was once the Chemin de Grasseuil but was renamed Avenue Louise Bourdes in 1930 after the family of shipping merchants who gave Villa Nellcote its name, and you're there. Not that you can see the house from the road. It stands surrounded by a jungle of trees—palm and cypress and pine as well as exotic tropical species from all over the world such as the banana and the baobab, whose unchecked growth the Little Prince feared so mightily in Antoine de St. Exupery's novel of the same name.

As Bruce Springsteen once sang, you could also just take a right at the light, go until night, and then, boys, you're on your own. Although Springsteen has publicly proclaimed *Exile On Main St.* as one of the albums that changed his life forever, his directions will do you no more good than those that precede them. The truth is, you just can't get there from here. At least not any more. As a destination, Villa Nellcote now exists only in the odd continuum of space, time, and memory. Still, it's a journey well worth making.

Even after you park your car in the curving gravel driveway before the great front doors, guarded on either side by a crouching stone female deity with lion's paws, you're still not there. Not really. See, you can't just drop in. That wouldn't be cool. You have to know somebody to go inside. You have to be invited. Calling first to say you're coming won't do it either. Quite possibly, no one will pick up the phone. Even if they do, they may be so out of it that they forget your message even as you leave it with them. Inconceivable as this may now seem, the telephone answering machine has not yet become a staple of modern life.

In every sense, Nellcote is a completely closed shop. A very exclusive private club with rules for admission that are clearly defined. In order to get in, you have to know someone who lives there. It also helps if you come bearing gifts, preferably a fresh supply of something currently being used at the villa on a daily basis. All those who wish to enter the court of the crimson king must first offer tribute. Nonetheless, it's still well worth the effort to get inside.

For as soon as you step through the two huge imperial front doors outlined in black and gold, each at least thirty feet high and made of glass through which whorls of black wrought iron curl like snakes to form a proscenium arch, you will know that you have left the ordinary world behind. Inside Nellcote, an alternate reality prevails. Much of it has to do with the physical space into which you have only just set foot.

The living room is large enough to accommodate the entire New Zealand All Blacks rugby team. From the center of the ceiling hangs a massive chandelier made of cascading crystal teardrops. In the raised gold filigree crown molding atop the walls, gilded angels and cherubs play hide-and-seek. A large rectangular mirror surrounded by ornate gilt fluting adorns the top of the large pink marble fireplace to your left. A dado runs waist high behind the overstuffed armchairs. Above glass-paneled *boiserie* doors, curving floral architraves float like clouds.

The dining room is to your right. As you might expect, it too is very grand. Two sets of doors, each topped with a pair of sculpted angels plucking at a harp, open from it to the living room. Over the long table at which people often sit for hours hangs yet another large crystal chandelier. There is a kitchen, but no one ever goes in there. Cooking at Nellcote is left to whoever happens to be the chef at the moment. On the other side of the living room are two small bedrooms with a bathroom that can only be reached from the inner bedroom. Over the course of the summer, a veritable who's who of rock 'n' roll royalty, circa nineteen seventy-one, will spend the night there.

Framed by an ornate black wrought iron railing to the right of the front door, broad marble steps with a carpeted runner lead up to the second floor. During their visit to the Cannes Film Festival in May, John Lennon and Yoko Ono decided to pay a visit to Nellcote. After downing an entire bottle of red wine on the verandah, John politely asked to be shown to the loo only to throw up before he got there. "At the foot of the staircase," Anita Pallenberg, the Queen of Villa Nellcote, would later recall, "there he was lying." While his genial host Keith Richards put the blame on "too much wine and too much sun," the fact that Lennon was also on methadone may have had something to do with the incident.

Up one flight of steps, past the curved oblong mirror on the landing, a second flight of steps leads to the master bedroom with doors that open out to its own grand private portico framed by four stone columns. There are five other bedrooms. The exquisitely beautiful bathrooms feature painted blue porcelain scenes of birds and flowers. Not that you will ever see any of this. In a house perpetually filled with people, virtually no one but Keith and Anita and their very close friends ever go upstairs. One does not even ask permission. Simply, it is just not done. And for very good reason.

Although our tour is nearly over, the best is yet to come. As always when the very rich take command of the high ground, they keep the view entirely to themselves. From the front, Nellcote looks like just another large mansion in the south of France. Keep walking through the living room and you come to the back doors. Thrown open to the light, they lead out to a broad porch framed by four huge white round pillars. Before you, the endless azure expanse of the deep water harbor of Villefranche lies gleaming in the sun. Along the shore on either side, the gaily colored rooftops of the surrounding towns can be seen.

Walk down nine broad marble steps, each wider than the last, and you find yourself in an undefined flat area set with a table and cushioned wicker chairs. To the right is a child's sand-pile strewn with toys. Beyond it is a very impressive stone battle-ment and wide marble steps that lead down to a small stony beach with artificial concrete cliffs and caves in which diving equipment or a small boat are often stored. The beach would seem to be private but in accordance with French law is in fact open to any citizen of the republic who can get there by some means other than coming through the house.

In every sense, the grandeur of Villa Nellcote reflects the gilded age in which it was built. Russian archdukes first began wintering at Nice in the 1890s. By the Roaring Twenties, wealthy Europeans and Americans like Gerald and Sara Murphy, the real-life models for Dick and Nicole Diver in F. Scott Fitzgerald's *Tender Is the Night,* started coming in spring and summer to enjoy the sun, the sea, and one another. In part to avoid English income taxes and so that he could live openly with his male companion, W. Somerset Maugham, then the highest-paid author in the world, made St. Jean Cap Ferrat his permanent home in 1929. Whatever anyone's initial reason for coming to the French Riviera may have been, it was the sheer physical beauty of the sur-roundings that kept them there.

Inevitably, the first thing you noticed when you walked into Nellcote was the light. It could be soft and smooth as melted but-ter in the morning yet by late afternoon become harsh as molten steel, transforming the endless expanse of azure ocean out back into a bowl of glinting Cubist fragments that were painful to the eye. No matter how late you stayed up at night in that house, and no one at Nellcote ever went to bed early, the light still woke you up long before you wanted it to. But then it was not a house designed for restful sleep.

Built to capture and hold the light, Nellcote was a literal hall of mirrors. Wherever you looked, you could see your own image reflected back at you from many different angles, some flattering, some so dismal that for a brief moment you might even begin to question the manner in which you had been living before deciding to go on doing whatever it was that had made you look this bad in the first place. Designed to serve as a haven by the sea, the villa became a cauldron in the boiling midday heat of summer on the French Riviera. The only escape was out back onto the terrace where meals were often served. On the broad steps below, you could sit in the shade as the day wore on and watch the light trace changing patterns on the glittering facets of the diamond-bright sea.

As in every great house, life at Nellcote that summer was very much a tale of upstairs/downstairs. A spiral staircase off the dining room led down into the first level of the cellar where there were half a dozen rooms, some huge, some tiny. The walls and ceilings were made of plaster. Most of the recording at Nellcote would eventually take place in the first room. Large and spacious, it had only two small windows that did not admit very much light or air, thereby making it ideal for a variety of purposes, some more nefarious than others. Which brings us to the putative dark and sordid history of Nellcote itself.

In the original manuscript of her memoir, *Even When It Was Bad . . . It Was Good,* June Shelley, who worked for the Stones that summer in the south of France, describes a visit she made to the "unpleasant woman" who owned Nellcote (her name was Madame Keller and she was Swiss). By the time Shelley went to see her, the Stones had already decamped for other shores and Shelley's task was to settle up with the woman for whatever damage had been done to the house while the band was there.

According to Shelley, local gossip had it that not only had this woman lived with a Nazi at Nellcote during World War II, but that many of the most valuable objets d'art in the villa were part of her Nazi boyfriend's illegal loot. Elizabeth Hiemer, who worked as the housekeeper at Nellcote for a decade before Keith and Anita ever came to live there, says that Nellcote was owned during the war not by Madame Keller but by the daughter of Monsieur Bourdes, after whom the avenue on which the villa still stands was named.

In *Exile,* a collection of photographs taken that summer by Dominique Tarlé and published in a limited edition by Genesis Press in England, Tarlé says, "The housekeeper, a German lady who had been living and working at Nellcote for many years, told me that at the end of the war many German soldiers tried to escape by hiding in the cellar at Nellcote." While it is true that Hiemer always spoke German with Anita, thereby becoming her confidante, she is in fact Swiss. Hiemer, who lived in Monaco during the war and was fifteen years old when hostilities ceased, stated during a recent interview (in which she spoke flawless French) that she had no recollection of German soldiers using the house for any purpose whatsoever.

In *Exile,* Tarlé also states that while rummaging about in the basement of the villa one day along with Bruce Byall, a tie-dyed, ponytailed roadie who lived for a while in a tipi in the garden at Nellcote, the two of them "found a box down there with a big swastika on it, full of injection phials. They all contained morphine. It was very old of course, and our first reaction was, 'If Keith had found this box!' So one night we carried it to the end of the garden and threw it into the sea—and were then concerned about the poor fish." Bruce Byall has no recollection of ever having found such a box or of throwing it into the sea. Which does not mean that it did not happen.

And then there is Andy Johns, who was just twenty-one years old that summer and pleased as punch to be working as a full-fledged recording engineer for the Rolling Stones for the first time, much as his older brother Glyn had done before him. "Even though I had been going in and out of the building hundreds of times," Andy Johns states in *Exile*, "I noticed one day that vents in the floors were decorated with swastikas." Bringing them to the attention of his host, Johns asked, "Keith, what the fuck is this?" As only he could, Keith replied, "Oh, well, this was the Gestapo headquarters during the occupation. But it's all right. We're here now. Fuck those people."

Years later, Johns picked up a book on the Gestapo that included a detailed account of the interrogation techniques they regularly used on anyone who fell into their clutches. "If you were picked up for jaywalking," Johns says, "they would run this list of tortures on you, the ball-crusher and the see-saw into the bathtub, just on the off-chance you might know something they were interested in. That basement was quite extensive so I'm fairly sure those bastards got up to some very bad things down there. Which would explain the bumps in the night and the power going on and off all the time and the generally weird vibe."

When she was asked if Nellcote had served as the local Gestapo headquarters during the war, Elizabeth Hiemer said she did not know whether the Germans had ever used the villa as an office during the war. She also had no memory of ever seeing swastikas in the floor vents of a house that she cleaned faithfully for more than a decade and then lived in by herself for six months after Keith and Anita departed for Los Angeles. Which does not mean that the swastikas were not there. Years later, Anita would tell author John Perry, "Nellcote had been, in the war you know, a big Nazi headquarters. There were still swastikas on the old heating system . . . ."

As Mick Jones of The Clash once sang, do you stay or do you go? If you go, there will be trouble. But if you stay, it will be double. You can pay your money and take your choice, but in the end, who you trust and who you choose to believe on any of these issues is strictly a matter of personal choice. With the possible exception of Stanley Booth, who did his time of service with the band and then spent years working on *The True Adventures of the Rolling Stones,* nearly everyone who has ever written about the Stones has chosen to follow the simple dictum first annunciated in John Ford's *The Man Who Shot Liberty Valence* (with a terrific theme song by the late Gene Pitney, for whom Mick and Keith wrote "When Blue Turns To Gray"): "When the legend becomes fact, print the legend."

But then in journalism, as in life, a great story always trumps the truth. Since the Stones are not about to sue anyone for what they write about them, it has always been open season on them in print. Our problem here is a bit more complicated. Guided by the hazy recollections of people whose memories are subject to not only whatever they ingested back then but also everything that has transpired in the thirty-five years since that epic summer in the south of France, we are about to embark on what will definitely be one very twisted journey through the past, where everything can only be seen through a glass darkly and even then may be nothing more than a fleeting silhouette of the truth.

So be it. For if all this is nothing more than a bit of magic theater, with the price of admission your mind, then the best advice for those about to get on board would be to buckle your seat belts as this is going to be one very bumpy ride. Whatever the real story concerning the Nazi presence in that villa may be, it does seem safe to say that just like so many of those who passed through there during the summer of nineteen seventy-one, Villa Nellcote itself was never quite what it seemed.

## The Players

**Keith Richards:** He is our hero. He is also our antihero. In itself, this is entirely postmodern. But then in many ways, so is Keith. In this particular rock 'n' roll passion play, he is our Jesus of Cool. A man so hip that he put the "s" back at the end of his own last name, thereby defying the edict of former Stones' manager Andrew Loog Oldham concerning the rules for attaining pop celebrity in the jelly-baby throwing, teenaged girls screaming, *Ready, Steady, Go!* era of the mid-sixties English pop scene.

With this one simple act, Keith empowered an entire generation of rockers who followed to call themselves by their rightful names.

Why is Keith so cool? To put it plainly, the man simply does not give a shit. All things that matter most to all the faceless, colorless individuals who control the world outside of rock 'n' roll are of no concern to him. Having spent his formative postadolescent years growing up in public as a Rolling Stone, Keith has seen and done it all—acid, Mandrax, cocaine, and heroin, not to mention also sex, offered up freely and willingly by women of all ages and classes as a reward for his undeniable talent and overwhelming success.

A working-class boy from Dartford who never really aspired to be much more than a Teddy Boy hanging out at night on a corner in some dismal new town in England until he discovered the guitar, Keith's great musical prowess and increasingly rebellious on-stage persona has by this point in his life already given him unlimited access to the wealthy and powerful. Having seen these people at close range, Keith knows that while some might be quite all right, most of them are just full of themselves and it as well.

Keith has no time for the crap. He does not care about the details. Money means nothing to him except when he wants to spend some more of it on whatever happens to tickle his fancy at the moment. More than anything else, it is his sense of weary resignation that makes him so attractive. Because the cards have always been stacked against him, Keith knows how the game is run. So what are you going to do about it, man? Get a gun and shoot the dealer? Well, yeah. And then what? Make your get-

away out the back door? Where the coppers will always be waiting to ice you just like they did to Bonnie and Clyde and John
Dillinger and every other outlaw who ever challenged the bloody
system? Forget about it. That was a game that could never be
won. Far better to just go about things your own way and let the
devil take the hindmost.

In his heart of hearts, Keith truly believed, as Bob Dylan
once sang, that to live outside the law, you must be honest.
Great. But what does that really mean? Keith is an outlaw but he
has a code of his own. He is fiercely loyal to his friends. He loves
his son. He loves getting high. More than anything, he loves his
guitar. At Nellcote, it is a physical extension of his body. The
man literally never goes anywhere without it.

While the Stones were recording *Goat's Head Soup* in
Jamaica, Andy Johns once saw Keith sleeping in bed with his guitar, which even he found to be a bit much. But that is just Keith
all over for you. A man who has long since gone beyond caring
what anyone thinks of him, Keith is both completely enslaved by
his own habits and as a free as any Buddhist monk performing
devotional prayers on a mountaintop in Nepal. Always, Keith
does what he pleases and leaves it to others to sort out the consequences. It is this trait more than any other that often puts those
around him into jeopardy.

By the time Keith comes to live at Nellcote, he has already long since left behind all bourgeois values. Always, the
man marches to the beat of a different drummer, one whose
name does not necessarily happen to be Charlie Watts. Even on
stage, it is Charlie who follows Keith rather than the other way
around. Keith is the one who sets the beat. He is the one who

creates the rhythm. Once Keith gets going with a guitar in his hand, all the rest of the band can do is open up all the stops, go full throttle to the end, and just hope like hell to keep up with him. It is not always pretty and it most certainly is not always perfect, but it is art.

Bar none (though Pete Townshend is right up there as well), Keith is the greatest rhythm player in rock. Without putting on any Negro affectations, he is also the blackest white man who ever lived. At close range, his charisma is overwhelming. In a 1974 interview, no less an authority than Marianne Faithfull, who slept with both Keith and Brian Jones before settling in as Mick Jagger's girlfriend, confessed, " . . . in the beginning, I was always really in love with Keith much more than anyone else, as a fan. He's the epitome of the Romantic Hero and, if you're a middle class girl and you've read your Byron, that's Keith Richard. . . . He's turned into Count Dracula now, but he's still an injured, tortured, damned youth. . . . That's the thing about the Stones. That they're dirty and awful and arrogant, and Keith is still like that."

Heady stuff indeed. But then as Rafael Sabatini once wrote of the hero of *Scaramouche,* his epic novel of the French Revolution, Keith was born with a gift of laughter and a sense that the world was mad. While in time, he will become what one of the Stones' women lovingly calls "an authentic pirate" (upon whom the actor Johnny Depp will model his portrayal of Jack Sparrow in *Pirates of the Caribbean,* with Keith himself set to appear in a cameo as Sparrow's father in the third installment of the saga), he is also vulnerable. Like every great hero, Keith carries within him a deep wound that he tries to heal by using whatever happens to appear before him at the moment.

In part, some of his pain may be caused by the actions of Mick Jagger, for so long his brother in arms and alter ego. Although Brian Jones taught both Mick and Keith that it was no big thing to have it off with each other's women because no female could ever come between the Rolling Stones, Mick had seriously crossed the line three years earlier. Day after day, as Keith sat brooding in his Rolls Royce outside the house in Lowndes Square in London where the movie *Performance* was being shot during the fall of 1968, Mick was carrying on a torrid affair with Anita Pallenberg, for whom Keith had written the plaintive ballad "You've Got The Silver" on *Let It Bleed*.

Anita herself had first come to the band as Brian's girlfriend/female mirror image only to leave him for Keith. Having it off with Mick, even before the cameras, was one thing. Mick's insistence on continuing to pursue Anita, who was also the best friend of Marianne Faithfull, then Mick's girlfriend, while all four of them were on holiday together in South America after the filming was something else again.

Two lesser or perhaps more ordinary men, despite how long they had known each other and how much brilliant work they had done together, would have come to blows and stopped speaking right then and there. Not Mick and Keith. The two were joined not only at the hip but at the pocketbook as well. They were also particularly English in their steadfast refusal to ever confront one another directly about anything. Like the slightly naughty schoolboys they still often seemed to be, each would instead snidely slag the other behind closed doors while continuing to work together in the studio and on stage. Mad as all this may have seemed to others, such was life among the Rolling Stones.

By the summer of nineteen seventy-one, Mick and Keith had already long since become the kind of killers that Andrew Oldham always insisted a pop star had to be, ready, willing, and able to eradicate anyone who stood in the way of their success. When Brian proved to be too difficult for them to handle, they greased the skids for his departure from the band and then went off to tour America with Mick Taylor in his place. Like a pair of great white sharks, Mick and Keith always had to keep moving forward in tandem so they could reap all the rewards due them. It was nothing they could change or even truly understood. Simply, it was just who they were.

Beyond any shadow of a doubt, Keith Richards is our hero. And the situation in which he finds himself trapped that summer at Nellcote is the source of all our drama. Without the help of his best friend and fellow songwriter Mick, who has already betrayed him with the woman he loves, Keith cannot complete the new album on which the Stones are working. Without the album, the Stones cannot tour America. Without the money they will earn there, they cannot survive as a band.

Despite all that Mick has already done to him and will soon do again, Keith has to find a way to live with Mick. Even now, it seems the kind of Faustian bargain they only offer you in hell—in the ninth circle, the one directly facing Lucifer, where all those who have committed treachery find themselves trapped for eternity in a frozen lake, doing penance for a lifetime of sin.

**Anita Pallenberg:** She is our leading lady. A woman of power who over the course of the summer at Nellcote will play many roles while remaining always the star of her own production.

As Christopher Gibbs, the well-known antique dealer and close friend who dressed the set for *Performance,* once said of her, "I think that in a more gracious age, Anita would have been called a witch." Anita is also our damsel in distress. She is our Lady of the Lake, the enchantress who imprisoned the wizard Merlin in either a cave, a tree, a tomb, or the Glass Tower so she could keep him for herself or watch him slowly die, depending on which version of the legend you choose to believe. And so it is with Anita. At the rock 'n' roll round table occupied by the Rolling Stones, Anita is the key. Whoever possesses her has the power. But as time will prove, no one can keep her for long. For in the end, she belongs only to herself.

At Villa Nellcote that summer, Anita was always the center of attention. How could she not be? Though the woman rarely went swimming, she could most often be found wearing a miniscule leopard-skin bikini that left nothing to the imagination yet made everyone wonder how she might look without it. No longer as physically stunning as she was in *Performance,* where she appeared naked or nearly so in all her scenes, the woman was still a natural wonder, not to mention a force primeval as well. Someone who knew her well back then described Anita as a "slattern." In the immortal words of Michael Philip Jagger, Anita could make a dead man come.

By no means was this the only source of her power. Ian Stewart, who began his career playing piano for the Rolling Stones only to be relegated to becoming their roadie because he looked more like a coal miner or a lorry driver than a pop star, once said it was impossible to ever hold a straight conversation with Anita because her mind was always racing so fast.

Depending on which substance you had just ingested that summer at Nellcote, her sudden, swooping conversational u-turns could seem mad, brilliant, or an eerie combination of the two.

A fairly representative example of what it was like trying to talk to her back then occurs during a scene in *Performance* when the subject under discussion is the current hair color of Chas, the gangster on the run played by James Fox. As Pherber, Anita notes that his hair has been dyed and that she fancied the red. Chas corrects her by saying it was the red that was dyed. Mistaking the word for "died," Turner, the utterly stoned rock star played by Mick Jagger, says, "Dead." "Dyed. Red," Chas repeats, still trying to get his point across. "Dyed it . . . dead!" Anita says, prompting Chas to repeat, "Red . . . red!"

Whatever anyone said to Anita that summer at Nellcote seemed to remind her of something that sounded just like it. Often, she would repeat a single phrase until the words themselves lost all meaning, becoming a series of notes in a riff that only she could play. Rather than ask what she was talking about, most of those at Nellcote simply took her pronouncements as received knowledge and then tried to work out their meaning after they had walked away from her.

Because she was so much more emotional than Keith and very volatile, talking to Anita that summer was like trying to handle quicksilver infused with nitroglycerin. There was no telling when her dark eyes would suddenly flash with anger and she would fly off the handle, sending a million pieces of deadly shrapnel flying in all directions at once. Now, she would be seen as a personality in the process of disintegration. Back then, she just seemed really far out.

And yet as someone else who spent that summer at Nellcote notes, "Although none of the standards of ordinary behavior apply to Anita, she knew how to behave. She's not someone who would insult people in public. She's far too well bred. She's a countess in her own right. Which means something in those terms."

Because Anita believed in conspiracies of all kinds, she was always looking for the inside dope on everything—from who had really killed John F. Kennedy to why an actress was chosen for a certain part to the rumor that the Mafia really ran the music business. Insofar as she was concerned, dark and sinister forces were working in secret harmony to rule the world. In an era when Mick Jagger had earned himself a place on Richard Nixon's enemies list for having the unmitigated gall to wear an Uncle Sam hat on stage during the Stones' 1969 tour of America, she may not have been so far wrong.

Closer to home, Anita was convinced that the Côte d'Azur was thick with thieves. She spoke constantly about the villa robbers who even now were planning to ransack Nellcote. At one point during the summer, her paranoia became so great that she persuaded someone working for the Stones to erect a barbed wire fence around the beach at Nellcote so no one could enter it from the adjoining property. Since by law, all beaches in France are public, the barbed wire had to be taken back down. In the end, her fear in this matter would also prove accurate.

Within the tightly controlled circle surrounding the Rolling Stones, Anita had first earned her position of power as the great love of Brian Jones' life. Together, they became the very first alpha couple of rock. Unable to be faithful to anyone for very long, they fought and fucked and paraded their ambivalent sexuality in public for everyone to see. When Brian finally became too difficult even for Anita, she left him to live with Keith, who by then had also fallen in love with her.

What first attracted Brian and Keith and Mick to Anita was her experience in worlds through which the Stones themselves had not yet traveled—her incredible fashion sense, her authentic movie star glamour, her continuing ability to get as high as anyone on the planet, her insatiable need for sex, her interest in the dark arts, and last but most certainly not least her utter refusal to take shit from anyone as well as the obvious pleasure she derived from shocking the bourgeoisie.

In an age when female liberation was still being born, Anita was a mover and a shaker on a level that few women before had ever attained. She was Lady Gregory, Brigitte Bardot, Colette, and George Sand all wrapped into one. Unlike Oscar Wilde, Anita's great tragedy was not that she put her genius into her life rather than her work. In her case, the two were one and the same. Acting in movies, like modeling, was just a way for her to display her power to a wider audience. Though she never played on a single track or wrote the words to any song on *Exile*, Anita was an authentic life artist who helped the Stones create themselves as the symbol of one generation's rebellion against another.

"Anita was a very powerful human being," Marshall Chess, then the president of the newly founded Rolling Stones Records, would later recall. "She was crazy and out of control but she was very brilliant and really had some kind of power over both Mick and Keith and she was very much an architect of their image. She herself had an architect mind. She was very much like Karl Rove."

All this served to make another woman's intrusion into the scene just that much more grievous for Anita. Michael Philip Jagger's brand new wife, Bianca Rose Perez Moreno de Macias (if in fact that was her real name) was a fabulous character straight out of Dickens, Little Nell by way of Nell Gwynne, who was not in the least impressed by Keith, Anita, or Les Rolling Stones. Rock music was simply not her thing. Which is why the theme song from *Love Story* would be played as she walked down the aisle with Mick that spring in St. Tropez. Bianca did not dress like a hippie. She did not want to live like a rock star. Bianca was not only getting married to Mick, she was also carrying his child. As such, she represented the most direct threat yet to Anita's position as the brilliant female sun around which the Stones have revolved for so long.

Always, Anita had to be the center of attention. She knew no other way. Anyone who distracted from this was bad and so had to be excised from her immediate circle by any means possible. Using all the wiles and weapons at her disposal, Anita threw herself wholeheartedly into this task. When voodoo spells proved futile, she began a whispering campaign behind Bianca's back, insisting that the Nicaraguan-born former girlfriend of actor Michael Caine and French playboy and record executive Eddie Barclay (who before he died would marry nine times) was in fact born a man and had then undergone a sex change operation.

Could it have really been so? At dinner one night in Paris during the 1920s, Ernest Hemingway sat down beside Zelda Fitzgerald only to have her lean toward him and, as though about to confide her greatest secret, say, "Don't you think Al Jolson is greater than Christ?" Later, Hemingway would write that Scott Fitzgerald did not write anything more that was good until after he realized his wife was insane. Nonetheless, Hemingway himself knew enough that night not to purse the issue any further. And so it was with Anita. You either took the woman at face value or you left her alone. With Anita, there was no middle ground.

Because Anita knew that Mick had always fancied black girls, sleeping with many of the female singers who'd backed up the American rhythm-and-blues artists with whom the Stones had toured England in the early days, she began plotting to have the black revolutionary Angela Davis released from prison in California, where she was then awaiting trial for murder. Once Angela was free, Anita intended to fly "the sweet black angel" to France so Mick would leave Bianca and marry her. If nothing else, it seemed like a plan.

Marianne Faithfull, Anita's closest friend, described her during the filming of *Performance* as "the dark queen under an evil spell, so gorgeous and dangerous." After Anita began her affair with Mick, whom Marianne loved and whose baby she was then expecting, Marianne still saw Anita "as very much the victim of all this, the vulnerable one who should have been looked after and protected. Her breakup with Brian the previous year had been devastating." Confirming what Christopher Gibbs said, Marianne also wrote, "Anita eventually took the goddess business one step further into witchcraft. There were moments, especially after Brian died, where she went a little mad."

So she often seemed that summer. Anita was beautiful and she was crazy and she was crazy beautiful. As the French say, *cherchez la femme,* meaning that at the heart of every story, including the tale of how the Rolling Stones made what some insist is their greatest album, there is always a woman. Look no further. In all her ruinous glory, here she is.

**Michael Philip Jagger:** Ah, Mick. What a piece of work is he. It would be tempting to call him the villain of our piece, but that would not be fair to anyone, Mick most of all. In truth, there were times that summer when he seemed as put upon as any desperate housewife trapped in a marriage from which there was no escape. Still, if you had to pick the one person most likely to emerge relatively unscathed from it all, Mick would be your man. When it came to survival, he was a genius. It was this primitive instinct that formed the core of his personality.

Unlike his good friend and songwriting partner Keith, Mick was not a natural man. Rather, he was a born showman who was always on. There was never a room too small for Mick to work. No audience was too tiny for him to entertain. In truth, his primary interest was always to amuse himself. Everything he did seemed carefully planned to elicit a specific response. Because Mick had an agenda, he was always prepared to play a dazzling variety of games to achieve his aim.

After the two of them parted company, Marianne Faithfull would write of him, "There's nothing truly mythic or tragic about Mick. He's too normal, too sane for any truly bizarre fate to befall him." In her view, his "compulsion to see life in a perpetual Sunday supplement" resulted in Mick always watching himself lead his own life without ever really feeling anything. During their final year together, Marianne felt as though she was living with a vampire, "a hollow voracious entity that constantly needed to replenish itself with things, people, ideas, souls. Mick's genius was in his lyrics, but his great talent has always been artifice, inflation and swagger . . . ."

Intellectually restless and easily bored, Mick was always looking for the action. Sexual fidelity, even to a woman he had only just married, was never his thing. On the road, Mick still liked to have it off with some young and fairly innocent looking girl he knew he would never see again. There were also ongoing affairs with women willing to be with him on any basis he preferred. Such were the perks that came with being the world's leading rock star. Or, as someone back then called him, "the leading molecule on the razor's edge."

Much like Keith and Anita, Mick would smoke it and he would snort it. On any given night, he could get as drunk as anyone in rock 'n' roll. It was only then that his anger emerged and he seemed truly out of control. But then, as one Stones insider recalled, Mick was "also sneaky. He was always doing more stuff than he let on but because he was doing it by himself and would never share his drugs with anybody if he could help it, no one knew. Let me tell you something. When he drinks, he is an addict as far as I'm concerned. He's an alcoholic. He's pathetic when he drinks."

No matter what he may have done the night before, Mick always woke up knowing what city he was in and exactly what he had to do that day. It was the way he was built, from the inside out. Within the tightly cloistered world of the Rolling Stones, over which he ruled with complete dominion, there was but one human being whom Mick could not control. And that was Keith.

Nearly everyone who has written about Villa Nellcote that summer puts Keith squarely at the center of the black circle from which the album was spun. Yet it is Mick who may be, if not the actual hero of this tale, then our most sympathetic character. For as Keith got high and dawdled for hours in the upstairs loo while the Rolling Stones sat sweltering in the basement down below, Mick was always waiting. He was waiting on a friend just as Keith had done as he sat in his Rolls during the filming of *Performance*. While turnabout may be fair play, it was still Mick who seemed to be suffering most during that endless summer at Nellcote.

But then it was Mick who had done most of the hard work to free the Stones from rock 'n' roll megabusinessman Allen Klein's financial clutches so the band could form their own label. Although the Stones then recorded *Sticky Fingers,* the single biggest album of their career, they could not tour America to support it. In order to do so now, they had to record another album. Until it was done, Mick found himself squarely under the thumb of his oldest friend.

In every way, they had always been different as night and day. A born winner, Mick set the record for the half-mile at his grammar school only to then proclaim running to be "a drag." As a teenager, he achieved a fair degree of local fame in Dartford by appearing on a weekly television show demonstrating his father Joe's fitness techniques for boys. Mick was then clever enough to be awarded a government grant to attend the prestigious London School of Economics. Always, his primary goal seems to have been to make money.

A born rebel and a rocker, the ultimate square peg who

never fit into any hole, Keith failed his eleven-plus exams and was sent to a technical school where he spent much of his time learning "how to ride a punch." Awful at sports, he got himself thrown out of the English equivalent of the Boy Scouts for drinking and fighting and was then asked to leave art school because of persistent truancy. After his parents split up, Keith did not see his father for twenty years. What both Mick and Keith did share (aside from various women) was their undying love of what Brian Jones liked to call "authentic R&B."

Still, unlike all those who would follow in their footsteps, Stephen Tyler and Joe Perry, Johnny Rotten and Sid Vicious, and Nikki Sixx and Tommy Lee just to name a few, Mick and Keith have never once had it out with one another in public. Between them, everything was always kept under the covers and between the buttons. Because all the hostility and anger remained unspoken and repressed that summer, it slowly built to a fever pitch, creating an atmosphere of tension so thick and palpable that you could have cut it with a dull knife. In light of their completely different personalities, how could it have been any other way?

Someone who could not live for long or create his music without madness swirling all around him, Keith *was* the chaos. Whenever life at Nellcote became too quiet, he would do something outrageous to stir it all up again just to give himself a badly needed shot of rock 'n' roll adrenaline. Without the chaos, Mick could not be in control. The legendary rock promoter Bill Graham once said that Keith could throw a towel over his shoulder on stage and become Errol Flynn in *Captain Blood*. Succinctly, he then added, "Mick is Mick. The most talented cunt in the business."

Which brings us at long last to our central question. What happens when Michael Philip Jagger, the unquestioned lord of the manor whose *droit de seigneur* has never before been challenged by anyone, suddenly finds himself a perpetual guest in Keith Richards' palatial mansion by the sea in the south of France? Mick cannot leave. At least not for very long. Whenever he does, work on the new album grinds to a complete halt. But even when Mick is there, there is nothing he can do to make Keith come up with new music to which he can write lyrics. Mick cannot stay but he cannot go. Clowns to the left of him, jokers to the right, and there he is, stuck in the middle with Keith. For Mick that summer, there is no exit. For him, the door to Villa Nellcote is both open and closed.

For someone accustomed to being the king, this is the definition of hell. As has been noted in print before, the original working title of *Exile On Main St.* was *Tropical Disease.* If anyone that summer at Nellcote was suffering from an odd form of rock 'n' roll dengue fever, it was Mick. Sick to death of it all he may well have been, but there was still no relief available to him. All Mick could do was suffer. At times, even to him, it must have seemed like eternity.

**The Ghost:** Played by Brian Jones, he walks the halls of Villa Nellcote in a long black veil. He visits the house when the hot winds wail. Nobody knows and nobody sees. Nobody but Keith. And Anita. And sometimes Mick. "Brian's death," Marianne Faithfull would later write, "acted like a slow-motion bomb. It had a devastating effect on all of us. The dead go away, but the survivors are damned. Anita went through hell from survivor's guilt and guilt plain and simple. She developed grisly compulsions. . . . Keith's way of reacting to Brian's death was to become Brian. He became the very image of the falling down, stoned junkie hovering perpetually on the edge of death. But Keith, being Keith, was made of different stuff. However he mimicked Brian's self-destruction, he never actually disintegrated."

Students of *Hamlet,* pay close attention. Neither Mick, Keith, nor Anita attended Brian's funeral. The psychic toll exacted on those who do not bury and honor their dead can never be overestimated, not even in the topsy-turvy world of the Rolling Stones.

**Note to Reader:** The supporting cast is huge. Fascinating though many of these people seem even now, they are essentially minor players and will be introduced as they appear on the scene.

## Costume and Design

We can't all hang out with the Stones at the Villa Nellcote, but at least we can look as if we do. In 1971, Mick and Keith and the boys communed in France to record 'Exile On Main Street.' Other rockers made the pilgrimage. Anita Pallenberg and Bianca came along for the ride. And men have been dreaming of their relaxed way of being, dressing, and loving ever since.

"Gimme Tax Shelter," *Men's Fashions of the Times,* Spring, 2002

Is it a union requirement that all those who write fashion copy must first smoke opium before they start putting words on the page? For if men have in fact been dreaming about what went on at Nellcote that summer ever since 1971, then not only the republic itself but the world at large is in far worse shape than any of us realize. How about their relaxed way of shooting smack? Enough with costume and design. On to the action.

**Anita Pallenberg** and son Marlon at a cafe in the harbor,
Villefranche, July 1971

# ACT ONE

1

**The Rolling Stones must** leave England. Not because they have offended the Queen, although if the truth be told, the boys have certainly done a bang-up job of that over the years, getting busted for urinating in public at a petrol station in Romford in 1965 just three months before Her Majesty personally presented the far more endearing and always completely cute and cuddly Beatles with their MBEs at Buckingham Palace.

After accepting the award, Beatle Paul, always the cutest of the lot, boasted in public of having smoked joints in the palace loo before the ceremony. Cheeky, to be sure. But it could not hold a candle to the slam-bang, pull-out-all-the-stops, set-them-up-and-then-take-them-down bust of Mick and Keith in February 1967 engineered by the *News of the World,* the lowest, most scandal-mongering English tabloid of them all. Although authorities were only able to charge Keith with owning a house where cannabis was being used and Mick for possession of four pep pills that really belonged to Marianne Faithfull, when those coppers trooped through the front door like a bunch of Shriners on convention, everyone was still high as a kite from the LSD they had taken earlier in the day. The lovely Marianne Faithfull was naked as the day she was born, save for a large fur rug in which she had wrapped herself after a bath so she could come downstairs to join the party. (Despite the rumors, there was no Mars bar soaked in LSD involved.) Nonetheless, the headlines in the English newspapers just about wrote themselves. *Rolling Stones! Drugs! Sex! Orgy! Naked Blonde!* It was enough to curl even Her Majesty's tightly lacquered hair.

After a farcical show trial that was more a generational clash than a true legal proceeding, Mick and Keith were found guilty and given unbelievably harsh sentences. The massive public outcry that followed included demonstrations in the streets of London as well as an extraordinary lead editorial in the *Times* demanding to know why the two leading Stones had been treated like enemies of the state. Forget the *News of the World.* This was the very gray and completely august *Times,* the newspaper of royal record regularly perused at court each morning over cold buttered toast, corn flakes, and kedgeree.

Although Beatle Paul may have offended regal sensibilities by smoking a number in the palace loo, Mick and Keith had demonstrated their utter contempt for the entire English establishment in open court and then had their sentences reversed on appeal. Not only had they thumbed their noses (i.e., "cocking snooks") in public at everything for which England had stood so proudly for a thousand years, but they had also gotten away with it all scot-free. No longer just pop stars, Mick and Keith were suddenly transformed into authentic cultural heroes whose pronouncements were taken as seriously as the latest bulletin from 10 Downing Street. Suffice to say that neither "Satisfaction" nor

"Get Off My Cloud" ever ranked very high on the royal top of the pops.

Still, it is not Her Majesty who is forcing the Stones into exile but the extremely dire state of their own finances. Although the band has made a packet during their many years on the charts in England and America, the Inland Revenue now wants to take it all away from them. Nothing personal, you understand. Just a matter of policy. In the income bracket in which the Stones now find themselves, the tax rate on earned income is eighty-three percent per pound, escalating to an astronomical ninety-eight percent per pound on unearned income. Going on tours and selling more records while continuing to live in England will do nothing for the band but generate yet more tax money for the Conservative Government led by Edward Heath.

And then there is the ongoing litigation with Allen Klein, the manager whom Mick and Keith personally chose to rescue them from Andrew Loog Oldham and Eric Easton. Thanks to a contract signed by Brian Jones when the Stones were just starting out, Oldham and Easton have for years been earning a dispro-portionate share of the band's record royalties. The Stones were so desperate to go with Klein that they signed with him for an advance of a mere million and a quarter dollars. The band now believes Klein is holding about seventeen million dollars that be-longs to them. Because Klein was clever enough to incorporate a separate branch of the Stones' publishing company in New York as an American entity under his sole control, the boys have to go to him whenever they need a farthing.

Rather than disburse funds, Klein prefers to "lend" the band money. In *The True Adventures of the Rolling Stones,* Stanley Booth quotes a memo written by Jo Bergman, then in charge of the Stones' office at 46A Maddox Street in London, in which she states that all the band's personal accounts are overdrawn, the Rolling Stones' number 3 account is overdrawn, seven thousand pounds are needed to clear the most pressing debts, and there are currently no funds available for running the office. At the same time, an official receiver in England has frozen large sums of the Stones' money pending the outcome of Eric Easton's suit against his former partner Oldham for breach of contract and inducing his clients to break the contract. In a separate suit, Oldham is also suing Klein over his creation of Nanker-Phelge Music in America.

While the only rule that applies in rock 'n' roll is that all sums of money owed by one party to another are always subject to dispute, not to mention also often a product of outright fantasy, it is still plain as day that the Stones' finances have hit rock bottom. As Mick Jagger will tell Roy Carr of the *New Musical Express* shortly before the release of *Exile On Main St.*, "So after working for eight years I discovered at the end that nobody had ever paid my taxes and I owed a fortune. So then you have to leave the country. So I said fuck it, and left the country."

The man behind this plan is none other than Prince Rupert Ludwig Ferdinand zu Loewenstein-Wertheim-Freudenberg, a descendant of the Bavarian royal family whose title is also a matter of some debate in certain circles. Along with Jonathan Guinness, Prince Rupert founded the merchant bank Leopold Joseph and is now its managing director. Inveigled by Mick into helping the band with their finances, Prince Rupert thought he had been given what Stones bassist Bill Wyman later called "the pleasant duty of investing surplus funds for a highly successful pop group" only to discover that the Stones were flat broke and "their assets did not cover their debts, mortgage payments, or daily expenses."

Even though Allen Klein still controls all the band's masters as well as the copyrights to their songs, the Stones soon decide to, as Wyman recalls, " . . . drop Klein and drop out of England—a heavy gamble but the only way, for Klein would certainly not willingly give us our freedom." Although the deal comes with certain conditions attached, none seemed particularly onerous at the time. Not if you are a Rolling Stone. The band has to stay in France for at least a year and agree to spend a hundred and fifty to two hundred thousand pounds. Roughly, this amounts to about half a million dollars. In return, no French taxes will be levied on what they earn. While they are there, a multinational offshore holding company based in Amsterdam and the Dutch Antilles will shelter and protect the band's money.

For those who can afford the passage, leaving England to live somewhere else because of the heavy burden of British taxation will soon become the thing to do. Still, the Rolling Stones are the first English band to decamp *en masse* for foreign shores. For the Stones, the decision makes eminent financial sense. Each of them currently owes the Inland Revenue more than a hundred thousand pounds. At the time, this amounts to a cool two hundred and forty thousand dollars per Stone, a sum far more astronomical back then than it is now.

As tax day in England nears, the Stones begin bidding farewell to their native land. On April 1, 1971, bassist Bill Wyman and his longtime companion Astrid Lundstrom fly to Nice accompanied by guitarist Mick Taylor and his companion Rose Miller, who just three months earlier gave birth to their baby girl Chloe. Lost in the hustle, bustle, and shuffle of leaving England for the south of France is the fact that of all the Rolling Stones, only Mick Taylor has no real need to go. As the newest member of the band, he has yet to make the kind of money that the rest of the Stones have already earned. Because Mick Taylor does not have a tax problem of any kind, his journey into exile makes no financial sense at all.

Just twenty-three years old as he boards a chartered plane to the south of France, Mick Taylor's future seems bright indeed. In time, he may become not only one of the great guitar players in rock but also a writer and a composer. If this were a Hammer Films production with dark music thudding loudly in the background and ominous portents popping up everywhere to fore-shadow certain doom for our hero, people in cinemas all over England would be up in their seats and shouting at the screen, "For God's sake, man, don't get on that plane!"

But it isn't. And so without another thought, Mick Taylor, Rose, and baby Chloe fly off to their brand new home in the south of France. For those keeping track of such matters, one of the many subplots that runs through the making of *Exile On Main St.* is the way in which Mick Taylor will be treated in the coming months, not just as a musician but as a human being as well.

And what of the other Stones? Charlie Watts, he of the sardonic face and unrelenting drumbeat, and his wife Shirley are already in France, having taken up temporary residence in a hotel in Cannes before moving to their rented house at La Borie in Thoiras, near Arles. Although Jo Bergman initially thinks Villa Nellcote would be just perfect for Mick, Bianca soon puts the kibosh on that by deciding the house is a bit too public and accessible for her taste. Instead, she and Mick have checked into the luxurious Plaza Athénée Hotel in Paris. In time, they will rent a villa in the walled city of Biot, a good forty-minute drive from Nellcote.

Naturally, Keith is the last to go. Never mind that he has no choice in the matter. No deadline known to man has ever impressed Keith Richards, much less one imposed on him by a financial advisor who may have a title before his name but in truth actually works for Keith. No one ever tells Keith Richards when it is time to go on stage. Keith goes on when he is good and ready and not a moment before.

As those in charge of this operation in the Stones office in London wait for Keith to leave, they begin to wonder if he will ever get it together. On a daily basis, he does not seem to be making much progress toward this goal. On April 5, the day on which English taxes are due, a team from the office arrives at Keith's house by the river at 3 Cheyne Walk in Chelsea to pack all his stuff into boxes and ship it to France. Wearing what looks to be a woman's thin cardigan with beaded pearls along the sleeves over a tight-fitting jersey and flared curtain-print drape trousers, Keith is then driven to the airport where he boards a BEA flight to Nice with his young son Marlon, then eighteen months old, and Jo Bergman and Shirley Arnold, longtime members of the Rolling Stones staff.

To look at Keith as he gets on the plane, you would never know that in the three weeks since the Stones completed their ten-day farewell tour of England, the man has been through two different drug cures, neither of which worked for long. From all accounts, Keith's long-running love affair with heroin began in earnest about a month after the Stones returned to England from the debacle at Altamont in December 1969. Purchasing pharmaceutical-grade stuff from someone who had stolen it from chemists in the north of England, Keith would use and then head for the loo where he would play guitar and write music for hours.

By the end of the recording process for *Sticky Fingers,* Keith was so out of it that he played no significant role whatsoever in the making of "Moonlight Mile," the final track. Accompanied by Anita, Marlon, and Gram Parsons, the brilliant singer-songwriter who was already an ex-Byrd and an ex-Flying Burrito Brother, Keith was in no better shape during the English tour. Traveling separately from the rest of the Stones, he failed to arrive on time for a single gig. But then that was just Keith all over for you. On stage, the man always delivered. What he did with his private life was his own concern. Which was exactly how all those atop the pyramid of rock who were using seem to feel about the matter.

In no particular order (the exact chronology has been lost over time), here is some of what had happened to Keith in the past three weeks. As our hero stepped out of the front door of his home on Cheyne Walk in London one day, a squad car screamed to a stop before him. Out came the requisite copper in blue who said, "Hello, Keith. How are ya, boy? All right? Not on the heavy stuff, are ya? Roll up your sleeve, will you? Let's have a look at your veins then. How's Anita and the baby? What's this? This smell like hash to you, Fred?" Thankfully, Keith was not holding at the time and so did not get busted. By this point in time, hauling various members of the Rolling Stones into the nearest police station for drug use had become the new national sport in England, right up there with fox hunting and football.

Although Mick had many friends in high places, among them the gay Labour MP Tom Driberg and Michael Havers, the Queen's Counsel who represented both Mick and Keith at the trial stemming from the bust at Redlands in 1967, he was no more exempt from such treatment than Keith. On May 21, 1969, Mick and Marianne were busted at Mick's home at 48 Cheyne Walk for heroin, LSD, and marijuana. Mick, being Mick, claimed that Detective Sergeant Robin Constable had framed him by planting the heroin in a white Cartier box on a tabletop. According to Mick, Constable then offered to sort the matter out in return for a bribe of a thousand pounds, a charge Constable denies to this very day while sorrowfully adding, "We shouldn't have arrested him. Anyone else!"

Just like Keith, Mick thought that most of the coppers involved in the business of busting rock stars for drugs, Norman "Nobby" Pilcher of Scotland Yard foremost among them, who had done Brian Jones, Eric Clapton, and Donovan, were on the take. It was Mick who paid out seven thousand pounds in bribes to make the Redlands bust go away only to get nothing in return. Or, as Keith noted one day on the back steps of Nellcote, "At least in the States, you know the cops are bent and if you want to get into it, you can go to them and say, 'How much do you want?' But in England, you can drop fifty grand and the next week they'll still bust you and say, 'Oh, it went to the wrong hands. I'm sorry. It didn't get to the right man.' It's insane."

Although Keith handles the inquisition outside his house that day with great aplomb, his behavior in any given situation is always subject to his mood as well as his relative level of intoxication. One night before disembarking for France, Keith downs a few margaritas and does a snort of cocaine and decides to visit Anita, then undergoing her own very harrowing detox in Bowden House, a private hospital located in Harrow-On-The-Hill. Leaping into the front seat of his pink Bentley with his friend Michael Cooper, the photographer who did the cover for *Their Satanic Majesties*, Keith jams a cassette of the as yet unreleased *Sticky Fingers* into his tape player, rigged with outside speakers so everyone can hear what he is playing, and off he goes.

Even at the best of times, traveling anywhere in a car driven by Keith Richards can be an adventure of major proportions. This particular night, it becomes Mr. Toad's wild ride. Driving like a madman, Keith bounces the Bentley off various curbs. He passes motorists on the wrong side of the road. All the while, he keeps honking his horn loudly so everyone will get out of his way. About to smash into a truck as he enters Harrow, Keith whips the steering wheel so suddenly to one side that he crashes the Bentley through an iron fence into the middle of a traffic circle. With the front of the car completely wrecked, steam shooting out of the radiator, and the tape still blasting, Keith and Michael Cooper make a run for it.

Going through a gate into a quiet English garden, they begin digging a hole in the ground in which to hide their stash when suddenly the door to the house opens and out steps Nicky Hopkins, the brilliant session man who only just played piano for the Stones on their English tour. Politely, Nicky asks them in for tea. Leaving the wrecked car for someone else to sort out, Keith and Michael Cooper go inside to bathe their cuts and bruises while Nicky phones for a limo to take them to Bowden House. When Keith calls Anita to tell her what has happened, she screams hysterically at him, "Just get me some H or I'm checking out of here right now. This minute."

And then there is the night at the Marquee Club on Oxford Street in London, where the Stones are scheduled to film a television special until Keith takes exception to the large banner hanging on stage with the name of the club on it and swings his guitar at the head of Harold Pendelton, the owner of the Marquee, whom he has never liked. Fortunately, he misses and the gig goes on as planned.

Still, as he boards the plane for Nice, Keith seems just fine, thank you very much. The proof of the pudding is that the flight itself passes without incident. When the plane lands in Nice, Prince Rupert, currently staying at the Hotel Majestic on La Croissette in Cannes, is there to greet Keith along with various French accountants and attorneys, all of whom are referred to not as *Monsieur* but *Maitre* in accordance with French tradition.

Plump, genial, extremely civilized, and looking not unlike the great English actor Robert Morley, Prince Rupert is every inch the merchant banker in a fine suit and an expensive shirt from Jermyn Street. Pleased as punch that Keith has finally gotten himself out of England, all those present feel confident that the next chapter in the true adventures of the Rolling Stones will now go smoothly. As always, there is but one small fly in the ointment. Back in England, Anita still has ten more days to go in Bowden House. Until she is clean enough to get on a plane and join Keith in the south of France, there is no knowing how he will adjust to the change in his surroundings.

Driving to Nellcote from the airport in Nice, Keith seems surprisingly up and bright and chatty, enjoying the scenery on what is a fine spring day in the south of France. As the car moves along the RN7 toward Beaulieu and St. Jean Cap Ferrat, Jo Bergman, a diminutive woman with impossibly frizzy black hair who first learned how to do this sort of thing by working for Marianne Faithfull back in the days of swinging London, cannot help but wonder whether Keith will like the house that he has never yet seen.

Outside Nellcote's great front doors, gravel skitters beneath the wheels of the car as it comes to a stop. Keith gets out with Marlon, followed by Jo and Shirley Arnold. Before anyone can knock, the young French couple who have been hired to look after the cooking and the gardening come to welcome the new lord of the manor. Although they do not have very much English, the French couple are nothing if not polite, extending their hands to Keith in smiling welcome. "Nice," Keith says succinctly, looking over their heads at his new home.

In the lexicon of the English working class, this phrase can mean anything from "This is bloody wonderful!" to "I've never seen anything so fucked in me entire life." At the moment, however, Keith definitely seems amused by everything. As he walks through the front door, someone flicks a switch and the huge chandelier in the living room comes alive, blazing away with brilliant light.

Does Keith like what he sees? Is Monsieur pleased, or *non?* He should be. This is like walking into Louis the XIV's private salon at Versailles only to discover that the large throne in the middle of the room has your name in gold letters on the back. More to the point, does Villa Nellcote belong to him? Is it a place where Keith can live in harmony with his muse and write the kind of music without which the Stones cannot record their new album? Does Villa Nellcote perfectly suit his royal rock 'n' roll tastes?

"Who hired the decorator then?" Keith asks, smirking at the sheer outrageous grandeur of it all. "Bloody Marie Antoinette?"

In every sense, this is Keith the actor reading lines that no one else could deliver half as well. Never mind that the rent on Nellcote is an astronomical twenty-five hundred dollars a month and that the house has been leased for him with an option to buy just in case he decides to stay in the south of France. For Keith, it is never the money. Rather, it's the vibes that really count, man. The feeling Keith gets when he meets someone new or walks into a hall he has never played before. The only substantive question anyone ever asks Keith is, "Is everything cool?" Meaning, "Is everything cool with *you*?"

Slowly, the grin on Keith's bony street urchin face grows so wide that it threatens to split his skull in two.

"I'll take it," he says.

Keith is happy. Naturally, so are Marlon and Shirley Arnold and Jo and even the French couple who barely grasp the significance of the scene that has just been played out before them. Keith Richards has spoken. The message he has conveyed is that everything is in fact very cool with him. Just like that, Villa Nellcote becomes his brand new home.

## 2

**Straight away,** Keith picks up the phone in the living room to call Anita back in England. Because Keith speaks no French at all, Jo Bergman has to place the call for him. After what seems like an eternity, Anita picks up at the other end. As he talks to her, Keith is bubbly and funny and full of life, as only he can be when he is delighted about something new.

On and on he goes, telling Anita how much he likes Nellcote and more importantly how much he thinks she is going to like it. He describes the big back porch where Marlon can play and all the trees and the killer view. "It's a great house," Keith tells her. A great house for kids and rock 'n' roll, which is really all he cares about right now. When she finally gets to see this place, Keith feels certain Anita will like it as much as him.

Keith is really selling the house to her now and for a very good reason. From the other end of the phone, he is getting a never ending string of complaints in the heavy Germanic monotone Anita employs when she is out of sorts, out of it, or just really pissed off. Nellcote sounds fine to her but she wants to be there *now*. Not in ten days' time. But the only way she can come to France is clean. Keith has underlined this point by going through detox first so Anita could look after Marlon while he did. Now that he is returning the favor, Keith expects nothing less from her.

"Soon," Keith tells her. "Before you know it, you'll be here."

Although this is precisely what you are supposed to say to someone in detox, Anita seems to know this as well and so goes right on complaining. According to Spanish Tony Sanchez, whom Keith always treats like a close friend but who has been described by Marianne Faithfull as the "dealer by appointment to the Rolling Stones," Anita is at this point in time far more addicted than Keith. Back when she was still hanging out with Marianne and reading *The White Goddess* by Robert Graves,

Anita would sometimes skin pop speedballs, a mixture of heroin and cocaine, three or four times a day. Or so Tony claims.

As her supplier, the man should be in a position to know. But because this is Spanish Tony, there is no telling just how accurate anything he says may be. *Up and Down with the Rolling Stones,* the snarky, tell-all memoir of his time of service with the band that Tony wrote strictly for the money, often reads like a child's garden of misinformation, a fact duly noted by Keith who in time will describe the book as being much "like Grimm's fairy tales" in that every chapter begins with the way things really were until "you turned the page two or three times and he went off into fairyland. Maybe he would incriminate himself if he told the real story."

But then Tony, a smaller and far less powerful version of Keith, with shirred dark hair and the sharp-boned face of a hawk, seems to have always gotten it wrong when it comes to his relationship to the Rolling Stones. Although he could often be found in close proximity to the lord and lady of the manor at Nellcote, Tony was never cool enough to hang out with Keith and Anita without having to render services in return.

Even Marianne Faithfull, who slept with Tony in exchange for the jack of heroin he brought her each night before she went on stage to play Ophelia beside Nicol Williamson in a production of *Hamlet* directed by Tony Richardson at the Roundhouse in London, describes him as "a dreadful person. You only had to see him eat to know how loathsome he was. He was a lowlife, a small-time spiv, but a weakling at the same time. He was enchained as anyone else, completely hung up on his own particular sickness." As someone who spent most of the summer at Nellcote would later say of Tony, "If you wanted something, fine, but you couldn't have him living in the house. The guy was just unbearable."

Nonetheless, Tony or "Spanish" as Keith sometimes calls him, does make Villa Nellcote his home away from home for long periods during the summer. In this drama, his role is that of the classically unreliable narrator, the witness whose testimony must be heard but remains subject to constant doubt. Even if Tony's drug-addled memory played tricks on him and he did all he could to hide the truth about himself in his book, this does not mean Tony did not get at least some of it right. Still, everything he says must be taken with a grain of salt, as opposed to a gram of cocaine or heroin, two substances with which he was also familiar.

In terms of Anita's drug use before she entered Bowden House, what can be verified is that she was already using heroin during the filming of *Performance* in the summer and fall of 1968. "By the completion of filming," she would later say, "I was heavily into drugs. I thought I was being very surreptitious about it all, but Donald (Donald Cammell, codirector of the film with Nicholas Roeg) made me return to shoot an extra scene— the one where I inject B-12. He must have been on to me."

In Bowden House, Anita is being given Mogadon tablets as part of what was then known as the sleeping cure. "They put you to sleep for seven days and you go through withdrawal while sleeping," she would later tell John Perry, "or you're supposed to. Spanish Tony was always coming by with a gram of coke and it just didn't work. I was bashing my head and there were all these sharp corners by the bed so I was bruising myself all over and eventually—you know—I just took off."

According to Spanish Tony, Anita showed up at the flat he shared with his girlfriend Madeleine d'Arcy on the morning after Keith crashed his Bentley into the traffic circle. Dope-sick and convinced the cure was not working, Anita demanded that Tony find her some heroin right away. He returned a few hours later only to learn she had thrown up. Her hands were trembling "as if her body were being racked [sic] by a series of electrical shocks." After snorting some heroin, she fell into a deep sleep. She returned to Bowden House that night but was back on Tony's doorstep the next morning pleading for more.

And so it went for the next four days until Anita's physician phoned Keith to tell him Anita now had more heroin in her bloodstream than when she had been first admitted and there was no point in attempting a cure if she was not prepared to stay in the hospital during the day. Keith lectured Anita until she agreed to do so.

At this point in the proceedings, it seems likely Anita was given Hemineverin, the English trade name for chlormethiazile, a powerful antipsychotic medication that acts as a tranquilizer and was then sometimes prescribed for recovering alcoholics. It was an overdose of this drug in suppository form that killed The Who's drummer Keith Moon in 1978. When the Hemineverin does not work, Anita tries to numb her pain by snorting wholesale amounts of cocaine brought to her with flowers by Spanish Tony, an experience she would later describe as "the WORST thing I've ever done in my life!"

During her stay at Bowden House, Anita renews her acquaintance with Susan Ann Caroline Coriat, whom Anita first met in the south of France before the filming of *Performance* when she was hanging out with Donald Cammell and his Texas-born girlfriend Deborah Dixon. A direct descendant of Thomas Coryate, the seventeenth century English diarist and travel writer, Susan, called "Puss" by those who know her best, is a high-born heiress whose two sisters are both countesses.

Twenty-four years old, dark, beautiful, and exotic looking, Puss is the mother of two young sons currently being cared for by her former husband after a series of mad adventures while traveling overland with her from India through Afghanistan, Persia, and Turkey to the Greek island of Pátmos. Due in part to a struggle over family money and to protect Puss's extremely fragile mental state, her mother has had Puss "certified," a legal term meaning that a doctor has determined her to be in need of psychiatric treatment and confinement after a breakdown. She was then sent for treatment to Bowden House.

Intensely attracted to one another, Puss and Anita party together with drugs supplied by Spanish Tony. The two women soon become lovers. Diagnosed as schizophrenic, Puss is subjected to electroshock treatment. Although this completely freaks Anita out, she asks Puss if her former husband, who has some experience in such matters, could possibly bring an exotic wedding present to Keith for Mick Jagger in the south of France. When Puss herself is discharged from Bowden House, the plan is for her to join the party at Nellcote.

Whether Anita tells Keith about any of this as they talk on the phone, no one can say for sure. Even though this detox, quite possibly her first, has been utter hell for Anita, Keith has been through it more than once and knows that it is just yet another part of the price you pay for using. Standing in the grand living room in Nellcote holding the phone to his ear as Anita continues to complain to him, Keith no longer seems to be really listening. For a moment, he considers putting Marlon on the phone. The child cannot yet really talk so there is not much he can say to his mother. More likely, the sound of her voice will only serve to upset the boy. Between Keith and Anita now, the distance is more than physical. Keith is well and Anita is sick. Until Anita is clean, there is nothing Keith can do to help her. Saying he hopes to see her soon, Keith hangs up the phone.

By any standards, the conversation between them has been a disaster. Keith, however, does not seem in the least upset. Along with Jo Bergman, Shirley Arnold, and Marlon, he troops into the grand dining room for his first meal in his brand new home. Recognizing this as their audition, the young French couple have pulled out all the stops. She has cooked herself to utter exhaustion, a fact made evident as her husband begins coming through the kitchen doors with one course after another.

Quickly, the meal becomes one of those mad pantomimes that always occur when people turn themselves inside out to please the Rolling Stones when in truth all the boys themselves ever want is the real thing. A little authenticity, if you will.

"Peas?" Keith says, looking down at his plate and then at Jo as though all this is her doing.

"Yes indeed," Jo Bergman says. "I believe they are."

"From a tin?"

"Quite possibly."

"Bloody *peas?*"

"Here in France," she explains. "They call them *petit pois.*"

Like every other whey-faced kid with bad teeth who grew up in postwar England eating only what came in a tin or a Cadbury's wrapper, Keith spent his entire childhood staring at dinner plates upon which two veg had been cooked until they were absolutely dead. One of them was always peas. From a tin. It is not just Keith either. On a ferry to Germany one day, Ian Stewart angrily refused to tip a German waiter, saying, "Because of you lot, I didn't get any bananas until I was seven."

"Bloody peas from a tin, Jo?" Keith says. "I can't eat these. Marlon neither. Christ, we need real food. Know what I mean?"

In the south of France, it is still early spring. If you want peas, you have to get them from a can. Rather than tell this to Keith, Jo says, "They are green, Keith."

"No," Keith says. "Not fresh or from a bloody tin. No peas." Gesturing to the male half of the young French couple who is now hovering by the table like a satellite in the sky, Keith says, "You tell him."

"M'sieu Keith," Jo says. "*Il n'aime pas les petit pois.*"

M'sieu Keith does not care for the peas? Fine. What would he like instead? Perhaps the asparagus hollandaise that the young man's wife is so fond of making or baby carrots from a jar that can be braised lightly with spring onions from the larder in the cellar? Turning to Keith, Jo translates his response.

"Chips," Keith says.

"I beg your pardon?"

"Chips," he says again.

"Chips," Jo repeats, in order to give herself time to think.

"Tomorrow night for dinner, I want chips."

"Just chips and nothing else?"

"Fish and chips," Keith says. "Meat pies. Yorkshire pudding. Roast potatoes. Real food. And no bloody peas."

"Right," Jo says, translating all this into French so the male half of the couple will understand.

"But of course," he replies in French. "This will be done just so."

Off he goes into the kitchen. As the door shuts behind him, Keith tosses one last word like a hand grenade at his retreating back. "*Chips!*" he says yet again.

So much for fine French cuisine. Here at Nellcote, Keith intends to live as he does everywhere else. In time, he will transform this house into something that resembles a cross between a backstage dressing room and a half-ruined hotel room on the road. Because Keith is a true blue rock 'n' roller, he knows no other way to live. Now that he is here, everything in and around Villa Nellcote is about to get just as funky as funky can be.

## 3

**Four days later,** Keith decides to buy Anita a present. Accompanied by the ever-present Jo Bergman, he goes shopping on the very fashionable La Croisette in Cannes. Popping into Cartier's, he picks out a ring of white gold or platinum on which two snakes made of sapphires and rubies coil around one another with their beady eyes staring out at the world. When it comes time to pay for his purchase, Keith looks at Jo who picks up a phone, calls Prince Rupert at his nearby hotel, and tells him they need thirty five thousand francs (seven thousand dollars) pronto. Instructing Jo to put the manager on the phone, Prince Rupert speaks directly to him in fairly flawless French and everything is soon arranged. Because this is the way business has always been done here on the French Riviera, the bill will be sent to the Majestic.

As they walk along La Croisette feeling like a pair of kids who have just gotten away with something slightly illicit, Keith begins tossing the elaborately wrapped little box up and down in the air like a red rubber ball. Up and down it goes. Seven thousand dollars up, seven thousand down. Like everything else Keith can afford, the price he paid for the ring means nothing to him now. But then what else is money really for?

When Anita finally arrives at Nellcote, Keith gives her the ring and she loves it. But as soon as Anita puts it on her finger, she takes it off again. The ring is very cool, but Anita does not intend to wear it in public because of the aforementioned villa robbers who it is well known are looking even now for a house to pillage and loot. Her feeling about the ring may also have something do with Le Mistral, the hot desert wind that blows from the northwest across the French Riviera in violent bursts, carrying with it grit and sand and dust. When Anita arrives at Nellcote, she can hear Le Mistral "howling through the chimneys and there was just me and Keith setting up camp there . . . I felt spooked out. I was very, very spooked out. Like a premonition of what was to come, a feeling, a foretaste of coming disaster."

Although Keith has bought Anita the perfect gift, he cannot force her to wear it. Sometimes she does. Sometimes she hides it in a drawer. Better than anyone, Keith knows that no one can tell Anita what to do. No one ever has, and no one ever will. For Keith, this is but part of her charm. What really matters right now is that Anita has arrived in stunning shape. Like Keith, she too is now clean. Anita is a clean lady. As with so much else in the life they share together, this condition will not last long.

According to Spanish Tony, Keith and Anita's brief honeymoon with sobriety ends with the arrival at Nellcote of Jean de Breteuil, called "Johnny Braces" by Keith and Tony because of the fiery red suspenders he wears. An aristocratic playboy and dope dealer whom Marianne Faithfull describes as "one step higher up on the evolutionary scale than Spanish Tony," Jean de Breteuil's lineage in France dates back seven hundred years. One of his ancestors is Gabrielle Emilie Chatelet-Lomont, a great beauty and scholar who was Voltaire's mistress and translated Sir Isaac Newton's *Principia Mathematica* into French.

Currently, the de Breteuil family owns all the French language newspapers in North Africa. When he is in America, the hashish and opium Jean de Breteuil supplies to his rich and famous clients, the already deceased Janis Joplin among them, reportedly comes from a Moroccan chauffeur attached to the French consulate in Los Angeles. Born with one green eye and one yellow eye, de Breteuil has for the past two years also been carrying on an affair with Jim Morrison's wife, Pamela.

With him on his visit to Nellcote, de Breteuil brings a small quantity of very pure pink Thai heroin in a woman's powder compact. According to Spanish Tony, Keith snorts some through the gold tube he wears on a chain around his neck and promptly passes out, thereby proving just how good the stuff really is. After he comes to, Keith asks de Breteuil to phone his dealer in Marseilles and have him drop in at Nellcote to provide a regular supply. In return for this favor, Keith kindly offers to let de Breteuil live rent-free for two weeks in his house on Cheyne Walk in London.

While he is there, de Breteuil begins an affair with Marianne Faithfull. In early July, she accompanies him to Paris, where they spend the weekend at L'Hotel. At one point, de Breteuil gets a call from Pamela Morrison, whom he immediately goes out to see. Returning to the hotel room in a state of agitation, de Breteuil beats up Marianne before telling her Jim Morrison has just over-dosed on heroin supplied to him by de Breteuil. "Jean saw him-self as dealer to the stars," Faithfull will later write. "Now he was a small-time heroin dealer in big trouble. He was very young. Had he lived, he might have turned into a human being." Knowing he must leave France before the authorities discover Morrison's body, de Breteuil flies off to Tangier to join his mother the comtesse.

Most certainly getting the chronology wrong here, Spanish Tony writes that not long after de Breteuil's visit to Nellcote, two burly Corsicans, sweating through their Daks lightweight suits, arrive at the villa carrying two identical black fiberglass executive attache cases in their hands. After a brief exchange of pleas-antries, the bigger Corsican clicks open his case to reveal a poly-ethylene bag the size of a two-pound sack of sugar. "Pure heroin from Thailand," he says. "Uncut and the very very finest qual-ity." The heroin is so pure that it has to be diluted with glucose or it will kill anyone who uses it. Keith and Spanish Tony mix a few grams with three times as much glucose powder. Told that the price is nine thousand dollars, Keith goes upstairs and counts out the cash. At Nellcote, the supply lasts less than a month. Or so Tony claims.

Twenty-eight years later, Anita tells John Perry, "I remem-ber one day I walked into the living room and there were these two guys sitting there, cowboy hats, cowboy boots—guess it was the big fashion in those days—and one says, 'Oh, we are from Marseilles, we brought you some gifts' and out of the boot came like half a kilo of smack. I said, 'No, we don't do that' and kicked them out—it was like . . . there were already massive amounts of stuff floating around."

Because of its color, the pink smack from Thailand is referred to as "cotton candy." When John Perry asks Anita about it, she says, "Good? Oh, fantastic. It was pure. It was totally pure. We had one bag of smack and one bag of cut. Do-it-yourself kind of thing. I mean it was lucky nobody died on the premises really. . . . We were all set to behave, but I remember exactly, they all just came and kept on coming, with masses and masses of stuff. And you can only say 'no' so many times."

Disingenuous as this statement may be, it is in perfect keeping with the role Anita now seems to really believe she played that summer at Nellcote—the long-suffering mistress of the villa who struggled mightily to provide regular meals for the Stones and their hangers-on as the band worked on an album that could have been done in half the time if not for all the drugs being used by Keith and Anita.

The truth is nobody forced anyone at Villa Nellcote to use heroin that summer. You had to *want* to do it. And if Nellcote had not been an hour's drive from Marseilles, then the dope would have come from somewhere else. For wherever a junkie goes, there is always heroin to be found. Notwithstanding Spanish Tony's claims, the truth would seem to be that at this point in time at Nellcote, Keith and Anita were still clean. Which is not to say they would not soon begin using again.

# 4

On April 16, not long after Anita arrives at Nellcote, the Stones celebrate the release of "Brown Sugar," the first single from

*Sticky Fingers,* with a reception at the international yacht club in Cannes. The song, which Mick Jagger wrote about his sexual affinity for black women, will in time come to be thought of in some circles as a paean to heroin.

Denying this rumor, Keith will say, "Apparently, what they get in Los Angeles, it's light brown with brown lumps in it. I don't know where that stuff comes from or what it is." Continuing to discuss the matter with the kind of expertise that can only come from personal experience, he adds, "These people don't know what they're getting. If you don't know what you're getting, you don't know what you're putting into yourself. And if you don't know that, you're a dummy. Nobody would eat meat with maggots crawling out of it but people will shoot up some shit they don't know about. Don't take my example. Take Jimi Hendrix. Or not. Depending on where you are and how you feel."

The party itself is quite the gala affair. The guests include Ahmet Ertegun, the legendary founder and president of Atlantic Records who along with his wife Mica is a full-fledged member of A-list high society in New York; Eddie Barclay, the fifty-year-old founder and longtime head of Barclay Records, well known on the French Riviera not just for his lavish parties but also, as his obituary in the *New York Times* will note, "his white suits, jaunty boutonniere, and David Niven mustache"; saxophone player Bobby Keys, the original good old boy from Lubbock, Texas, whose association with the Stones goes all the way back to the 1964 Texas State Fair; and Stephen Stills, one of the founders of the Buffalo Springfield who was then living in England while pursuing a solo career during yet another hiatus in the on-again, off-again career of rock's first super group, Crosby, Stills, Nash, and Young.

In little more than a year's time, Stills, an amazingly gifted singer, songwriter, and musician who ranked right up there with the most difficult figures in rock, would be sitting hunched over in a parked car outside a hotel in Denver. In a rasping voice, he would be whispering about stabbing Keith Richards with his expensive hunting knife for having had the incredible gall to deny him a line of blow after he had gotten everyone in Keith's hotel room high on cocaine. Keith then told Stills to leave the room immediately, thereby officially making him persona non grata with the Stones, a band with whom Stills had hung out not only in Los Angeles and London but the south of France as well.

(Memo to Stephen Davis, author of *Old Gods Almost Dead: The 40-Year Odyssey of the Rolling Stones:* It was not, as you incorrectly wrote in your book, the "overweight, glamour-deprived Gram Parsons" whom Keith threw out of his room in Denver after "Gram threatened Keith with a knife after having been denied all the cocaine in the room, and that he was told to stay away from the tour." It was Stephen Stills. Next time you want to check a fact about the Stones, please feel free to call me in the office.)

(Memo to A.E. Hotchner, author of *Blown Away: The Rolling Stones and the Death of the Sixties:* Love your salad dressing, man. Wish I could say the same for your book.)

(Memo from Turner, aka Michael Philip Jagger. Come now, gentlemen, your love is all I crave. You'll still be in the circus when I'm laughing, laughing in my grave.)

At some point during the party at the yacht club in Cannes, Mick throws a glass of wine in the face of a photographer who has been bugging him all night long. Stills, Charlie Watts, Keith and Anita, Bobby Keys and his wife Judy, Ahmet, and a raft of other close friends and associates then adjourn to Bastide St. Antoine, Bill Wyman's house in Grasse where everyone stays up all night having themselves just the finest of rock 'n' roll good times.

The Stones and Ahmet Ertegun, who is distributing their brand new album through Atlantic Records, most definitely have something to celebrate. In a week's time when *Sticky Fingers* is released, the album will go straight to the top of the American charts and stay there for an unprecedented twenty-five weeks, making it by far the single most successful album the Stones have ever produced. As the initial release on Rolling Stone Records, no one could ask for more. Featuring classic songs like "Bitch" and "Brown Sugar," *Sticky Fingers* becomes the album of the summer, blasting out of the back seats of convertibles at the Frosty Freeze and A&W Root Beer stands all over America. In Europe, it can be heard in every beachside disco and bar from St. Tropez to Mykonos and back again.

The Stones are now on a roll. As they start getting ready to record their new album in a venue still to be determined, all the signs and portents seem favorable. Commercially, *Sticky Fingers* is going to be far bigger than *Beggar's Banquet* or *Let It Bleed*, the two masterpiece albums that preceded it. All they have to do is start recording it.

Before this can happen, Michael Philip Jagger, who more than once has loudly proclaimed that he will never settle down and get married, throws a spanner in the works by announcing that he plans to wed the lovely Bianca in first a civil and then a religious ceremony in the nearby very hip, very yé-yé village of St. Tropez. Until the festivities are concluded, no one can be bothered about the new album. As always where the Stones are concerned, life takes precedence over art.

# 5

**Why is Mick Jagger's** decision to marry Bianca of such supreme importance in the scheme of things? Funny you should ask. Mick's wedding matters because it announces to the world that a generation that for so long has been at odds with the normal rules of behavior is not only getting older but actually giving in. It matters because in one of those oversized books charting the newsworthy events of the 1970s day by day, Mick's wedding is the only rock-related occurrence deemed worthy of mention during the first two years of the decade. Most importantly, it matters because Mick's wedding drives the most serious wedge yet between himself and Keith.

Look at it from Keith's point of view. You don't get married, man. That's what *they* do. All the utterly straight and boring people who live in the conventional world. Sure Bill Wyman was married, but he left his wife and now lives with Astrid. Charlie Watts got married years ago in a registry office, but that's just Charlie for you, not so much a rebel and a child of the sixties as a cool fifties jazz cat who has always marched to his own idiosyncratic beat.

Marianne Faithfull was pregnant with Mick's child, but he never married her. Paul McCartney never married Jane Asher. Clapton never married Alice Ormsby-Gore. Brian Jones may have fathered as many as seven illegitimate children, naming more than one of the boys "Julian" after the great Cannonball Adderley, but he never got married. Not even once. Back when Brian and Anita were together, neither of them would have ever seriously entertained the concept. It was simply too straight, too conventional, too entirely bourgeois for words.

Keith has never married Anita, but Marlon is their son and they love him just as much as if their union had been legitimized by state and church. Yet in St. Tropez in the merry month of May, Michael Philip Jagger is about to wed Bianca, she of the dark sultry eyes and cruel insolent mouth, always a sight to see, whether in a broad Daisy Buchanan hat with the front flap pinned back or a brilliant iridescent green scarf with a peacock feather on it wrapped around her forehead, sitting calmly backstage as utter chaos swirls around her, the elongated ivory holder through which she smokes her cigarettes bobbing like a miniature pointer in her hands.

Granted, Bianca is a killer queen of the first order, great to look at and impossible to control but not at all rock 'n' roll, being far more interested in all the social niceties Mick himself mastered long ago. Nor can anyone ignore the obvious physical resemblance between them. As Marianne Faithfull will later write of the wedding, ". . . in May of 1971, Mick had finally given in to his narcissism and married . . . himself!"

While her opinion may be somewhat influenced by a twinge of jealousy, the media quickly makes Mick's decision to wed into a public declaration that his life as an artist who does whatever he pleases without caring what anyone thinks of him is now officially over. And despite how Keith may feel about all this in his heart of hearts, there is really nothing he can do but accept

Mick's offer to act as best man and show up on time at the wedding with all the other guests.

Under the tutelage of Abbé Lucien Baud, the pastor of St. Anne's Church in St. Tropez, Mick has been studying Catholicism for a month so he and Bianca can be married at the altar after a civil ceremony in the town's council chamber. For reasons known only to him, Mick waits until the Stones' first rehearsal in France on May 5 to tell the band of his plans. On the day before the wedding, as though the thought only just occurred to him, Mick casually calls Bill Wyman to invite him and Astrid to the reception. Because he has not been invited to either ceremony, Bill is a bit miffed. All the same, Astrid and Rose Taylor buy a tandem bicycle as a wedding present for the couple.

Although Mick initially wants only close friends at the reception, seventy-five guests board a chartered Dan Air Comet plane from London to attend the wedding. Among them are Nicky Hopkins and his wife Linda, Mick's parents Eva and Basil Jagger, Paul and Linda McCartney, and Ringo and Maureen Starr. Currently not on speaking terms with one another, Paul and Ringo sit at opposite ends of the cabin along with film director Roger Vadim, photographer Lord Patrick Litchfield, Eric Clapton and Alice Ormsby-Gore, Ronnie Lane, Ian MacLaglan, Kenney Jones, Ronnie Wood, Marshall Chess, Jimmy Miller, Glyn Johns, Stephen Stills, and backup singers Doris Troy and P.P. Arnold. Concerning the flight, Anna Menzies of the Stones' office will later say, "If it had gone down, there would be no music business."

As always, Spanish Tony is along for the ride. Over the phone, Mick has asked him to bring three grams of coke from

England to the wedding, saying, "I'm not going to get through this gig without it." Enlisting a friend to act as his mule, Tony delivers the goods to Mick at the Hotel Bibylos in St. Tropez after (or so he claims) Keith and Anita commandeer his personal stash for their own use. In light of the extravagant wedding gift that Puss' husband has brought, Tony may have gotten all this wrong as well, but it is hard indeed to imagine why else he would have been on the plane.

According to Tony, the groom himself is in a somewhat pensive mood as he considers his pending nuptials, saying, "The whole fucking thing is more hassle than it's worth." Specifically, Mick seems to be referring to the furious row he had with Bianca concerning the prenuptial agreement he insisted she sign so that should they decide to part company at some point in the future, she will not be entitled under French law to fifty percent of everything he owns. After a good deal of arguing, she finally agreed to this arrangement.

Although Mick seems to think he has done all he can to keep the wedding a secret, the tabloid press in England has already gotten word of the event and descended en masse to cover it. Before the chartered jet takes off from Gatwick Airport, reporters interview everyone in sight, Spanish Tony included. Like a pack of dogs at a fox hunt, they demand to know everything about what is not just the pop wedding of the year but the decade as well.

Although the civil ceremony is scheduled to begin at four, both bride and groom are late, thereby giving the Mayor of St. Tropez, Marius Estezan, ample time to field questions and pose for the horde of press people in the council chambers. Twenty minutes pass. When Les Perrin, the long-time, long-suffering Stones' press officer, calls Mick at the Hotel Bibylos to tell him about the scene, Mick yells, "Get rid of them! If there's going to be all that crowd, I'm not going to be married."

With the help of Jerry Pompili, the former house manager of the Fillmore East who first worked for the Stones on their farewell tour of England, and Mick's personal assistant Alan Dunn, who began his life on the road with Dusty Springfield and now handles logistics for the Stones whenever they tour, Perrin tries to clear the hall. To his utter dismay, Perrin soon learns that because this is France and the ceremony is taking place in a government building, everyone by law has a right to be there. Raising the stakes, Mayor Estezan then announces, "If the bride and groom are not here by four-thirty, I shall go and there will be no wedding." When Perrin phones Mick with the news, he says, "Fucking hell! I wish to God I'd never said I was going to get married in the first place."

Mick and Bianca finally arrive at the council chambers only to be greeted by more than a hundred photographers, reporters, and cameramen in a state of fevered excitement who jostle for position in the blazing heat so they can record this moment for posterity. The scene is utter insanity. Cameras flash as press people shout and scream questions at Mick and Bianca in a variety of languages.

According to Spanish Tony, Mick mutters, "Fuck this. I'm not going through with it." Much to the delight of the photographers, Bianca then begins to cry. Perrin, who seems a bit overwhelmed in a situation demanding some sort of emotional rescue, whispers in Mick's ear that he has to get this over and done with now. Mick tells the photographers to take their pictures and then leave them in peace. "They got their pictures," Spanish Tony would later write, "and stayed anyway."

Wearing a wide-brimmed picture hat trimmed with rosebuds and a white pants suit designed by Tommy Nutter that reveals an astonishing amount of décolletage, Bianca enters the council chambers and signs the register as "Bianca Rose Perez-Mora." She lists her age as twenty-six, although when she first met Mick eight months earlier, she reportedly told him she was not yet twenty-one.

After the bride and groom go inside, Jerry Pompili takes up a position outside the front door of the council chambers alongside the St. Tropez chief of police, a thin balding guy whom Pompili would later describe as "a dead ringer for the French movie actor Jean Louis Trintignant." It is only then that the best man finally arrives for the ceremony. For reasons known only to him, Keith is wearing braided black tights and a white long-sleeved jersey under a green combat jacket. "Keith came walking up to the door," Pompili would later recall, "and the chief of police grabbed him. They were standing there with their hands around each other's throats screaming in their respective languages and I had to break it up. The cop had no idea who this guy was. You know Keith. He looked like he was going to play a gig."

Once he actually makes it inside, Keith sits with Anita and Marlon on the bride's side of the aisle with actress Nathalie Delon, former wife of French film star Alain Delon, and Roger Vadim, both of whom are friends of Bianca from her days in Paris with Eddie Barclay. Now that the best man is present, the wedding can proceed. Mayor Estezan performs the civil ceremony and then it is time for everyone to go to the Church of St. Anne, where Bianca will be escorted down the aisle by Lord Litchfield as the theme song from *Love Story* plays. Tommy Weber (pronounced "Webber") is also there along with his two young sons, eight-year-old Jake and six-year-old Charlie, also known as "Boo-Boo."

Although Anita later tells John Perry that Tommy Weber came to the south of France with "a whole lot of people" who claimed "they'd driven the whole way" in a gypsy caravan stolen four months earlier from the English folksinger Donovan at the Glastonbury Festival, Weber had nothing at all to do with that caper and instead flies into Nice from London via Ireland. Although to this point in his life Weber has but a nodding social acquaintance with cocaine, he brings with him as a wedding gift about a pound of the white powder concealed in money belts strapped to the bodies of his two young sons.

While today such behavior might be viewed as child abuse, among those at Nellcote who favor the drug for recreational use, this ploy wins Tommy Weber unlimited respect. It also does nothing to diminish his welcome or shorten the length of his stay. Thirty-five years later, his son Jake would recall that he had no fears for himself or his brother because he knew they would not be searched as they went through French customs. Rather, he was worried about his father who in his mind was simply "performing a favor for a friend." At the civil ceremony, Jake and Charlie are pressed into service as pageboys.

Although Father Lucien Baud seems somewhat unnerved by Bianca's nipple-baring attire, he somehow manages to get through the ceremony with his religious values intact, saying,

"You have told me that you believe youth seeks happiness and a certain ideal and faith. I think you are seeking it too and I hope it arrives today with your marriage. But when you are a personality like Mick Jagger, it is too much to hope for privacy for your marriage." No truer words have ever been spoken. Before the day is over, Keith will have four fights trying to attend his best friend's nuptials.

Because he has judged the church to be "not defensible," Jerry Pompili remains outside like a soldier on guard to cover the front door so people will not walk in as the ceremony is performed. As Mick and Bianca leave the church, Pompili and Alan Dunn escort the happy couple to a waiting Bentley parked about a hundred and fifty feet down the street. Intent on getting the shot that will earn them worldwide fame, the paparazzi flock toward the car and crowd in as close as they can. Elbowing one another for position, they push and shove and curse.

Because he literally cannot open the door of the Bentley for the bride and groom, Pompili shoves aside an Italian photographer. The photographer retaliates by smacking him in the head with his camera. Blood streaming down his face, Pompili promptly grabs his assailant and flings him against the quarterpanel of the Bentley so hard that he actually dents it. The car then pulls away. With the official business of the day over, the party can now begin.

At the Café des Arts, as many as a thousand people, Brigitte Bardot among them, are ready to celebrate. Still covered in blood, Pompili is working the party when Keith grabs him and says, "Okay, we're gonna have a big jam on stage. See if you can get everybody involved in doing this." Considering the talent assembled at the party, this could be the supreme meeting of English rock superstars on a single stage to celebrate the marriage of the most famous English rock superstar of them all.

Leaving Keith in his own private little space in the balcony, Pompili goes off to assemble the musicians. Naturally, everyone he asks says they will be only too happy to join Keith on stage. When he comes back to tell Keith the good news, Pompili discovers the best man is fast asleep. Keith has passed out. For the first time in the history of the Rolling Stones, the show goes on without him.

After Terry Reid does a few songs, Mick gets up on stage to sing with Doris Troy, P.P. Arnold, Steve Stills, and others. As the night wears on, Basil and Eva Jagger depart without ever having given their son his present. Not at all pleased by the way her brand new husband has ignored her, Bianca returns by herself to the Hotel Bibylos. At some point during the night, Keith Moon climbs in through the window of her bridal suite. Later, Bianca will say, "My marriage ended on my wedding date."

Back in England, Marianne Faithfull, who by all rights should have been walking down the aisle with Mick today, is in a black cab headed to Paddington Station after her weekly visit to a doctor in London who shoots her "full of Valium." Looking out the cab window, she sees a large black newspaper headline reading, "MICK AND BIANCA WED IN FRENCH FRACAS." Making a beeline for the station bar, she downs three vodka martinis, gets blind drunk, and staggers into an Indian restaurant where she promptly collapses face down into the curry. The owner of the restaurant calls the cops who lock her up for the night so she can sleep it off. Charged with drunk and disorderly conduct, she is fined one pound. Already "hanging by a thread," she soon takes up full-time residence on that wall in St. Anne's Yard in Soho.

And then there is Keith Richards, not just the best man at this affair but also the rock 'n' roll Man of Steel, who no matter how much he puts inside himself before the Stones step on stage to perform, still always somehow manages to play as though his life depends upon it. For the first and only time, Keith has missed a gig. Not just an ordinary show but the wedding of his best friend and partner in musical crime, Michael Philip Jagger.

While the act itself seems fraught with symbolism, everyone at the reception, Mick foremost among them, is far too busy partying the night away to even notice. It is only during the coming months as the split between Mick and Keith widens that this begins to take on added meaning. Once the festivities are over, all the wedding guests except for Eric Clapton and Alice Ormsby-Gore board the chartered plane for a groggy ride back to London.

Clapton remains behind because he is "clucking" (a Cockney slang term for craving heroin while trying to withdraw) so badly that he literally cannot get on the plane. Alice Ormsby-Gore keeps ringing Nellcote and saying, "Oh, God, he's in such trouble. Keith, can't you do something?" Tommy Weber, who knows virtually nothing about the junkie life, takes pity on them and says, "Christ, you can't leave them like that." Keith, who at this point is still clean and understands that he is now being asked to score for someone else, replies, "If you want to do it on your own, you can take the driver and go to Marseille and sort him out. But you'll soon find that he'll be on your back forever.

He shouldn't have come out here if he didn't have his shit together." Clapton is then provided with enough white powder to get him "well enough" to board a plane and leave the country.

While all this goes on, Mick is off on his honeymoon. In keeping with his current standing as an A-list member of the international jet set, Mick charters a one hundred-and-twenty ton, ninety-seven-foot-long yacht staffed by a crew of six for a ten-day honeymoon cruise to Corsica and Sardinia. Although the Rolling Stones have now spent nearly six weeks in exile, they have yet to record a single note of their new album. While Mick is off enjoying his first taste of wedded bliss, no work of any kind can be done. Until he returns to the south of France during the final week of May, all anyone can do is wait.

# 6

**While it may be true** that misery loves company, if you happen to be Keith Richards, it's also hard to have a really good time without some of your closest friends and even a few casual acquaintances around to share it with you. At Nellcote, an extended rock 'n' roll version of an upper-class British house party that will last throughout the summer has only just begun. All the guests seem to be having so much fun that none of them give any indication of ever wanting to leave. But then why would they?

At Nellcote, no one has to get up each morning to rush off to work before the boss discovers they are not yet at their desk. No one pays any rent. No one would ever think of offering to chip in for groceries. Everyone has nothing but time on their hands. Which is why they all show up for the long and leisurely lunch served on the back patio where people often sit for hours as countless bottles of ice cold *blanc de blanc* and fuming hash joints make the rounds.

Because there is no place in the world any of them would rather be, there is no need to hurry. Here at the center of the hip universe, the only requirement is that you amuse your hosts in a manner that will prolong your stay. As they all sit there laughing in the warm spring sunshine on the back porch of Nellcote, apparently without a care in the world, let's go around the table and meet a few of the regulars, shall we?

In terms of sheer physical splendor, Tommy Weber tops the list. Long blond hair hanging to his shoulders, Tommy can usually be found walking around the villa barefoot in loose trousers and a flowing shirt that he may not have remembered to button up the front. Down on Nellcote's rocky little beach, he can also be seen sunbathing in the nude, thereby establishing beyond all doubt that he is one of the truly beautiful people on the planet. Although no one seems to notice it at the time, Tommy and Anita look so much alike that they could be twins hatched from a single egg. Together, they make a stunning pair.

A fabulous character straight out of the pages of F. Scott Fitzgerald's *Tender Is The Night*, Tommy, then thirty-three years old, is a true English gent with impeccable manners who was born in Denmark and then brought to England as a child by his mother after World War II.

After growing up on a family farm in the English countryside where Charles Darwin once lived, Tommy attended Haileybury and Imperial Service College in Hertfordshire, an exclusive public school whose illustrious alumni include Prime Minister Clement Atlee, the playwright Alan Ayckbourn, and world champion Grand Prix racing driver Stirling Moss. Moving to

London, Tommy became one of the most eligible bachelors in town until he met and fell in love with Puss, then seventeen years old.

The two were soon married and Tommy began racing professionally, driving Ferraris, Mini Coopers, and both the Lotus Elan and BRM. He was about to enter Formula One competition in Monte Carlo when he broke his neck in a traffic accident. Acceding to his wife's wishes, Tommy agreed to give up racing. Getting involved in the music scene, he put together the Nigerian-Ghanian rock band, Osibisa. Following in the tradition of the family firm, Weber, Smith, & Hoare Ltd., which for two hundred years had brought tea and spices into England through their London wharves, Tommy then began opening up "veins" to move high-grade hashish from Afghanistan to the west.

After he and Puss parted company, Tommy, by his own admission, "set his sights on a few of the top girls in the world and eventually managed to get most of them." Having only recently kept company for three years with Charlotte Rampling (the two met during the filming of Luchino Visconti's *The Damned*), Tommy has come to the south of France with his two young sons to reconcile with his wife. Once Puss arrives at Nellcote, the plan is for her and Tommy to put their family back together again. That Puss may actually be coming there to see Anita does not occur to Tommy until many years later.

One day not long after Mick's wedding, Tommy takes sax player Bobby Keys up to his chateau in the hills, yet another place where the Stones originally think they may record their new album. When Tommy returns to Nellcote, Keith takes him aside and says, "Look, I've got a real bummer for you." After leaving Bowden House, Puss went to see the public trustee appointed to safeguard her money. Because she had been certified by her mother, the public trustee refused to give Puss her passport, thereby making it impossible for her to leave the country. Years later, Tommy Weber will say, "That broke her heart, that her mother should have done that." Having just been to see her psychiatrist, "who had given her enough drugs to keep her cool for two or three months," Puss "checked herself into a hotel with a couple bottles of champagne and started going through her medication."

The tough news Keith has for Tommy is that at the age of twenty-four, Puss has killed herself. "Listen," Keith says, "obviously you must stay here with the boys for as long as you like." As Tommy will later recall, "And that was how our relationship changed completely. Anita and Keith were simply marvelous because I was totally fucked up."

Although everyone seems to know about his tragic loss, Tommy Weber is still not everyone's cup of tea at Nellcote. Andy Johns, who many years later will note that unlike Tommy, he actually had a job to do that summer, considered Weber to be nothing more than "a very typical, very dodge-y weasel boy." Rose Taylor calls him "a sycophant—definitely just another of the court jesters." Truth be told, it is Spanish Tony, who much like Will Rogers seems never to have met a man he does not like, who has absolutely nothing good to say about Tommy.

"The only visitor I took a dislike to was a man called Tommy," Tony will later write. "He claimed to be an Old Etonian and, if ludicrously exaggerated accents are anything to go by, he probably spoke the truth. He also said he was an ex-racing driver, which impressed Keith." According to Tony, Tommy accompanied Keith to the Monte Carlo Grand Prix where they "staggered drunkenly around the track together with Anita, swigging tequila from a bottle and singing ribald songs." What Tony never mentions in his book is how jealous he was of Tommy for having insinuated himself so quickly into Keith's inner circle. But then in every way, Tony saw Tommy as his great rival. Not that the two men had very much in common.

How were Spanish Tony and Tommy Weber different from one another? Let us count the ways. In an earlier and far more chivalrous age, Tommy would have been a knight of the realm. Tony would have been the dark henchman in a hood who took care of matters better left unmentioned in the dank dungeon below the castle floor. Tommy was a charming rogue, a hail-fellow-well-met who by dint of his birth and noble bearing had always been a member in good standing of the league of gentlemen. Tony would not have looked out of place hawking cheap umbrellas on the sidewalk outside Marks & Spencer on a rainy afternoon. At Nellcote, Tony had to fight like a hungry dog for every scrap of attention from Keith and Anita. Tommy, who had grown up in great houses, was always a welcome guest at the table.

Keith demonstrates just how much faith he has in Tommy by giving him the job of setting up Radio Rolling Stone, a "pirate" radio station that will broadcast music all over Europe from midnight to six A.M. using the high-powered equipment on a mountainside slab in Monte Carlo that had been built by the Nazis during World War II. Like so many of the mad fantasies floating around Nellcote that summer, the plan will eventually come to grief. Still, it is not the kind of assignment anyone would have entrusted to Tony, whose services, while always required, were plainly far more limited.

Between Spanish Tony and Tommy Weber that summer in the south of France, a form of actual class warfare is being fought. Not that Tommy ever seems to notice. He is far too busy telling yet another incredible story about having only just discovered a new version of the Gospel of St. Thomas in some papers he got off the very same chap who financed the Dead Sea Scrolls expedition. One sunny afternoon, Tommy returns to the villa and casually mentions he only just had it off with Rory Flynn, the daughter of Errol Flynn, the legendary star and famed despoiler of women, on board the yacht belonging to Errol's son, Sean, a combat photographer then missing in action in Vietnam.

Tommy first ran into Rory back in London where she inveigled him into helping her try to sell the yacht so she could go to Southeast Asia to search for her brother. Although Tommy has done his best to help her, so many people are claiming ownership of the vessel on which harbor dues have not been paid in decades that no one knows what the yacht itself might be worth. All the same, the waterlogged vessel soon becomes one of the regular stops Keith and Tommy make whenever they take visitors on a spin along the coast to see the local sights.

Whatever else you might say about Tommy Weber, he was always good for a bit of amusing conversation to help make the time pass more quickly. And while it is true that Tommy has absolutely nothing to do with the actual recording of the album about to be made at Nellcote, he does play a central role in nearly everything else that happens there, including the incident that causes our hero to begin using once again. But more about that later.

Another guest at the table is Olivier Boelen, a thin hand-some man with short dark hair whom Keith and Anita first met while hanging out with the remnants of the Living Theatre in Rome. Boelen, who is Dutch, is now organizing an event entitled "No More Curtain Calls" featuring The Bauls of Bengal sched-uled to be performed in Calcutta in September that he feels cer-tain all the Stones will attend. Boelen will soon leave Nellcote, only to return again at the end of July. At that time, his sexual proclivities will give the local gendarmerie good reason to believe there is more than just music going on at Nellcote. Tommy Weber remembers him as a "highly intelligent, well educated Dutch gentleman, and another aristocrat" who was "bent as a corkscrew."

Moving on, we come to a man in a white one-piece racing suit covered with automotive decals who looks far more like a Formula One driver than Tommy Weber. This is "Stash," whose real name is Stanislaus Klossowski de Rola. Keith and Stash go all the way back to October 20, 1964, when The Bobbie Clarke Noise, a band with Stash on percussion featuring vocalist Vince Taylor, a seminal English rocker in the Gene Vincent mode, opened for the Stones at the Olympia in Paris. In 1965, Stash and Bobbie Clarke moved to Hollywood where Clarke replaced drummer Don Conka in the group that eventually became Love, featuring the mercurial Arthur Lee.

Stash and Keith became even closer during the halcyon sum-mer of 1966 when Anita and Brian Jones shared a flat on Court-field Road behind the Gloucester Park tube station in London. In that flat, the art dealer Robert Fraser first turned Brian, Anita, and Keith on to LSD. All the lamps in the living room were covered with scarves, the paint was peeling off the walls, and clothes, magazines, and newspapers were scattered everywhere but everyone was so young, good-looking, and utterly brilliant, especially when they were high, that the flat itself soon became the place to be in London.

Other denizens of a scene that even to the participants sometimes seemed straight out of Oscar Wilde included the antique dealer Chrissie Gibbs, Marianne Faithfull, fashion model Suki Poitier, Sir Mark Palmer, and Tara Browne, the heir to the Guinness fortune. In the early morning hours of December 18, 1966, with Suki Poitier beside him, Browne, thought to have been high on acid, drove through a traffic light in Redcliffe Square in South Kensington. As he swerved to miss an oncoming car, Browne slammed into a parked lorry. His death not only put an end to the idyll on Courtfield Road but also served to inspire John Lennon to write in "A Day In The Life" about a man who blew his mind out in a car because he didn't notice that the lights had changed.

On May 10, 1967, Stash was busted with Brian Jones in that flat but all charges against him were eventually dropped. At some point, Stash had a brief affair with Marianne Faithfull. For a while, he lived with English actress Fiona Lewis in Tommy Weber's house in Chester Square. Before coming to Nellcote, Stash has been traveling through Ceylon, Thailand, Laos, and India, where he studied with Lama Anagarika Govinda, the German scholar who wrote the introduction to W.Y. Evans-Wentz's translation of the *Tibetan Book of the Dead*. In Stash's words,

Govinda "was very much instrumental in my turning back towards western esotericism, after a lengthy plunge in Tibetan secret doctrines." Upon his return to Rome, Stash received a call from Keith and Anita saying they had this great villa in the south of France where they would be recording this summer. Heeding the summons, he has now also become part of their brand new scene.

At Nellcote, Stash is always treated like royalty, and with very good reason. Rumor has it that he is directly related to the last crown prince of Poland and so can never return to his native land without fearing instant death at the hands of the Communists who now rule that country with an iron hand. In fact, Stash's father is Balthus, the world-renowned painter of young girls trembling on the brink of womanhood, whose genius as an artist apparently also includes imagining he was born a count.

Tommy Weber remembers that "Stash would come and lay down these amazing fantasies and everyone loved him because he livened the place up. You'd laugh at and with him. But he was also extremely well-educated and you could learn a lot from him. At that time, he was into that whole Tannhauser thing." Tannhauser being the wandering thirteenth-century knight, poet, and singer of courtly love songs who escaped "the snares of Venus with the help of Our Lady" but was "refused papal absolution" by Urban IV until his papal staff suddenly burst forth in flowers, thereby indicating "divine grace."

Although Stash himself seems like one of the *minnesingers*, German lyric poets of the twelfth to fourteenth centuries of noble birth who received royal patronage to compose songs about courtly love, he is in fact trying to turn his own updated version of the myth of Venus and Tannhauser into a movie. Yet another of his projects is a film adaptation of *Moonchild,* a novel written in 1917 by Aleister Crowley, the practitioner of black magic usually referred to in his time as "the wickedest man in the world," whose writings are just becoming all the rage among the underground literati in England and Europe.

While Tommy Weber, Olivier Boelen, and Stash all contribute to the mise-en-scène at the villa, none perform any specific function for the Stones. The same cannot be said of Marshall Chess, son of the great Leonard Chess, founder of Chess Records in Chicago. All summer long, Marshall will come and go from all over the world to Nellcote like someone commuting to work from a nearby suburb. As the newly anointed President of Rolling Stones Records, his time of service with the band has only just begun. Diminutive in stature but wired as all get out, he is a never-ending source of boundless energy, eyes and teeth flashing as he laughs loudly at every outrageous idea the Stones come up with, saying, "*Yeah!* That's *great!* Let's *do* it!"

Thirty years old and newly divorced, Marshall is at the moment in charge of everything that concerns the Rolling Stones, from the making of their new album to finding someone who will take them out on tour in America once it is done to ensuring that Keith finally sits down to finish the extensive cover interview for *Rolling Stone* magazine that will establish him as a true star and the authentic rock 'n' roller in the band.

To a man, all the Stones love Marshall, and not just because of his background. When Marshall was just a kid working in his father's mailroom at Chess Records, Michael Philip Jagger would regularly send away from his home in Dartford, England, for the latest release on Chess. Growing up half a world away from one another, the two were united even then by their undying love for the blues.

Because Marshall gets what the Stones are all about on every level, there is no problem too big or too small for him to solve if it concerns the band. Which is how he has always felt about them. When the Rolling Stones came to record at the Chess Studios at 2120 Michigan Avenue in 1965, it was Marshall who drove Brian Jones around the city. No one in Chicago had ever seen hair that long on a guy and people kept shouting, "*Homo!* Who's that fucking *homo* with you? Dick-sucking *homo!*" Even then Marshall knew the Stones were special. That he is now in charge of their future blows his mind on a daily basis.

Born with the energy of a crossfire hurricane, Marshall is a fixer, a plugger, and a pusher. As he proved conclusively during their recent ten-day farewell tour of England, Marshall can not only function under pressure but also have a hell of a good time while doing it. Only Marshall can hang out with both Anita and Bianca and leave them laughing. Only Marshall can stay up all night partying with Keith and then get on the phone to Los Angeles early the next morning to get the latest sales figures on *Sticky Fingers*. When it comes to having a good time at Nellcote, he fits in perfectly with all the other guests. Or, as Tommy Weber will later recall, "Marshall Chess behaved beautifully there. The other times he'd been with the Stones, he had just seen them in the studio and on the road. There, his eyes were wide open. He was still sort of hypercritical of people but he was a good man. And a tough guy too."

Although no one knew it back then, this time will eventually come to be known as the garden period at Nellcote, the calm before the storm that begins once the Stones actually start recording there. As Dominique Tarlé notes, ". . . at first it had been a British family on holiday, then a huge party on holiday, then a large group of musicians and technicians working on an album. It was the same story, but changing in shape." That Keith himself was still clean during this period has much to do with the festive mood in the house.

At the moment, Nellcote is quite the happy place to be. All day long and well into the night, great music blares from Keith's stereo, everything from rough Jamaican reggae ("Funky Jamaica" by the JA Horns, a track which Keith absolutely adores and plays over and over again) to classic old soul, blues, and rock 'n' roll. Marlon and Jake and Charlie are always underfoot, and the living room usually looks like a bomb hit it. With nothing to do but have fun, every day is a brand new adventure. Keith may decide to take his red Jaguar XKE for a death-defying drive in the hills. He may hop into his newly purchased two-thousand-dollar speed boat (rechristened *The Mandrax*) for a ride across the bay, only to find himself suddenly pummeled so badly by rough seas that a boatload of French fishermen and the Gallic equivalent of the Coast Guard have to haul him back home. He may stop on a rocky beach to skim stones with Marlon or sit for hours at the dining room table playing the lick from "The Jerk" by The Larks over and over on his Gibson Hummingbird guitar as big money promoters from America try to talk business to him.

Late one night as Keith picks up the debris in the living room, he notices a pill lying on the floor. Although there is no saying who dropped it there or what it in fact may be, a leaper, a creeper, or a black bomber (but most certainly not a vitamin of any kind), Keith picks up the pill and examines it for a brief moment. Popping it into his mouth, he then goes upstairs to bed. As Stash will later note, Keith is tanned and looking well and up every morning by ten to greet the brand new day. Surrounded by good friends and a few casual acquaintances, the man is clearly having the time of his life. As always where the Stones are concerned, things are going so good that something bad has to happen. And so it does.

# 7

**Perhaps life at Nellcote** has become too peaceful for Keith. Perhaps he just feels bored. Perhaps, as Spanish Tony would have us believe, Keith is simply reacting to what happened the night before. Perhaps it is just a case of French Riviera road rage that spins so quickly out of control that no one is at fault. Whatever the reason, the never-ending need for chaos with which Keith Richards seems to have been born suddenly kicks in with a vengeance and all hell breaks loose.

According to Tony, it all begins one night after dinner at Nellcote. Lest anyone doubt that we are now entering purgatory and the road we travel will be littered with lost souls, consider if you will the two women who dine this evening with Keith, Spanish Tony, Tommy Weber, and Anita. One is Madeleine d'Arcy, "a beautiful blond dancer" for whom Tony left his wife and two children some years earlier. In a photo he took of her that summer, Madeleine stands by the front door of Nellcote in an impossibly short mini-dress and a pair of stacked platform high-heel hooker shoes. Her bare legs are strong and muscular. Her hair is thick and lustrous and she has a huge smile on her face. In her right hand, she holds what may be a flower, but the quality of the photo is so poor that it is impossible to say for sure. Undeniably attractive, she also seems spectacularly happy.

Two years later, she will be turning tricks in Brighton for fifteen pounds a night to support her heroin habit. Her dead body, bruised and battered beyond recognition, will be discovered by her close friend Marianne Faithfull. "She had been taking methadone in an attempt to withdraw from heroin," Tony will later write, "and somehow the drug had driven her into an inexplicable frenzy. She'd banged her face again and again against a bedside cupboard until she was battered, bloody—and dead."

Beside himself with grief, Tony shoots heroin for the first time two weeks after her death. In "Lady Madeleine," a song on her 1977 album, *Dreamin' My Dreams,* Marianne Faithfull will sing about walking down the avenue and missing Lady Madeleine and Spanish Tony not knowing what to do, his strange world having all fallen through as he wonders if his love was in vain, even as she thinks he might go quite insane.

Also sitting at the dinner table at Nellcote that night is Michele Breton, a very thin and boyish looking French girl with short cropped hair and shockingly full breasts who along with Mick Jagger and Anita appears naked in the bathtub scene in *Performance.* Just seventeen years old when the film was shot, she will never make another movie and seems to have been cast in the role of Lucy primarily because she had already participated in a ménage à trois with writer and codirector Donald Cammell and Deborah Dixon. As had Anita.

But then the gist of *Performance* was art imitating life even as it created the kind of real-life melodrama on the set that no screenwriter could have ever imagined. As the film scholar

David Thomson would later note, Anita was "not just the most obvious lead for the film but its most threatening sensibility. It was in Pallenberg's being and her own devouring glances that *Performance* felt like the cast were acting out their own psychodramas."

Stoned on hashish and psychedelics during filming, Breton will spend the next five years of her life drifting around France and Spain. Busted for possession in Formentera, she lives for a year in Kabul shooting morphine. During this period, she sells her passport as well as all her belongings. Deciding to give up intravenous drug use after an LSD trip, Breton goes to India where she is hospitalized for three months. She then returns to Kabul, travels to Italy, and eventually settles for thirteen years in Berlin where Mick Brown, an English writer working on a book about *Performance,* finds her in 1995. "I've done nothing with my life," she tells him. "Where did it start going wrong? I can't remember. It's something like destiny."

Blissfully unaware of what their future holds, Madeleine and Michele accompany Tony, Keith, Anita, and Tommy after dinner is done to Tony's bedroom where, in his words, they all decide "to unwind by gulping down a few Mandrax tablets followed by hefty swigs of Courvoisier. The combination produces oblivion almost as quickly as a bonk on the head from a cowboy's gun. In less than an hour, all six of us had flaked out on my vast Louis XIV bed."

Regaining consciousness at five in the morning, Tony hears "whispers and faint gigglings from two people on the other side of the bed." Thinking at first that it must be Keith and Anita, he discovers instead that it is Tommy and Anita, who then begins to gently moan. "I could feel the bed shake as Tommy climbed stealthily onto Anita," Tony writes, "and then they were making love, gently at first and then violently. All the time, Keith and Michele snored on in blissful, drugged unawareness." When the pounding stops, Tony falls asleep once more. In the morning, he wakes up "to find Keith and Michele stretching themselves and gradually coming to." Tommy and Anita are nowhere to be seen. When asked if any of this is true, Tommy Weber will later say, "I can't remember any of these things. It could have happened but I really wouldn't have been that vulgar."

Nothing much is said about anything at breakfast, and then Keith and Tony roar off in Keith's XKE to have a look at a speedboat for sale in the neighboring harbor of Beaulieu. According to Tony, Anita, Tommy, Michele Breton, and Dominique Tarlé follow along behind in a rented gray Dodge driven by Dave Powell, Keith's chauffeur and aide-de-camp. As Tony and Keith head for the harbor, Tony takes it upon himself to tell Keith in a very Victorian manner that while they were all passed out the night before, Tommy took "a liberty" with an unconscious Anita. "He had his hand up her dress," Tony says, "and he was fondling her. It wasn't anything serious, but I thought you should know so you can tell the guy to piss off when we get back to the house this evening."

While it is true that Tony literally cannot bear the sight of Tommy and would be more than happy to do anything in his power to damage his standing with Keith, his comments may have far more to do with business than friendship. Tommy is now so completely ensconced at Nellcote that Tony views him as a direct threat to his livelihood. Although Tommy will later say, "I wasn't part of any supply route there at all," this seems to be precisely what Tony is thinking at the time. Neatly killing two birds with a single stone, he drops a dime on Tommy and then entreats Keith not to let anyone know the source of the story. "Sure, man," Keith says. "You can trust me."

Arriving at Beaulieu "in a shower of warm summer rain," Keith and Tony go looking for the harbormaster's office so he can direct them to the person selling the boat. Suddenly, another brand new Jaguar, this one an XJ6, tries to squeeze past them in the narrow road. There is an ugly ripping sound as the other Jaguar's bumper scrapes along the side of Keith's car. "All of Keith's pent-up anger seemed suddenly to explode," Tony writes. Through the open window of the car, Keith screams, "What do you fucking think you are fucking well doing?' Ignoring the "sputtered apologies" of "the genteel Italian couple in the XJ6," Keith then adds, "You fucking stupid foreigners. I'll smash your fucking heads in."

Before Tony can stop him, Keith pulls "a huge German hunting knife" from his leather satchel, jumps out of the car, and screams, "You stupid fucking idiot!" at the "old man" driving the other car. Explaining that it was just an accident, the man's wife plaintively asks Tony, "What's wrong with your friend? Is he a madman?" Hearing the commotion, Jacques Raymond, the harbormaster, whom Tony describes as "a broad-shouldered six-feet-two giant of man" comes out of his office. Ushering the Italian couple inside, he waves Keith away, which only serves to further enrage him. "That's right," Keith yells. "You fucking foreigners stick together. What the hell do you think you are playing at?"

The fact that Keith himself is a foreigner here, not to mention also a stranger in a very strange land, apparently does not occur to him at the moment. In light of the news Tony gave him on their way to the harbor, Keith's own state of mind may be less than clear. Since the harbormaster speaks no English and Keith does not know a word of French, Tony does his best to calm things down. It is then that Keith brandishes the knife.

As even Tony takes great pains to make perfectly clear, it is not as though Keith actually means to stab the harbormaster. Rather, he is just trying to establish that in this particular fight, he is the alpha dog and does not intend to be trifled with. Entirely missing the message, the harbormaster lets fly with a roundhouse right. Down goes Keith. As he lies on the ground, Keith screams, "Get him, Tony, fucking kill him!" Before Tony can respond, the harbormaster charges him, intent on landing yet another knockout punch. Ever the loyal foot soldier, Tony responds by hitting the harbormaster in the face, thereby "knocking the Goliath onto a table."

Getting to his feet, Keith rushes out to the XKE. According to Tony, Keith returns a moment later with Marlon's toy Colt .45 pistol in his hand, thereby pioneering the concept of using a fake weapon to further inflame a real situation. Pushing the Italian couple to the floor, the harbormaster promptly pulls out his own revolver. Unfortunately for Keith, the harbormaster's gun happens to be real. Terrified that the harbormaster may turn the gun on him, Tony grabs the toy pistol from Keith's hand, flings it to the ground, and begins shouting in French that Keith has no pistol. In fact, he has nothing at all.

Going to his phone, the harbormaster makes a call. Seconds later, the sound of approaching sirens can be heard. Even if the local gendarmes do not shoot Keith and Tony, they will most certainly arrest them. Both men dash for the safety of their cars. As they do, Keith tells Tony to take the XKE while he hops into the Dodge. Knowing Keith will never get away from the law "in that old bus," Tony wonders why Keith chose to give him the XKE. Keith's logic becomes crystal clear when the harbormaster points to Tony and informs the gendarmes that this is the man who tried to shoot him. Since Keith and Tony have similar hairstyles and they are both English and this is the south of France, his confusion is understandable.

Deciding to flee the scene of the crime before anyone starts asking questions he would rather not answer, Tony slams the XKE into gear and peels out in a cloud of blue smoke. Hurtling back to Nellcote at a speed he conservatively estimates at between a hundred and forty and a hundred and fifty miles an hour, Tony roars up the driveway, leaps out of the car, bolts the villa's big wrought iron gates shut, puts the Jag in the garage, and waits.

Fifteen minutes later, Keith returns in the Dodge. "Jesus, man," he says admiringly, "That made the Monte Carlo Grand Prix look like a practice session." In other words, even though Tommy Weber has been a professional racing car driver, it is Tony who is clearly the true outlaw here, the cunning wheelman who exhibited street smarts when life and limb were on the line. Or so Spanish Tony would have us believe. And now we come to the real story of what happened that day.

"I was actually in the harbor with Jake and Charlie and Marlon," recalls Tommy Weber. "I think the three boys were in the E-type and I had my car as well. One of the port uniforms tried to grab Keith and took a swing at him and he missed Keith and nearly hit Marlon. At that point, Keith pulled out a .38. And then a whole battle started." Tommy's son Jake, who was waiting in the car at the time, distinctly remembers being told that it was Keith who opened up the harbormaster's face by punching him with his right hand, the one on which he wore his heavy silver skull ring, thereby proving that his signature piece of jewelry was not only ornamental but also of great use in a brawl.

"I," says Tommy Weber, "knowing the complexity and the politics of the whole thing, get the kids in my car and take them back up to Nellcote to 'clean the place up' before we have a big, big bust which is obviously going to happen. Even though we had protection from the local prefect, we didn't have enough protection from the Customs and this was the harbor. So I knew it was really serious. Keith and Spanish Tony were having a lovely time having a serious 'Western brawl' with all these uniforms. Later, I'm told they thought I was running out on them but I knew they were quite capable of looking out after themselves.

"So I took the three kids to get them out of the situation and also to get up to Nellcote to warn Anita and everybody there to clean up whatever was lying about because we were going to get a spin. And that was exactly what happened. I took the .38 and dumped it in the harbor and Keith told the police that it was Marlon's toy gun. I was the one who took the gun off Keith in the harbor. I had to disarm him or he would have used it."

In Spanish Tony's version of the story, Keith finishes congratulating him on his amazing getaway and then goes inside the villa where he gets on the phone to the Stones' local lawyers. Three of them immediately race over to the villa to plot the best course of action. After much discussion, they decide to contact the police. Later that night, an officer appears at Nellcote with a writ ordering Keith and Tony to appear at the police commissioner's office at ten the next morning. After he leaves, Keith pulls Anita aside and begins to harangue her for having it off with Tommy the night before. He also lets it slip that Tony was the one who told him the story. After chanting evil spells at Tony, Anita calls him a "filthy squealer."

Some time later, Tommy accuses Tony of trying to get rid of him so he can have Anita all to himself. "You filthy bastard," Tony says. "If she was my old woman, I'd knock your head off." Fortunately for Tony, Keith then walks into the room. "You should be doing this, Keith, not me," Tony says. "It's your woman he fucked." Realizing he has just incriminated himself in front of Tommy, Tony desperately tries to recover by saying, "Well, you know what I mean, don't you?" Tony then challenges Keith to do something about it right now. Turning on his heel, Keith stalks from the room.

At breakfast the next morning, Keith tells Tony that he just read about Errol Flynn getting caught in a similar punch-up during his time on the French Riviera. When Flynn was ordered to report to the police commissioner, he refused to go and they had to come to his house to see him. Deciding that whatever was good enough for Errol Flynn will certainly work for him, Keith chooses not to go with Tony to the police commissioner. At the meeting, the police check Tony's papers and charge him with assault.

When the police come to Nellcote to speak with Keith that afternoon, he explains that because of the harbormaster's unprovoked attack, Marlon banged his head on the ground and he now intends to sue the man for assaulting his young son. The Stones' lawyers and the police then get together to discuss the matter. How much money changes hands during this meeting, no one can say for certain. That evening, however, the chief of police comes to dine at Nellcote. Keith provides him with a few auto-graphed Rolling Stones albums. And, as Tony writes, "that was the end of that little problem as far as he was concerned."

Since it was Tony and not Keith who hit the harbormaster, the Stones' lawyers urge him to take the blame for the entire inci-dent. Before the case can be heard in court a few weeks later, Tony leaves the country. The Stones' lawyers plead guilty on his behalf and Keith pays his twelve thousand dollar fine. Or so Tony claims.

Bill Wyman, always a far more reliable source, writes that Keith "got into a spot of bother with the law when his car was in a collision with another containing two Italian tourists." Keith then got in a "furious row" and demanded "immediate compen-sation in dollars. They refused and the argument escalated into a fight." Accused of "injuring a French port official," Keith had to go to court in Nice where both he and the harbormaster "pre-sented medical certificates proving that they had been injured." Keith was charged with assault and battery and "was told he would go to trial" but the charge was withdrawn "after Keith went to the magistrate's office and apologised—but the French police had marked Keith's card."

A few weeks later, Keith tells a reporter from *Rolling Stone* magazine, "We had a car crash down here and settled it and some little bureaucrat from the local harbor has to butt in so someone mentioned, 'Oh, that's one of the Rolling Stones.' 'Is it?' BANG. Someone leaps in. Telephones flying. And when someone hits them back, it's pistols. 'They've got a gun. Call the police.' Mention the Rolling Stones and get a smack in the face."

And, despite what Tony claims transpired in that very crowded bed at Nellcote the night before the punch-up, Tommy goes right on living at Nellcote. But then as a couple, Keith and Anita have already weathered so many storms of every conceivable nature that physical fidelity would seem to be the least of their concerns. All the same, doing it with someone else while your partner lies passed out in the same bed does seem a bit much even for them. But then as Keith once said from the dock at Old Bailey, "We are not old men. We are not worried about petty morals."

In terms of the Rolling Stones and their women, no truer words have ever been spoken. With the exception of Charlie and Shirley Watts, whose marriage seems completely traditional, and Bianca, who would never engage in such shenanigans with people for whom she has so little regard, nearly all those in the Stones' inner circle will in time have it off with one another. Although some of the couplings seem so unlikely as to challenge the laws of physical probability, they happen nonetheless. Some are just furtive one-night stands on the road. Others develop into full-blown affairs that drive everyone crazy.

Considering how small the Stones' inner circle actually happens to be, the sheer logistics of arranging such extremely dangerous liaisons would stagger the talents of a NASA engineer. Still, long before such behavior becomes a cultural norm, the Stones' women seem completely emancipated, taking their pleasure when and where they please. And if anyone should wonder why these people choose to engage in such risky business so close to home, the simple answer is because they can.

Fueled by drugs as well as the kind of freedom that only comes with unlimited privilege, the Stones and their female companions are also completely isolated from the real world. Back when kings and queens still ruled the world, those who lived at court disported themselves in a similar manner. Or, as Marshall Chess will later say of the Stones, "In their rock and roll world, it was understandable. It's very hard to explain because it was like you had entered another world. It was like going to Mars. An alternate reality."

Still, if for no other reason than to get Keith off the street before he does some real damage to himself and others, the time has come for the Rolling Stones to begin work on their new album. Which does not also mean that it is about to happen.

# 8

**On June 7** after a four-day drive from London, the Rolling Stones recording truck, also known as the mobile, finally arrives at Nellcote. For a solid month before leaving on his honeymoon, Mick would pile along with Keith, Jo Bergman, and Ian Stewart into Jerry Pompili's vintage 1964 Volkswagen bus, the hippie vehicle of choice not only in America but all over Europe as well, to journey into the French countryside to look at places where the band might record. "Of course," Pompili would later say, "no one liked anything. We wasted a month and then in the end they decided to do it in Keith's house. Typical Stones."

As Andy Johns will later note, it was not as though there were unlimited choices available. "There was that one studio in France called Le Chateau," he recalled, "which was fucking awful. I worked there years later and they wouldn't have liked it. The accommodations were bad. The loos were always backed up and while you were trying to eat your dinner, you could smell the sewage. No. They would have had to go to Paris but they wanted to live in the south of France. So, we've got the truck? Bingo!"

In large part, the truck exists not just because the Stones

have wasted so much money over the years by booking expensive studio time by the hour only to then show up late or not at all for sessions but also because of the residual guilt Mick and Keith still feel about allowing Andrew Oldham to boot Ian Stewart out of the band in 1965 because he neither looked nor acted like a pop star. "I think by way of making it up to him," Johns will later say, "they built the truck and said, 'Here ya go, Stu. You run this.' The idea being that if it made a profit, Stu would get a fair old chunk of that. And I think had he not died, they would have given him the thing. And he could have had his own business."

A huge, vaguely Fascist looking British Leyland van painted in camouflage colors, the truck has a top speed of sixty miles an hour and weighs twelve and a half tons fully loaded. Purchased for two thousand pounds, the truck has been acoustically treated, air-conditioned, and outfitted with recording equipment modeled on the system used at Olympic Studios in London, long one of the Stones' favorite places to record. The board is a custom-made twenty-track Helios console. Four large Tannoy speakers, each about four and a half feet tall, serve as monitors. There is a sixteen-track 3M tape machine and an eight-track Ampex. There are also a talkback system and a black-and-white camera, both of which are meant to enable whoever sits at the board to see and communicate with the band as they play. Because neither work very well, Andy Johns spends most of the summer running from the truck into the basement at Nellcote so he can talk to the musicians.

By the time work on the truck is done, the Stones have pumped an astronomical sixty-five thousand pounds into building what Johns will later call "the first proper mobile in Europe." The band then uses it at Stargroves, Mick's country estate in

England, to record tracks that appear on *Sticky Fingers* as well as "Sweet Black Angel," which eventually makes its way onto *Exile On Main St.*

"Originally," Andy Johns will later recall, "Stu was supposed to find another house where we'd park the truck and people would show up. Because he couldn't find anything, he looked at the basement at Nellcote and they all thought, 'Yeah, this would probably work.' When I got there, I looked and I went, 'Geez, this could be a little tough.' And it turned out to be—a little tough."

Before recording can begin down there, Ian Stewart first has to deal with the echo. Because all the rooms are empty and the walls are made of plaster, the overall effect is like shouting inside a cave. Stu solves this problem by buying a large amount of the thickest, cheapest carpet he can find. He then carpets the walls, ceilings, and floor of the room in which he expects the Stones will record. "We started off in this one room down near the kitchen that I thought would work and it didn't work at all," Johns says. "Sounded fucking dreadful. So I moved them to another room. It was still very tough recording there. Trying to get a sound at that place was like pulling teeth. Unlike Mick's house in England, which was very easy."

Once the mobile has been parked by the villa's front steps, it has to be plugged in. Following the dictum first annunciated by Chip Monck, the lighting designer who firmly believed that in order to make rock 'n' roll happen, it was his God-given right to tap into any available source of electricity, legal or otherwise, Stu hooks up the mobile to a nearby utility pole. What Stu does not know is that French voltage tends to zoom all over the place.

"It was Stu's idea to do that with the electricity," Johns

recalls. "The utility pole was outside the villa on the road. They ran a line through the garden to the truck. The idea was, 'Oh well, let's just tap into the electricity supply on the street. Then it'll save Keith money.' Of course the electricity was going on and off constantly. Everything, all the guitar amps as well as all the recording gear, were hooked up to the truck so if there was just a slight variation in the voltage coming in—Bing!—the breaker on the fuse thing would go. Unbelievable. False economy. We were conspiring against ourselves, I suppose. By working there."

Shortly after the mobile arrives, what in retrospect will prove to be the most significant event of the summer occurs. Keith and Tommy Weber decide to spend the day driving go-karts around a local track. Based on Keith's driving record in England, it should come as no surprise to anyone that calamity results. Deciding to have a go at Tommy, who in any vehicle is the better driver, Keith takes a running shot at him with his go-kart. "It definitely felt like murder," Tommy recalls. "He was trying to knock into me. He drove straight at me and the thing flipped. He didn't realize what happens when you pull one kart over the wheels of another. It goes up and the kart turned over. I was still trying to slow the cars down and I had him with his head in my lap, the go-kart on top of him, and his back scraping along the tarmac. His back was like raw steak. A little later he looked at me and he said, 'Okay, Tommy, I think it's about time you went to the doctor and get him to get us some you know what.' Which everyone had been staying away from. And that was the beginning of it. The go-kart accident instigated the opiates."

Since the Rolling Stones make it a practice never to go anywhere without having a physician around on whom they can depend, their local doctor by this point has already been sending around what in France is called a *piquer* (someone like a district nurse) to administer injectibles at Nellcote. To this point in time, the substance being injected is Vitamin B-12. Back then, this practice was all the rage for those with money on both sides of the Atlantic in high-pressure situations who could not be bothered to exercise in order to keep the old immune system up.

"Keith was absolutely in physical pain," says Tommy Weber. "And he knew what it was about. And he knew what it was going to do. He saw it in the world. He was actually pissed off that he had to be the person who had to keep all these people in line, including Mick, who was the whipping boy. When you realize that, you understand that Keith was free. He could go as far as he wanted to. He could allow Mick to take all the judgment of the straight world while he was able to really try and find out what the fuck was going on with the music, the recording, and the whole meaning of it."

Confirming Tommy's account, albeit in far less specific terms, Bill Wyman will later write that after the go-kart accident, Keith looked bad and hurt worse. In terms of working on the new album, there was also some "downtime" while Keith recovered.

At long last, we have the true time line of how it all went down at Nellcote thirty-five years ago. Until shortly after the mobile arrived in France on June 7, Keith and Anita were clean. To be sure, they were smoking hashish and snorting cocaine and downing an entire bottle of tequila at a single sitting, but heroin, despite what Spanish Tony claims, had not yet entered the picture.

Whether it is just a simple desire to numb the physical pain that causes Keith to begin using again or the realization that with the mobile parked outside the villa, the time has finally come for him to begin work on the new album and that in order to do so, he will not only have to go down into that dank basement each night but also plumb the hidden depths of his own musical soul, an expedition he does not feel he can undertake without serious chemical assistance, no one can say for sure. "That was why he said it," Tommy Weber explains. "Obviously, it had been weighing on his mind and he'd been trying not to start himself back up again. Knowing that the work was there and the work required that level of decadence. I don't think it was being in an altered state to make the music. It was more the way of life. 'It's only rock 'n' roll, but I like it.' I *like* it. It was the liking, the decadent state, that gave them that fantastic self-confidence to create that incredible work."

Whatever his real reasons may have been, Keith was the one who placed the order. And so the madness at Villa Nellcote that summer began in earnest.

# 9

**At some point** during the second week in June, the Stones actually begin playing together for the first time at Nellcote. From then on, Bill Wyman remembers them working every night from eight until three in the morning for the rest of the month. However, "not everyone turned up every night. This was, for me, one of the major frustrations of this whole period. For our previous two albums we had worked well and listened to producer Jimmy Miller. At Nellcote things were very different and it took me a while to understand why."

Down in the cellar, the Stones discover another problem— the humidity that tends to collect in the basements of large houses on the French Riviera during the summer. "You must have heard the stories about how impossible it was to work at that place because of the humidity," says Andy Johns. "The guitars would go out of tune halfway through a song. Always. You'd stop them or they'd go to the end and you'd go, 'We have to do that again because we're going out of tune.'"

Despite these problems, everyone still believes that recording the album at the villa is a brilliant plan. The reason for this is simple. In the deck of cards that is the Rolling Stones, Keith has now become the grinning joker. Although he was the one who always railed the loudest at Brian for turning up so stoned at sessions that he would sometimes fall asleep on the floor, thereby forcing Keith to record all the guitar parts on his own, he now lives in a time zone all his own.

Since Keith has already proven there is no knowing when or if he will ever arrive at any session on time, and getting him from one place to another, most especially when he has other things on his mind, can be a nightmare of major proportions, how better to solve this problem than by making his home into the Stones' new recording studio? When the Stones need Keith to record at Nellcote, all Mick will have to do is knock loudly on the pipes and Keith will come scurrying down the stairs with guitar in hand, eager and ready to join the band. Wholeheartedly, Keith himself has signed on to the plan. When asked if the Stones really mean to record their new album at Nellcote, he grins and says, "Yeah, right in my own basement, as it turns out. After months of searching, I end up sitting on it." No truer words have ever been spoken.

With serious work on the new album just beginning, yet another unfortunate motoring incident occurs. Tommy Weber, who has not slept in two or three days, is driving Olivier Boelen's rental car on the Grand Corniche at four in the morning when he becomes convinced that Puss, whose spirit is still within the forty-nine day grace period before it leaves the earth for good, is in fact at the wheel. Insofar as he can tell, the two of them are on the track at Lake Garda or Nurburgring. Just as they would do back then so he could learn the course before a race, Tommy is wearing a blindfold and telling her what section of the track is coming up as she drives.

In truth, Tommy has fallen asleep behind the wheel. He finally wakes up only to see a rickety old French truck bound for market heading right toward him on a narrow, twisting road on which there is only room for one vehicle at a time. As he comes to, Tommy is telling Puss where to hit the truck so both vehicles will not go careening over the mountainside when they collide. "She was pulling me into the next bardo," he recalls. "But then there was someone screaming *'Tommy! Tommy! Tommy!'* and I finally realized it was me driving, and this truck was literally bearing down on me. I hit the truck exactly where I was telling Puss to do it and we entangled and everything was fine."

Bailing out with all the dope, Tommy eventually makes his way down the mountain to the first building he finds which turns out to be a nunnery. He runs inside screaming, "Morphine! *Morphine!* I want *morphine!*" and of course "the old dears sit me down and give me morphine very sweetly." After Jimmy Miller and horn player Jim Price come to fetch Tommy a few days later, they take him to see the ever-useful local doctor who puts a plaster cast on Tommy's broken wrist.

Never one to let an injury keep him down, Tommy then goes water skiing in the bay with the cast wrapped in plastic in order to impress a young woman whom his son Jake remembers as looking a lot like Raquel Welch. "I was in the boat with the kids," Tommy recalls, "and we had one of those huge ferries bearing down on us. And we all had to dive in the water to get out of its way. It just wouldn't stop. I think Keith had taught Charlie how to swim and maybe Jake as well. It was very lucky we survived that. Thanks, Keith."

For those who think the scene at Nellcote could not possibly become more surreal, consider the real version of the story Anita will tell many years later in which she distinctly remembers building a raft with Bobby Keys during the early days at Nellcote and then rowing out at night into the bay to see what was happening on the American naval vessels anchored there. "We used to do that lots," she tells John Perry, "rowing out in the night . . . check the Americans out, shoutin' up to the sailors, see what they had." ("What they had" being of course a euphemism for illegal contraband that could be smoked or sniffed.)

While the concept of Anita and Bobby Keys building anything that could hold water for more than a millisecond is more than enough to boggle the mind even now, the actual story is far more fantastic, the sort of experience that can only occur when people who live together are getting high on a daily basis, thereby putting basic reality itself in doubt. It all starts one morning on the back patio at Nellcote as Anita peers through a pair of German optic artillery range finder binoculars so powerful that she often uses them to look right into Aristotle Onassis' bedroom on his massive white power yacht, the *Christina*.

Bobbing at anchor at the bar of the harbor out beyond all the battleships and the biggest yachts in the world is, yes, wait for it, an actual galleon, replete with sails and a clanking lantern, which looks much like the abandoned and derelict brigantine, the *Mary Celeste,* or perhaps the *Flying Dutchman* of yore, the lost ship doomed to sail for eternity around the Cape of Good Hope in Africa. Excited as all get out by this amazing apparition, Anita implores Keith to come check it out. Keith, who has already had quite enough of Anita's enormously rich fantasy life, not only declines the invitation but also offers the opinion that she has gone off her head. At the moment, he has far better things to do than stare at ghost ships silhouetted against the morning sky.

Turning to Tommy, Anita says, "Look, you've got to see this. I've been trying to tell Keith but he won't listen to me." Tommy, who has already spotted the galleon through the World War I binoculars, says, "Yeah, I presume it's just a joke." Anita says, "No, it's the real thing. I've had a real good look at it." Never one to pass on any sort of adventure, Tommy says, "Well, we've got to get on it." Without missing a beat, Anita replies, "That's exactly what I was thinking."

Heading down to the harbor, Tommy and Anita enlist the aid of some friendly locals to commandeer a fishing boat tied up at the quay and begin chunk-chunking out toward the galleon. Naturally, the sea begins to rise, becoming rough and choppy. Halfway to the ship, which no one is yet completely convinced is actually there, the fishing boat runs out of gas. Because Anita simply will not take no for an answer, turning around is not an option. Like the master and commander he was born to be, Tommy says, "It's okay, boys. All hands to the oars." Rowing hard as they can, they draw ever nearer to the galleon, which they now see has to be at least seventy feet long but sits so high in the water that it could never be boarded without someone lowering the gangplank.

With the galleon's lantern clanking loudly above their heads as they bob about in the fishing boat, Tommy starts banging on the side of the vessel with an oar, trying to raise somebody on deck. But no one is on board. Never one to be daunted by logistics, Anita says, "Let's get on this." Tommy replies, "Are you sure? It's very rough." Anita says, "Of course. What do you mean?" She then starts calling him *un lache,* a French slang term for "coward." Tommy, who has already been told by Anita that his real drug of choice is alcohol, thinks she is saying, "You lush. Like a drinker." Still, he manages to reply, "I'm not going to jump aboard that. Not if my life depends on it." Anita responds, "Well, I will. My curiosity depends on it." And then she tries some "suicidal jumps."

Because the sea has become far too rough for such activities, Tommy and Anita finally realize there is no way either of them can get on board. Turning the fishing boat around, they row back into the harbor and return to Nellcote. "We never swam out at night to a naval ship," Tommy says. "This was it. The galleon. It was an *old* naval ship. The *Mary Celeste.* The *Flying Dutchman.* And the story just got mixed up. But it was truly one of the most wonderful experiences of my life. Like something out of Homer. Because by dawn, the galleon was gone. *Gone.*"

Back at the villa, Anita tries to explain to Keith where she and Tommy have been. Not surprisingly, he does not believe her story. A somewhat violent altercation between the two of them ensues and Anita says, "That's it. I'm not standing another moment of this. C'mon, Tommy." Grabbing Marlon, she joins Tommy and his sons in his car. Going directly to the bank, she empties some of the Stones' accounts and they both then repair to Tommy's house in the hills. Tommy, who has been after

Anita since he first laid eyes on her years ago, could not be more pleased.

Until Keith comes looking for him. While this visit could be yet another opportunity for Keith to demonstrate his pugilistic skills, not to mention also his marksmanship with a handgun at close range, he never actually makes it to Tommy's house, stopping instead for a meal at a nearby hotel on the Route Napoleon. Having been through this sort of thing before, Keith then departs, leaving it to Tommy and Anita to sort themselves out. Although Tommy considers Anita to be "the most incredibly beautiful super woman," he soon comes to realize that she is not only way out of his league but is also using him to get Keith's attention. After Anita tells Tommy that he is too "boring" for her, he takes her back down the hill to Nellcote.

Fortunately for all concerned, Keith himself happens to be in St. Tropez at that moment, a blessing in disguise for Tommy who admits that if he had run into him, he would have been "shitless." In time, everything between the three of them settles down and works itself out in a completely civilized manner. "I thought Keith would never speak to me again," Tommy recalls, "but he was cool and charming at all times. I would come down to Nellcote every now and then and see everybody but I could tell the house was getting more and more decadent. They didn't need me and I was putting the radio thing together so I was more or less a visitor and not a resident anymore."

Tommy continues to pursue the Radio Rolling Stone project until August when the son of the head of Radio Monte Carlo with whom he has been working, "a partaker," OD's in an apartment in Monte Carlo. "We waited long enough to see that the rescue people were there," Tommy says, "and I thought, 'Well,

the writing's on the wall. Things are getting very odd at Nellcote.'" Grabbing his sons, he says, "Come on, we're off." Going
to his house in the mountains, Tommy "buries the necessities."
Leaving his car at the airport in Nice, Tommy Weber boards the
next plane to Paris, flies to Portugal, and spends the next three
years traveling the world with his two young sons, never to
return again to France.

# 10

**On July 6** as the Rolling Stones finally go to ground in the basement at Nellcote, beginning two weeks of endless jamming that
will not yield a single track that can be used on the new album, a
black plague of death brought about by the unbridled use of
heroin sweeps through the international rock 'n' roll jet-set in
Europe. With the drug itself as the connective tissue that binds
together all those in this particular social class who are using it,
there is far less than six degrees of separation between the Stones
and the first casualties in what will soon become an endless litany
of drug-related death.

It is but a few short months since Jean de Breteuil stood in
the living room at Nellcote offering up his Corsican connection
in Marseilles so those at the villa could have access to a regular
supply of smack. When he returns to London, de Breteuil stays in
Keith's house on Cheyne Walk where he begins an affair with
Talitha Pol Getty, the exotic beauty who at the moment is
estranged from Jean Paul Getty Jr., the son of the richest man in
the world.

Five years earlier, the Gettys were the most fashionable
couple in the world, well known among the cognoscenti in London and Paris for throwing fabulously stoned-out hippie jet-set

parties at their palace in Marrakesh where Brian Jones was a house guest and John Lennon and Paul McCartney came to celebrate New Year's Eve. In one of the iconic photographs of the era, the Gettys, young and beautiful and unbelievably rich, stand on their rooftop terrace in kaftans with the Atlas Mountains behind them.

According to Spanish Tony, Jean Paul Getty Jr. is now "so chronically addicted to heroin that he was snorting a gram a day without managing to achieve any noticeable effect." While going through withdrawal in Rome, Getty falls in love with another woman. Deciding to leave her husband, Talitha Getty flies to London where she begins her affair with de Breteuil. Planning to return to London in less than a week, Talitha Getty leaves for Rome. Along with Marianne Faithfull, de Breteuil flies to Paris where he supplies Jim Morrison of The Doors with the heroin that causes his death on July 3.

Nine days later, Talitha Getty is found unconscious in her husband's penthouse apartment on Via Della Ara Coeli in Rome. Thirty-one years old, she dies three days later without ever regaining consciousness. Although the cause of death is listed as barbiturate and alcohol poisoning, it is later revealed she died from a massive injection of heroin. A month later, de Breteuil dies of apparently the same cause.

At some point during July, Ginger Cooper, born Felicity Meredith-Owens but nicknamed "Ginger" for the color of her hair, who lives with the photographer Michael Cooper but has never married him, takes her own life, apparently while undergoing rehab in Bowden House. Not long after, Michael Cooper comes to visit Keith and Anita at Nellcote. Although he looks tanned and healthy, his hands shake as he drinks constantly from a bottle of liquid methadone. "God," Anita says to him, "you look so healthy outside but you must be rotting inside."

Eighteen months later, Michael Cooper, who as his son Adam will later write, had already gotten "off the heavy drugs" and was "trying to sort his life out," takes an overdose of Mandrax, washes it down with a bottle of Scotch, and ends his own life. According to Spanish Tony, Keith and Anita are "bitterly upset." Concerning his father's suicide, Adam Cooper writes, "I have often been asked why he did it. The answer I give which I truly believe to be the case was that it was an accumulation of so many factors—the heady decade of the 60s was over and the initial dreams and expressions of the youth had not materialized. Vietnam was in its full throes and getting worse, the Stones had exiled, and Michael, sensitive as he was, was dragged down by it all. Very sad, as I am convinced that if he had managed to hang on, he would be doing something of great creativity and importance today."

Although people are dropping like flies, no one seems to get the message. "I remember Jim Morrison dying that summer, yeah," Andy Johns will later say. "But it doesn't get through when you're on the stuff. I don't think anyone really thought about it. There was also that thing that this is part of the price you have to pay. During those years, lots and lots of people died. It was just like, 'Oh well, too bad.'"

At Nellcote, Keith and Anita keep right on using. According to Tony, they are now subsidizing their regular supply of heroin from the Corsicans by also buying from "les cowboys," whom Jerry Pompili remembers as "these local guys from Villefranche that Keith befriended because we all used to go hang out at Albert's, this restaurant, hotel, and whorehouse too I think, that was right on the port. They were young guys in their twenties—anywhere from four to seven or eight of them—I could never keep track. I considered them more petty thieves than anything else. Hustlers who would sell a woman, contraband, cigarettes, whatever."

"I was the person who found and employed them," Tommy Weber recalls. "I was the go-between. Between them and Keith and Anita and the band. They were just local guys sort of hanging around like groupies and we thought we'd make use of them and so they became the assistant gardeners and cooks, just to make them feel important and get them to obey orders and basically keep them under control. And they would also go down to score in Marseilles because they knew all those things. I could see if you caused trouble with them, they could be trouble. And that was exactly what happened when I left Nellcote, or so I'm told. That was what Keith and Anita saw as part of my value. I knew the coast like the back of my hand because I'd lived there all my life on and off and consequently I knew how extremely dangerous these Corsican French bandits could be."

Although the cowboys are now firmly in place at Nellcote, the sheer volume of drugs being used on a daily basis at the villa keeps increasing so rapidly that demand soon outstrips supply. After being sent back to London to avoid going to trial for the Beaulieu punch-up, Spanish Tony is ordered by Keith "to send some of the dope he had hidden at Cheyne Walk out to him." For the first time, Tony is "frankly scared. International drug smuggling is taken slightly more seriously than mass murder in most of Europe, and I had no desire to spend the rest of my life rotting in a French jail."

After spending several days "puzzling over the best way to

handle the chore," Tony decides to go shopping at Hamley's, London's premier toy emporium on Regent Street. Inside a toy piano, he conceals an ounce of cocaine. Without saying a word to the driver, Tony slips the toy piano into a van containing records, rugs, and furnishings bound for Nellcote. When the shipment arrives, Keith calls Tony at three in the morning demanding to know why he has not sent him anything, only to be told he can find what he is looking for by unscrewing the keyboard of the toy piano. Taking direct action, Keith smashes it open so he can access the contents.

As though to confirm that where the transport of illegal substances across foreign borders is concerned, there is no limit as to the elaborate schemes that the human mind can conceive, a Stones insider on his way to London stops by to say good-bye to Keith at Nellcote one day only to be asked if he can bring some grass back with him. "I said, 'What are you, crazy?'" the insider will later recall. "And he said, 'No, no, no. There's a perfect way to do it.' He told me to go to Harrod's and buy a two-pound box of chocolates. Then take it home, steam the cellophane off, and carefully open it up. There are two layers. Take out the top layer and throw the bottom layer away and put anywhere between a quarter to a half a pound of grass on the bottom and then get all these English pennies and use several of them to get the weight just right. Then carefully put it all back together, re-glue the cellophane on, take the receipt back to Harrod's, and have them gift-wrap it with a nice little card. Then I carried it under my arm through Customs. It was a gift-wrapped Harrod's box of chocolates. They would never have thought of opening anything like that."

Considering the level of drug use at Nellcote, it should come as no surprise that nothing much gets done in the basement during the first half of July. As Bill Wyman will later write, "For two weeks we recorded jam sessions and most of those nights were dull and boring. Recording in Keith's basement had not turned out to be a guarantee of his presence. Sometimes he wouldn't come downstairs at all."

Even when he does, Keith will often pop in for just a moment and then explain he has to go upstairs where no one dares follow him so he can put Marlon to bed. "Even Mick would never go up there," Andy Johns will later say. "It was as if hell existed upstairs, ironically enough." What makes this all the more frustrating is that Keith can usually be found in the living room, the kitchen, or out on the back porch from four until six or seven each day playing his guitar by himself.

"Just a riff going round and round and round," Johns recalls. "Then he'd disappear. He loved to play but not when I had the tape rolling. So he would disappear and if you did manage to get all them hooked up and trying to do something, it would go for maybe an hour and a half, two hours, then Keith would go, and this was the euphemism, 'I have to put Marlon to bed.' Which meant he was going to go upstairs and have a fix. And of course he would nod off in bed. And we'd all be sitting there. Two, three in the morning. And everyone was too scared to go up there."

Rose Taylor, who often spends the night at Nellcote waiting for Mick Taylor to be done recording so she can drive them both back home, recalls, "Keith would be carrying Marlon asleep and up he'd go with him to bed. And then you wouldn't see him for hours. He was so discreet. I never saw Keith do anything but drink Jack Daniel's and smoke joints. I had no clue at all. They had to be this way because of the law. I suppose they were geniuses at concealment. Discretion, with a capital 'D.' And it had to be that way because this was what was going to blow it for everybody, ultimately."

After putting up with it for as long as he can, Andy Johns finally takes a stand one night and says, "Look, one of us has to go up there and wake the bastard up." Along with producer Jimmy Miller and Mick Jagger, Johns then finds himself standing at the foot of the stairs at Nellcote in what he calls "trepidation, as it were, literally almost drawing straws. Mick went, 'I'm not fucking going up there.' And I said, 'Well, neither am I.' So it fell to poor old Jimmy. 'Oh, okay.' And he went up there. Keith had nodded off and he still had the needle stuck in his arm. So that was exactly what was happening."

As Bill Wyman will later write, "Keith was getting out of it a lot and in retaliation Mick wouldn't turn up some nights. The principal spectators at these games were me, Charlie, and Mick T. Stu . . . was equally frustrated and his 33rd birthday on 17 July was probably one of the least memorable for him."

Which brings us back once more to the central thread of this drama, the continuing story of Mick and Keith struggling against all odds, virtually every illicit drug known to man, and one another to begin work on their new album. To be sure, Mick has done nothing to help the process by getting married and then disappearing from the scene to enjoy his honeymoon with Bianca. But even once he returns, Mick seems like an outsider. Every now and then, looking somewhat lost, he turns up at Nellcote in the afternoon, sits down at the piano, and does his best to get Keith involved in writing some new songs. All to no avail.

As with everything in their lives, Mick and Keith even approach the craft of songwriting from opposite ends of the spectrum. Like the successful businessman he could have been, Mick likes to sit down with pen and paper during the day to work out what the Stones will record that night in the studio. Not Keith. As he will tell Michael Watts of *Melody Maker* once the album is finally done, "I can't sit around on a song for too long. I like to get in the studio and write it there. Mick, on the other hand, likes to have it all worked out and rehearsed before he goes in. That's the basic difference between us. I get bored quicker."

Extremely sensitive yet also completely indifferent to one another at the same time, Mick and Keith begin an endless game of cat-and-mouse in which the ultimate goal seems to be to see who can piss the other one off the most. "Mick would be in the basement," Anita will later tell John Perry, "and Keith would not go down there. Keith always likes to give Mick a hard time, you know." As every English schoolboy knows, turnabout is fair play. So if Keith is giving Mick a hard time, then that is exactly what Mick will give him in return. As June Shelley will later note, "The pressure was not so much to get the record done as it was that Mick was not there when they needed him."

In his defense, Mick now has some issues of his own. To wit, the rigors of married life. One day, Mick decides that he wants to buy a motorcycle. June Shelley finds him a Suzuki but because Mick will have to wait three days to pick it up, he goes out and buys one on his own. Eager as a schoolboy to try out his new toy, Mick returns to the lovely home he shares with Bianca in Biot only to learn that his wife, who is by now quite pregnant and not feeling all that well, has gone upstairs to rest. So he asks Nathalie Delon, who is staying with them at the time, if she would like to hop on back for a ride. Off they go on the back roads of the French Riviera to visit Bill Wyman in Grasse.

When Bianca wakes up from her nap, she comes downstairs and asks, "Where's Meek?" Looking around, she asks, "Where's Nathalie?" A long moment passes before someone says, "She went with Mick." Bianca says, "Oh?" Turning around, she goes upstairs, packs a bag, and tells Alan Dunn, Mick's aide-de-camp, "Take me to the airport right away." Dutifully, Dunn drives her to the Nice airport where they book a flight that she misses, quite possibly on purpose. Before leaving the house in Biot, Bianca has told the housekeeper where she is going so the message will get to Mick.

After booking herself to Paris on the next flight, Bianca sits down behind a pillar on the upper level so she can see Mick when he comes into the airport. When Mick returns from his completely innocent ride through the French countryside with Nathalie Delon, the housekeeper informs him that his wife has gone to the airport. Naturally, he follows her there. When Mick arrives, he and Bianca have somewhat of a scene and she decides not to get on the plane. As June Shelley explains, "She was just starting to show and not feeling all that great and it was extremely hot and Mick had dared to go off with another woman. It was about control. Not that she suspected him of anything. And also Nathalie was her friend. So how dare Nathalie do that to her? Go on the first ride with Mick on the new motorcycle."

At some point in the proceedings, someone comes up with

the bright idea of having all the Stones stay at Nellcote so they can get some work done. Since Mick Taylor has never learned to drive, it takes Rose forever to bring him to Nellcote and then take him back home at four in the morning. Bill and Charlie also live a good distance from the villa. So the plan makes eminent sense to one and all. According to Spanish Tony, Bianca, who absolutely refuses to go near Nellcote, declares, "I never want to see that cow Anita again. I'm staying in Paris, and you can do just what you like." Off she goes once more to the Nice airport. This time, she does not miss her flight.

Mick then begins flying from Paris to record at Nellcote only to return to the City of Light to be with Bianca. "It was a ridiculous arrangement," Spanish Tony will later write, adding, "Keith appeared not to notice." The Stones however are now spending so much time at the villa that they are being billed through their own office for expenses incurred while recording there.

After Mick spends three consecutive days at Nellcote, calling Bianca in Paris every night, she tells him to return at once or not bother coming back at all. When Mick tells her he will only be another day or two at the most, she slams down the phone. When he tries to ring her afterward, there is no reply. Five days later, he flies to Paris but cannot find her. In time, she returns to their suite at L'Hotel, the Left Bank Hotel favored by Oscar Wilde, who, as he lay dying there on November 30, 1900, said, "Either that wall paper goes, or I do."

Although the decor does not figure in their decision, Mick and Bianca leave L'Hotel at the end of July to fly to London, where Mick announces they are expecting a child in September. They then repair to Dublin for a summer holiday with the

Guinness family. As Bill Wyman will later write, "This further frustrated our recording process and Marshall Chess told me, 'In talking to Charlie, Mick Taylor, and Keith, I get the feeling that things are really moving at a slow pace. I am very concerned with this.'"

As well he should be. With Keith here and Mick there, nothing much at all is now going on down in the basement of Nellcote. Call it a stalemate. A Mexican standoff of the first order. With our two central characters no longer even in the same country, recording comes to a halt, thereby enabling us to turn our attention to the full-blown party at Nellcote, which now seems to be growing at an exponential rate.

# 11

**Ah, the dog days** of summer in the south of France. As a cauldron of scalding heat envelops Nellcote from dawn to dusk, making it virtually impossible to do much more than contemplate when you will next submerge yourself in the cooling sea, the tension between Mick and Keith keeps right on building without ever boiling over into the kind of violent storm that might clear the air and make it possible for work on the album to proceed. When Mick returns from his holiday, he finds two new guests in residence at Nellcote, the brilliant singer-songwriter Gram Parsons and his young wife Gretchen. Almost immediately, they become caught up in the crossfire.

Thirty-three years after dying from an overdose of heroin in a motel room in Joshua Tree, California, on September 19, 1973, just two months before his twenty-seventh birthday, Gram Parsons will be named to the eighty-seventh slot on *Rolling Stone* magazine's list of the one hundred greatest popular musical artists who ever lived. Immediately preceded by Tupac Shakur and followed by Miles Davis, Parsons' standing as one of the immortals of rock is vouched for by none other than his old pal, Keith, who writes, "Like I know the blues, Gram Parsons knew country music—every nuance, every great country song that was ever written. And he could express it all—in his song writing. But he also had intelligence and honesty. That's the kind of guy I like to hang with. Also, he loved to get stoned. At the time, that was an added plus."

By the time Gram Parsons comes to stay at Nellcote at the end of July, he is so out of it that it is sometimes hard to understand how anyone can communicate with him unless they are playing along as he sings. Jo Bergman, never one to judge anyone around the Stones too harshly, will later say Parsons was "a physical wreck, totally zonked out of his head."

Already an ex-Byrd (having left the group before they toured South Africa because Keith told him, "Man, we don't go there,") and an ex-Burrito Brother, Gram Parsons first began hanging out with the Stones at Stephen Stills' house in Laurel Canyon shortly before the 1969 American tour. His deep and immediate connection with Keith, not to mention the time he then spent at Redlands tutoring Keith in the subtleties of country music, resulted in The Flying Burrito Brothers releasing their version of Mick and Keith's "Wild Horses" before anyone ever heard the Stones do the song.

Because Gram literally begged Keith for the gig and then paid for his band to go there out of his own pocket, the Burritos played for half an hour at Altamont before Crosby, Stills, Nash, and Young took the stage. Gram and Michelle Phillips, the actress and former member of The Mamas and The Papas, were

the last two people allowed on board the helicopter that evacu-
ated the Stones that night. So it is not as though he does not have
his own history with the band.

On the English tour that preceded the move to Nellcote,
Gram and Gretchen Parsons were an integral part of Keith and
Anita's entirely self-contained traveling group. Unlike Keith, who
could ingest a staggering variety of substances without losing
control, Gram Parsons seemed so out of it at one show that
someone had to be delegated to lead him to the stage so he could
watch the Stones. Promptly getting lost, Gram Parsons and his
guide climbed endless sets of stairs to a door that they then
swung open only to find themselves standing on the balcony of
the cinema next door where *Myra Breckinridge* was playing on
an enormous screen in an otherwise empty house. Surreal as the
experience may have been, Gram Parsons had long since become
accustomed to being lost. Like Blanche Dubois, he often relied on
the kindness of strangers whom he believed to be his friends.

Still, when he was lucid, there was no one whom Gram Parsons could not charm. On that same tour, he sat at breakfast one
day telling Charlie Watts about the fateful night Bobby Keys had
found himself playing on one of Yoko Ono's recording sessions.
"People were sniffing Excedrin and bouncing off walls," Parsons
said. "She took Bobby in a corner and said, 'Imagine there is a
cold wind blowing and you are a lonely frog.' He just laid down
his saxophone and played marimbas and tambourine. 'Lady,' he
said, 'Yew shore got a strange slant on things.'" Then Parsons
added, "Yeah. Starting with yore eyes." Laughing softly, Charlie
Watts said, "Fantastic. Gram . . . fantastic."

Which was the way nearly everyone around the Stones felt
about Gram Parsons before he came to stay at Nellcote. More

than anything, the man was sweet. Unlike so many others in the rock scene back then, he did not seem to have a malicious bone in his body. And there was no denying his brilliant talent. No doubt at Keith's bidding, Marshall Chess was doing his best to sort out all the tangled record contracts Parsons had signed during his meteoric rise from the International Submarine Band to The Byrds to The Flying Burrito Brothers. Once Gram Parsons was free of prior legal entanglements, he was going to be signed to Rolling Stone Records. And then Keith would produce his album. Or so Parsons proudly told one and all.

Musically, the two of them were a match made in heaven. They were a psychedelic version of Don and Phil, the Everly Brothers. At Nellcote, they could often be found playing and singing their hearts out in the dining room or out on the terrace. Sometimes, Mick would join them. But when Gram Parsons was there, Mick was always the odd man out. "Mick and Gram never really clicked," Keith would later say, "mainly because the Stones are such a tribal thing. At the same time, Mick was listening to what Gram was doing. Mick's got ears. Sometimes when we were making *Exile On Main St.* in France, the three of us would be plonking away on Hank Williams songs while waiting for the rest of the band to arrive."

Although for years there have been rumors that Gram Parsons is all over *Exile On Main St.*, singing harmony in the background as the Stones recorded in the basement, Anita would later say, "I don't think Gram even went down there." Confirming this, Andy Johns recalls, "I didn't see Gram Parsons very much. He kind of kept out of the way." One night when Johns had some people down in the basement kitchen doing background vocals, Gram began shouting, "I can't hear anything with these fucking ear phones, man." Going to check on the problem, Johns discovered that, as he later remembered, Gram "didn't have a set of ear phones. He had the foot pedal from a Vox amp up against his ear. And I said, 'This might explain it.'"

It had to rankle Mick no end that Keith was perfectly willing to sit and play and sing with Gram Parsons for hours but then would fail to appear when the Stones were ready to record. And then there is the manner in which each of them prefers to write their songs. "As a songwriter," Keith will later say, "Gram worked very much like I do, which is knock out a couple of chords, start to spiel and see how far it can go. Rather than sitting around with a piece of paper and a pen, trying to make things fit neatly together." Which was precisely how Mick liked to do it.

"They've got two ways of working," Anita will later say. "Mick likes to write black and white ABC; with Keith it's just getting a feeling. Mick likes to write 'brrrrrm' and Keith is just like, all about sound. He plays what he hears and knocks up a song when it comes. So a lot of that was going on and Gram was always a bit like a pig in the middle."

Still, as Keith noted, Mick does have ears, and the Stones were already notorious for borrowing from anyone who could help them. It is no accident that "Torn and Frayed," the seventh track on *Exile On Main St.,* sounds like an utter rip-off of the Burritos, replete with steel guitar. "Sweet Virginia," the track which precedes it, much like "Wild Horses," also bears the unmistakable stamp of Gram Parsons' musical influence on the Stones.

While Gram Parsons himself posed no threat to Mick in any sense, his presence was a distraction. Sensing vulnerability,

Mick was quick to strike. Much like Donald Cammell, whom Keith would later call "a vicious manipulator of people," Mick liked to move human pieces around the chessboard. While it was usually sex that was his short-term goal, in the end it always came down to power. Unable to interject himself between Keith and Gram, Mick began to work his wiles on Gretchen.

Not yet twenty, Gretchen Burrell had met and fallen in love with Gram Parsons in Los Angeles when she was sixteen years old and working as a model while attending high school in Newport Beach. Two years later, she appeared in *Pretty Maids All in a Row,* directed by Roger Vadim. When she appeared nude in *Playboy* in a pictorial to promote the movie, Vadim told the magazine, "Gretchen Burrell has the best figure in the cast; her breasts are just right, like a happy compromise between Twiggy and Jane Russell."

"The surroundings at Nellcote were beautiful," Gretchen Parsons would later say in *Rolling Stone* magazine, "but the tension was relentless. You could cut the air with a knife." For starters, Anita did not take kindly to her. "I was aloof from all these California girls," Anita would later recall. "Gretchen was a bit moan-y, always reproaching Gram for being who he was. That was the vibe I got." And then there was Mick, whom Gretchen believed was trying to get to Gram by coming on to her. "He wouldn't leave me alone," she would later tell English rock writer Barney Hoskyns. "He was a little overbearing with me, and that would get Gram's goat, I think. I don't think it was about me, that's for sure. It just seemed too obvious."

As always, Gram Parsons compounded this problem by continuing to be his own worst enemy. Staying up for two and three days at a time with Keith while doing cocaine and heroin,

Parsons begins passing out. Since it is Keith's house and he has never taken kindly to anyone, Mick least of all, telling him whom he can or cannot have stay there, it seems reasonable to assume that it is Anita who finally broaches the subject, telling Keith she has had quite enough of both Gram and Gretchen Parsons as house guests. Parsons may also be using far too much of Keith and Anita's supply of heroin. In all likelihood, it is a combination of all these factors. Gram Parsons is using too much of their stuff, he is falling out all over the place, and, as much as Keith may love playing and singing with the man, their time together is doing nothing to help the new album get made.

Keith rings Linda Lawrence, then living in Ireland with her husband Donovan, who wrote the song, "Legend of the Girl Child Linda," for her. At the age of fifteen, Linda Lawrence fell in love with Brian Jones and then gave birth to his son, Julian. While living in Los Angeles, she was also Gram Parsons' girlfriend. "Could you please take Gram?" Keith asks her over the phone. "He's out of his head and he needs to be with somebody." She agrees to do so but never hears from the Stones again.

Jo Bergman is then asked, most likely by Keith, to take Gram Parsons to the airport and put him on the next plane to London. Before he leaves Nellcote, Parsons asks Michael Cooper if he and Gretchen can stay in Cooper's home in Holland Park when they get to England. Cooper says they can but then calls his assistant Perry Richardson with instructions that when Parsons comes to pick up the keys, Richardson should tell him they are lost. According to Gretchen Parsons, Gram is so upset at being booted out of Nellcote that he tries to overdose on the toilet one afternoon.

To those who were not there, this may not seem like a reason to kill yourself. But when you are suddenly handed your walking papers and exiled from the Stones' section of rock 'n' roll heaven, it can be very cruel indeed. Suddenly, your backstage pass to the hippest scene on the planet has been revoked. No longer one of the chosen few, you now have to shift for yourself to survive. Never mind that you were once a Byrd and then a founding member of the Flying Burrito Brothers. Never mind that Keith will later say of you, "There's not a lot of guys you don't mind waking up and they're there—for weeks—and it's a pleasure to have them around."

What Gram Parsons has never been is a Rolling Stone and so when the whip comes down, he is the one who has to go. The plan for Gram Parsons to be on Rolling Stones Records as well as the idea that Keith will produce his first solo album never comes to pass. Prodigious as Keith's grief at the loss of his good friend may have been, once Gram Parsons is asked to leave Nellcote, the two of them never see each other again.

Barefoot in a denim jacket, biker shades, and shorts that summer at Nellcote, Gram Parsons was the rock 'n' roll prince of Denmark. He was young Hamlet, destined to suffer the slings and arrows of outrageous fortune but far too stoned to take arms against a sea of troubles, choosing instead to move in silent and inexorable fashion toward the endless sleep of death. He was Romeo in blue jeans, banished (with the accent on the final syllable, please) from Verona, never to gaze again on the beauty of fair Juliet. As Shakespeare wrote, "Hence-banished is banish'd from the world/And world's exile is death: then banished/Is death mis-term'd: calling death banishment/Thou cutt'st my head off

with a golden axe/And smilest upon the stroke that murders me."
And so it was that summer at Nellcote for Gram Parsons.

# 12

**Unlike Gram Parsons,** Mick Taylor is, for better and worse, a
Rolling Stone. Even if he wanted to leave Nellcote, they would
not let him go. For Mick Taylor is one of them. As such, he has
to pay his dues. He has to pass the test that even Brian Jones,
who founded the Rolling Stones only to lose his band to Mick,
the woman he loved to Keith, and then his life as well, failed.
Much like Brian, Mick Taylor will in time also come to realize
that he cannot survive close and constant contact with Mick Jagger and Keith Richards.

In an interview with Barbara Charone in 1976, Keith called
Mick Taylor "a cold fish" who "wasn't particularly good for the
group." While hindsight may be 20/20, most particularly for a
Rolling Stone, no one seemed to feel that way about Mick Taylor
that summer at Nellcote. His playing on "Can't You Hear Me
Knocking?" and "Moonlight Mile" (a track on which Keith can
barely be heard) on *Sticky Fingers* had given the Stones' sound a
brand new dimension. While it may be true, as Keith also told
Charone, that Mick Taylor is a "lead guitarist, which completely
destroyed the whole concept of the Stones," Taylor himself
always seemed perfectly content to play whatever part he was
asked to perform in any song.

When Mick Taylor and Keith Richards sat on stage each
night on adjoining wooden stools holding acoustic guitars during
the 1972 American tour as Mick sang "Sweet Virginia" and
Robert Johnson's "Love In Vain," it was Mick Taylor who
seemed as pure and authentic a guitar player as England had

ever produced. "He must have been petrified," Andy Johns would later say of Taylor. "Because he was a bit like that. Nervous Nelly. And if you remember on the road, when it was time for his solos, he would just stare at the floor. I remember there was that quad movie thing we did and the version of 'Love In Vain,' just, the *bastard!* It's a serious tearjerker. I've never heard anyone who played like that. I never ever have. I'm just privileged to have been in the room with the guy." But, as Johns also remembered, "He was never really quite considered one of them, I should think. The funny thing is when I read interviews with Mick or Keith now, and they say, 'We don't understand why he left the band.'"

In every band, there is always one member, usually the youngest or most fragile, who is automatically assigned the role of scapegoat/sacrificial lamb. In The Beatles, it was George. In Cream, it was Eric Clapton. By dint of his age, just twenty-three, his quiet soft-spoken personality, and his epicene good looks; long blond frizzy hair framing the delicate, fine-boned face of a pre-Raphaelite angel, Mick Taylor is forced to play this part in the Rolling Stones during that summer in the south of France.

As the last one to have been invited to the party, Taylor is at a distinct disadvantage. Unlike Brian Jones, who was Keith's guitar mentor and surrogate older brother as they sat shivering together in their freezing cold flat on Edith Grove in London, desperately trying to make their two guitars sound like one, Taylor is distinctly a lead guitarist. It is a role that only came into existence after Cream went to America to play the Fillmore in San Francisco for the first time. Discovering they needed enough material to fill two sets a night, they turned Eric Clapton loose for solos that lasted longer than most of the songs he had recorded with his previous band, The Yardbirds. That Keith may have been, as Andy Johns also recalled, "just slightly jealous" of Taylor's playing also figures in the mix.

Back then in rock 'n' roll, all credentials were entirely personal. The way you lived was just as important as how well you played. Around the Stones that summer, no one exemplified this better than moon-faced Bobby Keys, who played saxophone in the honking, soulful manner of King Curtis and Plas Johnson back when it was the sax rather than the guitar that was the lead instrument in rhythm and blues.

Born on the same day as Keith, Bobby Keys actually recorded with the great Buddy Holly at K-Triple L radio in Lubbock, Texas. He appeared at the first Alan Freed show at the Brooklyn Paramount and played with Bobby Vee at the Texas State Fair before the Stones performed there during their first tour of America in 1964. Keys, who was twenty-nine years old that summer, seemed to have no intention whatsoever of making it to thirty. Though he had a wife, he spent most of the summer living with the actress Nathalie Delon in what June Shelley remembers as "a flat with funny furniture" not far from Nellcote.

One day at eleven in the morning, Mick, Bianca, and Jo Bergman dropped by to say hello only to discover Bobby Keys and Nathalie Delon eating baked potatoes with caviar while drinking Dom Perignon. According to Shelley, Mick looked at the two of them like they were completely out of their minds and said, "Even a Rolling Stone wouldn't do that." When Bobby offered to pour Mick a glass of the bubbly, his response was, "I'll have a beer." Live fast, die young, and leave a beautiful shadow was Bobby Keys' credo. Because he did everything to excess,

Keys was someone whom both Mick and Keith could appreciate, if not always understand.

In the cool of the evening after everyone at Nellcote had enjoyed their siesta, Bobby and Anita would sometimes go out together to reconnoiter the coast, looking for a high value place to burgle. Not that they ever did any actual breaking and entering. At Nellcote, it was always the thought that counted. Not to mention how far out on the edge you were really willing to go. In this, as in so much else, Mick Taylor was a kettle of distinctly different fish.

The son of a factory worker, Taylor grew up in the industrial new town of Hatfield, created in large part by the DeHavilland Aircraft Company in 1948, the year he was born. At the tender age of sixteen, he was invited by the seminal English blues musician John Mayall to join his legendary band, the Bluesbreakers. Replacing Peter Green, who had himself replaced a fairly decent lead guitarist named Eric Clapton, Taylor toured with Mayall for the next four years before deciding to leave the band. In June 1969, Mick Jagger asked Taylor to replace Brian Jones in the Rolling Stones.

What virtually no one knew at the time was that Taylor himself had serious doubts about his decision. "He could have done other things," Rose Taylor would say thirty-five years later. "He could have gone and joined Paul Butterfield. He could have done music he was more interested in than rock and roll. He could have played the blues. And jazz. He was taking classical guitar lessons. If he had done something he had been the boss of, it would have been better for him. Of course everyone said, 'Oh, you have to take this job. It's so wonderful.' In all the time he did it, he never ever thought it was wonderful. Ever."

In part, this is because by both temperament and personality, Mick Taylor is completely unsuited to play the role of Keith Richards' sidekick in the Stones. Unlike Ronnie Wood, who will take his place in the band, Mick Taylor is not a rock 'n' roller. Rather, he is a solitary soul who keeps to himself. It is no accident that he seems so comfortable with Bill Wyman, whom Mick and Keith always seem to tolerate without ever really liking all that much. Both Wyman and Taylor are completely dependable. Insofar as Mick and Keith are concerned, this does not automatically count as a virtue.

Rose Taylor, who first met the Stones while they were recording *Sticky Fingers* at Olympic Studios in London, remembers, "I couldn't believe how rude they all were. To each other, really. I was used to bands who all got on with one another and seemed to like one another. They didn't have the same camaraderie. Mick Taylor and Charlie and Bill seemed to be there all the time. And it was just always waiting. For Keith or Mick. It was absolutely always waiting for one of them to turn up."

As Keith would later say of Taylor, "He joined at a time when with any other band he wouldn't have been forced out of England, forced to live that kind of life that was alien to him. It was unnecessary for him 'cause he hadn't earned any money. We were being forced out on back taxes anyway. He was really an odd man out. There was no way he could feel part of the whole thing as much as the rest of us."

"Boys will be boys, I guess," Anita would later tell John Perry. "So Gram was on that end of it, you know, and Taylor on the other end of it . . . poor Mick. He was very, uuhhh, torn, you know? The whole thing was a nightmare. Aggression. Sexual aggression. It was like aggression on every bloody level. Taylor was constantly harassed by Jagger, in every way, I remember seeing him in tears." When Perry said he had heard rumors that Jagger had come on sexually to Rose Taylor, Anita responded, "Coming on to Taylor—you know, Jagger's bisexual—just giving him a hard time any possible way he could. It certainly wasn't easy for poor [Mick Taylor]. Some days he was too scared to go down to the basement . . . he'd lie in bed and chill out—hide under the pillows!"

As the summer wears on and tempers down in the basement grow shorter, Taylor often finds himself being criticized by Keith. "I remember Keith really humiliating him in front of people a couple of times in the south of France," Andy Johns would later recall. "'Well, look,' he told him, 'don't play on this. You play too fucking loud.' From Keith, right? 'You're great live but in the studio, you just don't make it.' Which was bullshit. Mick Taylor was always fabulous. One of the greatest musicians. One of the very greatest. I would always hang on his every note. A beautiful tone and his intonation. When he was on bottleneck, it was just all over. Just astounding. I've never heard anyone play with that sense of melody. Ever."

"I loved the play between Keith and Mick Taylor," Marshall Chess would later say, "because Mick was so melodic and Keith was so rhythmic. But Keith was definitely giving Mick a hard time. It was one of the reasons he left. That's a part of Keith's personality. Mick Taylor was playing stuff that he couldn't play. Mick Taylor had this very feminine, very beautiful, melodic lead. Keith could never have played the lead in 'Can't You Hear Me

Knockin'?' and Mick could never have played those hard rhythms. That was what made them a great band. That they were both playing different styles that meshed."

But then as Marianne Faithfull points out in her book, Mick and Keith always need someone to act as a buffer, a go-between, and a medium, a role initially filled by their first manager, Andrew Loog Oldham. "Ron Wood is perfect for this," she wrote. "Mick Taylor was less useful, and it's a role no one should ever have entrusted to Brian Jones."

Trapped in a situation he would never have chosen for himself, Mick Taylor continues to show up each night at Nellcote for sessions at which nothing is accomplished. Driven to despair by the slow pace at which the work is going, Taylor confesses over the phone one night to Charlie Watts that he has just about had it. Commiserating with him, Charlie says, "You're not the only one. I've tried to jump in the river but there was only four inches of water in it."

"We would not have been together all the time if they had been recording in London," Rose Taylor remembers. "I suppose in a sense it was like we were on tour in the south of France without going anywhere and there didn't seem to be any escape. If we had been at home, we could have had other people and the reality check of being with friends and family and all of that. It was very rarefied there. Tremendously isolating. It really was exile. It was. In every form."

Because Mick Taylor does not drive, Rose has to chauffeur him each night from their house in Le Tignet and then wait around all night long so she can drive him back home at dawn. While he suffers down in the basement, she sits and listens to Anita. "She would go on at me and tell me all the intrigues,"

Rose would later say. "She sounded completely batty to me but she would weave a spell with it all, you know. She would be telling me what Keith was doing with Stash and what this person was doing and they would find girls all around the house and I would think she was off her rocker. I think I was the new audience. Perhaps I was the chosen one. Fortunately, I can't remember anything she said."

"Mick and Rose Taylor," another Stones insider recalls, "were meat for the grinder. They were victims waiting to be used and abused. Mick was a sweet chap and Rose was very intelligent and very bright but also trying to fit into this amazing life because she realized this was the opportunity of his lifetime. Everybody respected Mick Taylor like they respected Nicky Hopkins. Because he was so lyrical and such a beautiful musician and he had somehow managed to retain the innocence."

The only track on *Exile On Main St.* on which Mick Taylor will receive a cowriting credit, yet another sore point that leads to his departure from the Stones, is "Ventilator Blues." As Andy Johns would later recall, "Sometimes, Mick Taylor would stop because he was out of tune. There was this one little tiny fan in the window up in the corner. Which didn't work very well. Therefore, 'Ventilator Blues.' It's one of my favorite tunes. It's about the fan in the window."

In that dank and humid basement where a single fan does nothing to cut the heat, Mick Taylor is as trapped as anyone at Nellcote that summer. Caught between Mick and Keith, there is nothing he can do but continue showing up each night to record while hoping the album will soon be done so the Stones can begin touring America. Until they do, Mick Taylor will not begin to earn the kind of money that Mick and Keith have already been making for years. Unlike Gram Parsons, Mick Taylor is a Rolling Stone. For him, there is nowhere else to go.

# 13

**Late one night** down in the basement as Keith is putting an overdub on "Rocks Off," the track that will eventually become the first cut on the album, he falls asleep. In itself, this is nothing new. As Andy Johns would later recall, "Keith used to nod out. He would play the intro and he'd be tacit for the first verse because he'd nod out and never come back in again. And I wasn't going to stop the tape and go, 'Wake up!' Because the talkback had busted, if I wanted to get their attention, I would run down the stairs and wave my arms and go, 'Oy!' So we would just sit there and let the tape roll. You would know you were getting close if Keith came out of the basement to listen to a playback. That meant we were getting somewhere. He knew what he wanted, oh yeah."

Regaining consciousness at three in the morning, Keith asks to listen to what he has just done only to fall asleep once more. Deciding the night is now conclusively over, Johns leaves the mobile, gets into his car, and returns to the villa where he lives with trumpet player Jim Price, easily a half hour to a forty-minute drive from Nellcote. When Johns gets there, the phone rings. "Oy!" Keith says, none too pleased at having woken up only to find everyone gone. "Where the fuck are you? I've got this idea for another guitar part." Johns promptly drives all the way back to Nellcote where at five in the morning Keith begins doing this rhythm track that, as Johns would later say, "was spectacular. Made the song work. It was excellent. Like a counter-rhythm part. Two Telecasters, one on each side of the stereo, and it's absolutely brilliant. So I'm glad he got me back there."

Still, with so little real progress being made down in the basement, time begins to weigh heavily on everyone. In rock 'n' roll as everywhere else, the devil soon finds work for idle hands. For want of anything better to do, Andy Johns and Jim Price, a veteran American-born session man who has been on the road with Delaney and Bonnie and Joe Cocker and recorded with George Harrison, decide to set up a casino at the villa where they live. "We bought a full-sized roulette wheel," Johns recalls, "and people would come by and we would play roulette until one or two in the morning and then it would change into poker. Sometimes craps. And we were making quite a bit of money on the craps and the roulette. We were the house. Keith came once. And he didn't want to join in. I think that was because he might lose. Or we might win. Which of course would have been an act of *lese majeste*. It was the time that he shot me up."

Johns, then twenty-one years old, has snorted heroin a few times but never injected the drug. "During the course of that project," he says, "I started using. Because it was easy to get. Marseilles was just down the road and you could get this China White that was very powerful for not a lot of money. So I started taking this stuff. I mean, it was so fucking boring most of the time. So much waiting around."

On the night that Keith comes to visit Johns and Price at their makeshift casino, Johns goes into his bedroom "to change my shirt or for some fucking reason and Keith had a needle and a spoon and I'd been brought up to think that was very inappropriate behavior. But I was along the path a little bit by now and I said, 'What are you doing?' And he said, 'Oh, do you want to do this too?' And I went, 'Yes. Okay.' And he went, 'Oh, this needle's fucked. It won't work. We'll go back to my place.' So we jump in his car and drive all the way back to Nellcote and he takes me downstairs and cooks something up and he didn't inject it in the vein. He just skin popped me. And went, 'Now, you're a man.' Which I thought, looking back on it now, 'How adolescent of him.' And how adolescent of me. 'Oh, I'll do this too.'"

Johns then goes back upstairs and is sitting in the mobile when Ian Stewart walks in, takes one look at him, and says "Andy, what's the time? Andy, what's the time?" "And of course," Johns would later recall, "I couldn't see. So I was looking at my watch and going, 'It's uh, I think it might be . . . well. . . .' And Stu said, 'You've been hangin' out with Keith, haven't you? Ohhhh dear, he's in trouble. I'm gonna tell your brother.'" One of Stu's oldest and closest friends, Andy Johns' older brother Glyn not only engineered the Stones' first demo but is also well known for his distinctly dim view of all forms of drug use, most especially the hard stuff. "And I said, 'Please don't.' So Stu picked up on it within ten fucking minutes. I said, 'Stu, no, I haven't done anything.' I just lied. He knew. I didn't become a junkie *per se* until a little later on. By the time we went to Jamaica to do *Goat's Head Soup*, I was deep into it."

Johns also recalls that Stones' producer Jimmy Miller started doing heroin at about the same time. "With heroin," Johns says, "you do a little bit your first time and it makes you nauseous. 'But hey, let's try that again!' It's so insane. And after a while, you start really liking it. And then you have to have it. And then it's too late. Once you get past the initial thing, once you're in and you're a proper junkie, it actually wakes you up and gives you energy and you get quite enthusiastic about doing things. Because you feel so fucking great. I mean, I've made some wonderful albums on smack. Because you become slightly obsessive. You're feeling very good about everything and so work becomes extremely attractive."

In time, Jimmy Miller will become yet another casualty of the drug scene at Nellcote. Near the very end of Traffic's "You Can All Join In," Dave Mason joyously sings about Jimmy Miller "rockin' to and fro." It was the brilliant work Miller did producing that album which first brought him to the attention of the Stones. A soul drummer who grew up in a showbiz background, Miller was recording black bands in New York when Chris Blackwell, the founder of Island Records, heard a George Clinton single that Miller had produced and brought him to England.

The first song Miller produced for Blackwell was "Gimme Some Lovin'" by The Spencer Davis Group with sixteen-year-old Stevie Winwood on lead vocal. Miller then did their follow-up single, "I'm A Man." He was working with Traffic in Studio B at Olympic Studios in London while the Stones were in Studio A recording *Their Satanic Majesties*. After Mick and Keith heard a playback of a track Miller was working on, Mick asked him to produce the Stones' next album. In fairly rapid succession, Miller produced *Beggars Banquet, Let It Bleed,* and *Sticky Fingers,* arguably the three greatest albums the band ever made.

"Jimmy was a gas," says Andy Johns. "His sort of shining moment with the Stones was *Beggars Banquet* when he brought them back from that disastrous *Satanic Majesties* period. Obviously, they knew they had to make a change because that record was just a joke, or most of it was. Jimmy's thing was that he could play drums and he understood grooves and he was very good at getting them. I was around when the Stones were doing

*Let It Bleed.* They'd come in and play bits and pieces of songs and Jimmy would get excited and he would lead them to the trough as it were. 'Why don't you try this with that?' I think it was as much inspiration as anything else. Because telling those guys specifically what notes to play, that was not going to happen." Setting the groove for all that follows, it is Jimmy Miller who begins "Honky Tonk Women" by playing the cowbell. He also plays drums on "You Can't Always Get What You Want," a track that seems far more extraordinary now than when it was first released.

Looking as though there was nowhere else in the world he would rather be, Jimmy Miller arrived in the south of France at the Nice airport in a cream-colored suit, a dark shirt, a loud striped tie, and a pair of snazzy brown-and-white saddle shoes. A very sharp black leather satchel hung from his left shoulder and he carried an attaché case in his right hand. With coiffed hair and a beaming smile on his broad, open face, he looked a lot like Michael Palin, one of the stars of *Monty Python's Flying Circus.*

Miller's ebullient mood would not last for long. As he later told Caroline Boucher of *Disc* magazine, "Seven weeks went by and we hadn't cut the first track. Every night, I would say, 'Has somebody got a song?' There were a lot of problems with that album, it was the one I was least happy with. I would have been happier if it had been a single album. I think that's the case with most double albums, but even so we chose the material out of almost twice as much stuff."

"When they first started working with him," Andy Johns will later tell writer Steve Appleford, "he was a lot of help. Then after a year or two, they kind of used Jimmy for what they wanted, and learned Jimmy's tricks, and started shutting him out a bit. So by the time of *Exile On Main Street*, they weren't listening to Jimmy very much, and it did him in. They weren't really rude, but they would ignore him a lot more than he would have liked." Nonetheless, Miller still made his own musical contributions to the album. He can be heard playing drums on "Happy," the tenth track on the album, as well as at the end of "Tumbling Dice," the first single released from *Exile On Main St.*

"After the breakdown on 'Tumbling Dice,'" Johns says, "Charlie was having a hard time of it, so Jimmy played. And I edited it on. So he really did have a fair amount of input. But by the time they were in the south of France, he was kind of on his way out. He would just sit there and they would do millions and millions of takes and his input consisted of remembering which takes he liked. 'Oh, we should listen to take ten. We should listen to take twenty and compare that with take four, I would think.' I didn't see him do much else. And then if I would get an interesting sound, he was getting nervous enough by that time to make out like he had come up with it. Which was pissing me off a little bit but hey, I wasn't going to make a big thing about it."

During the making of *Exile On Main St.,* Johns and Miller become quite close. "We were sort of like best mates and hung out and did everything together for a few years after that," Johns says. "But in the end, Jimmy got totally burned out because he became a junkie and never stopped. He lost his gift. That album was the beginning of the end for him." As Keith will later tell his biographer Victor Bockris, "Jimmy was great, but the more successful he became the more he got like Brian. Jimmy ended up carving swastikas into the wooden console at the studio. It took him three months to carve a swastika. Meanwhile Mick and I had to finish up *Goat's Head Soup*."

"I was part of getting rid of him," Marshall Chess says. "Because what I noticed was that they didn't really need him to make a great record. Maybe I was subconsciously trying to position myself. I saw that he wasn't really producing. He was more or less kissing their ass and adding stuff. I loved Jimmy and I hung out with him a lot. But it wasn't right. I didn't think they needed him as their full producer."

Although Miller would spend the next twenty years working with Blind Faith, Motorhead, and Johnny Thunders of the New York Dolls, he never again reached the artistic and commercial heights he had scaled while producing the Stones during their heyday. In 1994, Jimmy Miller died of liver disease. "When Jimmy Miller was dying," Johns says, "I went backstage to see the Stones and I said, 'Poor old Jimmy. What a shame. What's going on?' And Keith went, 'Oh fucking hell, man. We've given him fifty grand. And sod him anyway. You know the British Museum has one of those glass cases with my liver's name on it and they're going to have to wait a long fucking time for it.' He obviously realized he had an iron constitution."

Sadly, the same cannot be said for Miller. "Jimmy," Keith would tell *Crawdaddy* magazine, "went in like a lion and came out a lamb. We wore him out, completely. Same with Andrew Loog Oldham. Burned out like a light bulb." But then as Keith said when he was told Gram Parsons had died, "Gram was one of my closest friends. Unfortunately, many of my closest friends have died suddenly. . . . Once he'd moved back to LA or whatever to form his own band, I started hearing stories. Hollywood is the end of the line for so many people. It's a killer and if you're weak you can be sure it'll get you."

In other words, it is never the dope itself that kills you but rather the circumstances in which you are taking it. That so many of those around the Stones who thought they could live like Keith ended up dead long before their time never seemed to factor into the equation.

As Bill Wyman, the straightest of the Stones even as he begins smoking hash each day in the south of France, will later write, "It was certainly bizarre at Nellcote; it made *Satanic Majesties* seem organised. Andy Johns had to try to record guitar over-dubs while people were eating in the kitchen. It was like making one of those 1960s party records where everyone felt they should be involved. This chaos was not eased by Keith and Anita's lifestyle, which was becoming increasingly chaotic. It was obvious drugs were at the centre of the problem—whatever people tell you about the creative relationship of hard drugs and the making of rock 'n' roll records, forget it. Believe you me, they are much more a hindrance than a help."

Although Jimmy Miller certainly deserves to be remembered as one of the greatest rock producers who ever lived, virtually no one who listens to his music now on various greatest hits compilations has any idea who he was. Nameless and faceless, he has become just another name on the back of a repackaged CD case. Perhaps that is the way he would have wanted it. To be remembered for the music, and nothing else.

When Mick Jagger sings about going down to the Chelsea Drugstore to get his prescription filled on "You Can't Always Get What You Want," the final track on *Let It Bleed*, described by *Blender* magazine as "a song about heroin that became an elegy for the recently departed Jones [Brian] and for the 60's," he finds himself standing in line with Mr. Jimmy, and man, he looks pretty ill. They decide to have a soda, his favorite flavor, cherry red. Mick sings his song to Mr. Jimmy, says one word to him, and that is "dead."

# 14

**Let us now consider** the plight of Bill Wyman, who by actual count has slept with more women while on the road with the Rolling Stones than anyone else in the band. That he bothers to maintain a running tally is no accident. A born collector, Wyman keeps a detailed diary and has saved every last bit of Stones-related ephemera that ever passed through his hands—showbills, concert posters, ticket stubs, backstage passes, recording contracts, press releases, and perhaps even some of the jelly babies that crazed teenaged girls would fling at the Stones when they were playing church halls in the north of England. As Wyman will later note, it is as though he was born to be a librarian.

When he incorporates his extensive collection of priceless memorabilia into a massive book entitled *Rolling With The Stones,* Wyman makes it very plain that he was royally pissed off by all the drug-induced madness at Villa Nellcote that summer. Not that you would have known it to talk to him then. If nothing else, Bill Wyman was the silent Stone. Rarely moving as he played bass on stage, his face never betrayed what he was thinking or feeling. While still waters may run deep, Mick and Keith treated Wyman like a sideman rather than a fellow member of the band. Which was not to say that the man himself could not also be quite strange.

Unlike Wyman, most people trying to stop smoking cigarettes in the south of France that summer would not have done
so by replacing them with hash joints. Nor would they have
begun photographing women's breasts as a hobby. At dinner,
Wyman will sometimes ask the most attractive woman at the
table to slip into another room for a moment and remove her
blouse so he can snap a quick photo to add to his collection. At
one point, he rents a boat, anchors it off the nude beach in
St. Tropez, and then turns his back on the good-looking women
sunbathing topless on deck to, as June Shelley will later write,
"point his telescopic lens at strangers on the beach."

Although Wyman had some odd quirks of his own, he was
nothing if not completely dependable, showing up on time night
after night to record at Nellcote only to wait for hours as Mick
and Keith dither about. Understandably fed up with it all,
Wyman hires a yacht in September and goes off with his companion, Astrid Lundstrom, to enjoy a five-day vacation.

After he leaves, Keith promptly strolls into the basement at
Nellcote one afternoon and cuts "Happy," which will become
the tenth cut on *Exile On Main St.* The basic track consists of
Bobby Keys on baritone sax, Keith on guitar, and Jimmy Miller
on drums. "We were basically doing the sound check," Keith will
later recall, "making sure everything was set up for the session,
and track just popped out." As he tells his biographer, Victor
Bockris, "Sometimes, I'd be ready to play and some guys would
come over early. I had an idea for a song, but it was really like a
warm-up."

"I worked on 'Happy,'" Andy Johns says. "That was a bit
of a surprise. I wasn't expecting that. That went very well and
easily and no pulling of teeth at all. He just walked in and

recorded it. In the end, Keith was pretty much in charge. It was Keith who had final say. That was when I figured that out."

In time, "Happy" will come to be recognized as Keith's signature tune, the song that most completely expresses what he is all about. Not for him the wealth, fame, and social standing that Mick seems to crave so deeply. Keith just wants to keep on rocking until they have to pry his cold, dead fingers from the neck of his guitar. Plainly, the song also demonstrates the power of an artist to transcend the circumstances of his own life. For even as Keith is becoming enslaved by heroin, he still somehow manages to project the feeling that he is truly free, a working-class hero who needs nothing more than the love of a good woman to keep him happy. In fact, the song seems to have been inspired by a bit of news Keith had only just been given by Anita. Which we shall consider in due time.

When Wyman returns from holiday, having no doubt added to his extensive photo collection, he discovers that Keith has, in his words, "worked on a song called 'Happy' while I was away and it was very good. When I got back we listened to two tracks recorded earlier and I immediately realised that Keith had taken it upon himself to re-record my bass part on both tracks—I thought they sounded terrible and I told him so. Finding my outburst very funny, both Keith and Jimmy [Miller] started to take the piss. I went home really angry and, falling into the same trap as everyone else, didn't go back the next day. It was becoming clear that Jimmy, Andy, Bobby, and Mick T. were involved with hard drugs. I felt like I wasn't in the club—not that I wanted to join."

One track of course does not an album make. As the month wears on, recording grinds to a halt yet again as Mick begins spending more time in Paris with Bianca, who is about to give birth to their child. As Wyman will later write, "Mick was very worried about Keith. We talked about the situation without ever really coming up with a plan. All we could do was to try and keep going, hoping it would come together amid the chaos."

As though to illustrate this point, Andy Johns and Jim Price are now living with Bobby Keys and Jimmy Miller in Bobby's apartment on the ocean. "The poker game continued," Johns says. "We would just stop for work, as it were, not the other way around. These games were getting sillier in as much as, 'Oh, whoever has the lowest hand has to take four Qualuudes. Whoever has the lowest hand has to take a tab of acid.'"

One day, Johns looks out the window only to see that Jim Price has thrown a couple of albums he does not like into the sea. Going downstairs to his room, Johns returns only to see "a couch floating out to sea. And a dining room table." When Johns goes down "to this little tiny bit of beach to investigate," he feels something warm and wet falling on him like rain from the heavens above. "I looked up and there was Bobby with his dick over the balcony, pissing on me. Then they all started pissing on me. Then this degenerated into Bobby breaking into the wine cellar downstairs," which has been locked by the owners because, as Johns says, "there was some major shit in there, apparently."

Just then, the owners of the apartment, who lived below, return. "They looked out in the ocean," Johns remembers, "and there was half their furniture drifting off towards Africa, and so they thought they better have a look around. So of course they see the door to the wine cellar's been broken down and there's Bobby passed out in this sort of heap of broken wine bottles, rare vintages, et cetera. So we were asked to leave. Not surprising, as it was. We had to go. Boredom, yeah." Johns and Miller promptly move into the historic Hotel Negresco on the Promenade des Anglais in Nice so they can continue working on the album.

With summer over and most of the tourists gone from the south of France, the aimless rhythm of daily life at Nellcote is rudely shattered on October 1 when nine guitars as well as Bobby Keys' set of engraved black saxophones, a baritone, an alto, and a soprano, are stolen from the villa even as local security men sleep peacefully in the chauffeur's quarters above the garage. According to Bill Wyman, Keith is home at the time watching television but never hears a thing. "The haul," he will later write, "included Albert King's old Gibson Flying Arrow (which Keith used at Hyde Park), my Fender Mustang Bass, and Bobby's baritone sax."

As Anita later tells John Perry, "That was nasty—it was sort of an inside job, you know?" French record executive Dominic Lamblin confirms this by recalling, "When Keith had problems with the local dealers, they confiscated all his guitars. I know there was a note sent to us with a list of all the ones that had been taken. We were never able to find any. They had sent the list to us so that we could circulate it in the big musical instrument stores."

Without doubt, it has to have been les cowboys, who not only had access to the villa but to whom both Keith and Bobby Keys may have also owed money, who pulled off the heist and then pawned their haul for cash. Because Keith's guitars were fully insured for forty-four thousand dollars, he was able to replace most of them in time. Although Keith was in tears when he called Stones' guitar tech Newman Jones with instructions to purchase new instruments for him, the robbery itself was all about dope and money.

Far more significant than the actual loss is that at long last, the walls at Nellcote have been breached. While the house has never been all that secure, it can now no longer be defended. Just as Anita predicted so many months before, the villa robbers have come and taken not only the tools of Keith's trade but also the objects in all the world that are most near and dear to him. It does not take much thought to realize that where villa robbers feel free to tread, the police can also come.

For a few days after the robbery, the villa is shut down. As only Anita could put it, "The massive gates were closed, and big lights shining onto the street. We went to maximum security. Suddenly it became Auschwitz. We were even thinking of putting monkeys in the bread trees to enhance security . . . all sorts of crazy ideas. But TOO LATE, you know? As usual. Too much trust and faith in everything until you get ripped off. I mean we should've done that before—but that was the time and that was the vibe. We felt like King of the Castle anyway, you know? Nothin' can happen to us."

That Anita herself may have contributed to the current state of siege at the villa seems never to have occurred to her. But then by this point in time, according to Spanish Tony, Anita is not only shooting up three times a day but has also gotten into "turning people on to heroin for the first time." Taking the high moral ground, Tony adds, "I thought she went a little too far, though, when she persuaded the teenaged daughter of the chef at Nellcote to accept an injection of smack. The child was violently sick, and

I worried she would complain to her father." According to Tony, the chef soon found out about his "daughter's fix" and demanded thirty thousand pounds ($72,000) from Keith or he would "go to the police and tell them" that Keith had "held her down while Anita forced the needle into her arm . . . 'Fuck off,' said Keith. 'You're fired.'"

As always when Tony reports what he claims to have seen and heard at Nellcote, one hardly knows where to begin. Over the course of the summer, there were many chefs employed at Nellcote. Unable to put up for long with a household that demanded feeding at odd hours of both day and night, chefs came and went with stunning regularity. The one whom everyone remembers is Jacques, whom Keith always called "Fat Jack." Looking as though he just stepped out of an Eddie Constantine movie about the drug trade in Marseilles, Fat Jack wore a red bandanna around his neck and tended to sweat profusely at all times (especially when he was on acid, as one Stones insider recalled).

A jolly fellow who was always laughing, Jacques in another life could have been Falstaff, blathering and bragging in a local tavern while waiting for his good friend Prince Hal to arrive. In this incarnation, he was one of les cowboys to whom Keith had taken a particular liking. Everyone interviewed for this book, including those who were on staff that summer at Nellcote, insists that Jacques was far too young to have had a teenaged daughter. Nor did anyone remember a girl that age ever being at Nellcote. Which does not mean that someone who fit that description who may or may not have been related to Jacques in some manner did not pass through the house at some point.

While Anita herself was entirely capable of such an act, Tony seems to have gotten at least some of the details of this story wrong. Still, with the black seed of paranoia firmly planted in the hearts of all those living at Nellcote, no one is now immune to the disease. When, according to Tony, the Corsican dealers return with half a kilo of smack, they not only inform Keith that the price has suddenly gone up to twelve thousand dollars but also "treated Keith with a new aloofness."

Worried that the Corsicans may suddenly decide to kidnap Marlon and hold him for ransom, Tony writes that Keith now believes the time has come to bring in guard dogs and put up video cameras to protect the villa. Tony tells Keith it would be a lot easier if he just paid the Corsicans fifty thousand dollars to protect the boy. For a while, Keith seems to think this is an excellent plan. Then he decides it would be better if he and Tony applied for gun permits so they could be armed at all times. "Naturally," Tony writes, "owing to our earlier contretemps at Beaulieu, our applications were refused." As though Keith Richards ever needed a permit to own or carry a gun.

As Andy Johns and Jimmy Miller begin preparing rough mixes of as many tracks as possible so the powers-that-be at Atlantic Records will know that at least some work is being done on the new album in the south of France, the scene at Nellcote takes yet another turn toward the dark side. As Bill Wyman will later write, "But one night disaster struck when there was a fire at Keith's house. His staff quickly dealt with the situation. Keith's chauffeur said he broke down the bedroom door to find Keith and Anita lying on the bed, naked, with the mattress in flames around them. His first thought was that they were overcome with smoke, but they were completely out of it." In terms of what is now going on down in the basement, Wyman adds, "Keith was becoming even less communicative. Where he was always so decisive and to the point, he was now vague and withdrawn. Mick had an excuse for not being around as Bianca's baby was due at any moment."

On October 21, 1971, at the Rue de Belvedere nursing home in Paris, Bianca Jagger gives birth to a six pound, ten ounce baby girl named Jade. The proud father promptly calls Keith to say he will not be back at Nellcote for three weeks. While the arrival of a child in any circumstances is always a blessed event, the birth of Mick Jagger's daughter brings us at long last to yet another of the deep, dark secrets that lie at the very heart of the making of *Exile On Main St.*

# 15

**At some point** during the month of September, Anita discovers she is pregnant. Considering the way she and Keith feel about Marlon (and the fact that Anita was pregnant just before filming began on *Performance,* only to have an abortion so she could do the movie), this should be terrific news for all concerned as well as the cause for genuine celebration. Unlike Keith, who is inspired by the news to write and record "Happy," Anita does not seem all that pleased about her condition. To the contrary, she is quite upset and conveys her feelings in German to Elizabeth Hiemer, the housekeeper with whom she feels so comfortable. Taking aside June Shelley, who is now doing everything and anything for the Stones in the south of France, Hiemer asks her to help Anita, who has what Shelley will later call "this split feeling about the child because Keith wanted the baby very badly and it wasn't that she didn't want the baby, it was that she was afraid."

Someone who never lived at Nellcote might reasonably assume that Anita's fear stems from the fact that she is using and that this could harm her unborn child. But this soon proves not to be the case. Before too long, Rose Taylor, who has also been drawn into the loop, asks Mick Taylor for some money so Anita, who literally has none of her own and does not want Keith to know what she is doing, can have an abortion. Acting as go-between, June Shelley tells Anita that Mick Taylor is more than willing to give her the money.

Although the two women do not have a particularly warm relationship, Anita tells Shelley she has to do this because she doesn't think she is capable of handling a second child. Even though Shelley has seen the local doctor come to the house each day at a certain time and then go upstairs, no doubt to adminis-ter some sort of injection, Anita says nothing to her about drugs. Just that she does not think she can have the baby and so can June please buy her a ticket to Switzerland.

Shelley now finds herself in an awkward position. Because she is being paid by the Rolling Stones, she considers Keith to be her boss and does not feel it would be right for her to do anything behind his back. Whenever the Stones or one of their companions goes anywhere, it is Shelley who makes all the arrangements through an Italian travel agency. Unlike Anita, Shelley has her own credit card. So she can book the trip for Anita without ever talking to Keith. What worries Shelley most is whether Anita can actually do this on her own. When Shelley finally decides to talk to Keith about it, she tells him, "Anita wants me to buy her a ticket to Paris." Keith never asks why

Anita wants to go, which makes Shelley think the two of them have already discussed the matter in private. "Go ahead, June," Keith says. "Buy her a one-way ticket to anywhere she wants to go."

Shelley thinks about it for the next few days. She asks Rose if she could accompany Anita but Rose has a young child of her own to care for and so cannot go. Shelley then approaches Elizabeth Hiemer and says, "Do you think if I bought Anita a ticket, she could handle this thing on her own?" Looking Shelley straight in the eye, Hiemer says, "Yes, Madame June, I think she can do it. Help her. You must help her." On four different occasions, June Shelley buys Anita a ticket to Paris, London, and Switzerland. Each time Anita fails to make her flight, oversleeping or finding some other excuse not to go.

While to some this might just seem like typical addict behavior, Shelley realizes Keith has known all along that Anita would never get it together to go and so was only humoring her when he approved the ticket request. Precisely what else Keith knows is more difficult to say. For where pregnancy is concerned, only the mother can ever be completely certain about the father of her unborn child. The real reason Anita wants an abortion is that she believes she is carrying Mick Jagger's child.

Can this really be so? Or is it simply another delusion? As you might expect, the principals themselves remain spectacularly unavailable for comment. However, there is a good deal of circumstantial evidence to consider. While Keith has never been nearly so obsessed with sex as Mick, this does not mean that the man cannot hold his own in this department. During their 1972 American tour, the Stones found themselves staying with Hugh Hefner at the Playboy Mansion in Chicago. A never-ending succession of Playmates, Playboy Bunnies, and girls who just wanted to have fun, all as lovely as they were vacuous, flowed in and out of Mick and Keith's rooms in a never-ending stream with just one thing on their minds—sex with a Rolling Stone. As it turned out, the girls were not only comparing notes but also keeping a record of how it all went. "The girls told me they had a chart," a Stones insider who was there recalls. "And they said Keith was the best fuck of all of them. Of all the Rolling Stones. You know why? Because when you're on heroin, you don't come. You can fuck for two-and-a-half fucking hours." As yet another Stones insider would later confide, "Apparently, Keith is endowed like an ox."

Marianne Faithfull, who before she ever met Keith had what she would later describe as "a huge crush on him," then had "a wonderful night of sex" with him while they were both on acid in the flat on Courtfield Road in London. "My night with Keith," she would later write, "was the best night I've ever had in my life, as a matter of fact." Having always been "a little in love with Keith," she was now "totally bowled over." When they woke up together in bed the next morning, she found herself "fluttering around in a state of absolute rapture" only to have Keith tell her she ought to give Mick a call as he was the one who really fancied her, adding "He's not that bad when you get to know him, y'know?"

As she would also write, "It's curious that Keith lived through all this convoluted sexual stuff with these people and stuck around. He knew perfectly well what was going on. It perpetuated itself in the incestuous relationship between me and Mick and Keith and Anita. And at some level he must have found all this profoundly troubling. In the end he really couldn't bear it. . . . Which is probably one reason he eventually ended up doing so much smack. To block it out."

While performance anxiety of any kind seems never to have been part of Keith's makeup, getting high and making music were always what he cared about most. For reasons better left to a licensed sex therapist to explain, during that summer at Nellcote insofar as Anita was concerned, Keith seemed to prefer manual stimulation to the exclusion of all other forms of sexual contact. A Stones insider who was there clearly remembers Anita complaining in a very loud and public manner that Keith would not have sex with her. "She was getting fed up because he wouldn't bonk her," the insider would later recall. "And when you're a junkie, you don't do a lot of that. When you're young enough, you can still do it but coming is virtually impossible."

"I didn't know what had happened with Mick Jagger until Anita told me she'd had an affair with Mick during the filming of *Performance*," another Stones insider recalls. "Everybody knows about it now. But she was still continuing her affair with him when they moved to Nellcote." Which may be yet another reason Bianca could not stand to be at Nellcote and left the south of France to live in Paris. Even some of those who were at Nellcote find this scenario not only highly unlikely but also physically impossible. "I don't know how she could have managed to be with Mick," one says. "Well, when Keith nodded out maybe."

"It was tossed around whose kid it really was but never discussed in front of me," Marshall Chess would later say. "She thought it was Jagger's kid, yeah. There were major problems between Mick and Keith over it, yeah. A cold fucking wall went up between the two of them. Believe it or not, one of their weaknesses is that they will never sit and talk face-to-face about areas like that. They cannot deal with those kind of areas. Or one another. Or anyone. It's particularly English and more so when you become a star before you develop into a man. Because they were always surrounded by ass-kissers and secretaries before they grew up and learned how to handle their own life. They had other people taking care of their dirty shit. They never had to clean up after themselves."

With everything to lose and not much to gain, a fair question to ask might be why Mick Jagger, newly married and about to become a father, would endanger not only work on the new album but also the entire future of the Rolling Stones by continuing his affair with Anita at Nellcote. No one seems to believe Mick was in love with her. Rather, as someone else who was an integral part of the scene back then would later say of Mick, "He likes to fuck. He likes to be sexual. I think Mick fucked them all. The only one he didn't sleep with was Charlie's wife. It was like science fiction. Everything was different."

Turn the equation on its head for a moment and consider the fairly innocent bystander in this situation. How could Keith put up with it? After such knowledge, what forgiveness? If Keith knew what was going on between Mick and Anita, how could he go into the studio each night and work with Mick in such close proximity? No amount of dope in the world could dull that much pain. If in fact Keith was really in pain at all. As someone else who was there and knew what was going on at the time would later say, "Perhaps Keith just has a facility about not thinking about things he doesn't want to think about. Perhaps physical fidelity didn't mean that much to them. I don't know if Keith knew or not. Because you can't tell with Keith. You really can't. So I have no idea whether he knew about that at all."

Putting an even more bizarre spin on the situation is that when Anita finally gives birth to a baby girl, the child is named "Dandelion" after the song on *Their Satanic Majesties* in which Mick sings that dandelion don't tell no lies, dandelion will make you wise, tell me if she laughs or cries, blow away, dandelion. As though we are now in fact dealing not with Mick, Keith, and Anita but those original rock 'n' roll outlaws, the French symbolist poets Rimbaud and Verlaine, as well as Verlaine's young wife Mathilde, the child's name is an elaborate pun in French—not *Dandelion* but *dent de lion* as in the tooth of the lion, referring to Mick Jagger, a Leo.

Friends, no one can make this sort of stuff up. Even if they could, why would they? In any terms you might name, none of it makes much sense even now. But then where Mick and Keith and their women are concerned, almost nothing ever does. Purely for the record, let it be noted that the daughter born in time to Keith and Anita turns out to be in fact Keith's child. And, for reasons which may have nothing to do with any of this, she is now called Angela.

# 16

**According to Spanish Tony,** the French police arrive in force at Nellcote on the day after the Corsicans deliver what turns out to be their final shipment. As they move about Nellcote asking questions and taking statements, the gendarmes say they have come because the Corsicans have been seen visiting the villa. Since it would have been impossible for anyone, much less the police, to take up a position on the narrow road outside the villa without being noticed, this seems completely improbable

even now. Rather, as is almost always the case when a drug bust
is about to go down, someone has gone to the police and offered
to testify against those at Nellcote to whom they have only just
sold drugs or with whom they have just been using them. In
other words, someone has ratted out Keith and Anita.

"We always had 'the drill,'" Anita will later tell John Perry.
"Just in case. Bust drill. From the bedroom, out of the second
floor window onto the roof of the recording truck and out into
the garden. We had regular rehearsals. 'Cause there was a vast
amount of drugs there . . . and all these hoods from Marseilles—
these guys were dealing from our house, as well, that's what we
didn't realize, they were dealing from the premises. That's why
we got nailed with all that stuff."

While there would have been no reason for the Corsicans to
deal from Nellcote, they may have also been selling to les cowboys. Apparently referring to them, Anita tells Perry, "Within
forty-eight hours of firing those guys, the trouble started. They
went to their mums, their mums made them go to the police and
confess and involve everyone in the house. I myself had fourteen
years hanging over my head, me and Bobby [Keys]. I was accused
of trafficking. And then all the other people were incriminated as
well, but I think me and Bobby Keys, for some reason, were the
worst . . . 'cause, I dunno, they probably took a dislike to us. Me,
because I fired them, so that was the revenge."

Since Jacques, the chef also known as Fat Jack, was the
only cowboy regularly employed at Nellcote, no one else could
have dropped a dime on Keith and Anita. This theory jibes neatly
with another Stones insider's recollection that it was Jacques who
was bringing the heroin in from Marseilles. Had, as Spanish

Tony reports, Jacques ever tried to blackmail Keith for any reason whatsoever, Keith would have had no compunction whatsoever about sending him packing, believing he had little to fear from someone who could not go to the police without also incriminating himself. If in fact it was Jacques who rolled over on Keith and Anita to extricate himself from some far more serious legal entanglement, the strategy would in time prove to be completely ineffective.

Rene D'Amico, a local rock musician who visited Nellcote several times that summer (precisely for what reason, he does not say) and was a good friend of Jacques (whom he also describes as a friend of Tommy Weber despite the fact that Tommy only remembers him as "a hopeless fucking cook and a cowboy who was too young to have a daughter") later reports that Jacques himself went to jail for a while after Keith and Anita were no longer in residence at the villa. Since more than one person seems to have been talking to the police, Jacques may not have been either the prime suspect or the main informant but simply someone caught up in a spider's web of accusations. In any event, just as when Keith's guitars were stolen, it is all about dope and it is all about money.

Armed with depositions from five people who claim they have seen Rene D'Amico using heroin at Nellcote, gendarmes come knocking at D'Amico's door in Marseilles. Because under the Napoleonic code, bail is not granted to those awaiting trial in France, D'Amico is put in jail for six months. Along with all the others who have been charged, he then appears before the same judge before whom Keith testified after the Italian tourist run-in. Although D'Amico is granted probation, the judge by that point cannot have been all that kindly disposed toward either Keith or the goings-on at Nellcote.

As Anita also tells John Perry, "And then there were other incriminations, such as, there was this Oliver [*sic*] guy from the Living Theatre, he came down and apparently he slipped some Mandrax to some local youths and tried to rape them . . . so there were all those incriminations of corrupting minors, I mean it was mega-trouble." While Olivier Boelen did often take good-looking young men to his room at Nellcote for sex, he seemed like someone far more inclined to seduction than rape. There were however boxes and boxes of Mandrax, the European equivalent of Qualuudes, known for good reason in England as "randy mandies," available that summer at Nellcote. As one Stones insider recalls, "We were giving them to people like sweets."

By dint of their lifestyle, their drugs of choice, and those to whom they have thrown open the front door of their home, Keith and Anita have finally managed to inflame the locals beyond the point of reason. On the French Riviera, aptly described by Somerset Maugham as "a sunny place for shady people," where all forms of aberrant behavior have always been tolerated so long as the bill is paid on time, this is not all that easy to do. Now that it has happened, Keith and Anita will have to deal with the consequences. Sort of.

Unlike those who have nowhere else to go, Keith and Anita cannot wait around for the police to arrest them. Once this happens, no amount of high-priced French legal talent can help them, for they will find themselves sitting in jail for an indeterminate amount of time until they are brought to trial. Aside from the fact that they are both using and Anita is now nearly two months pregnant, this simply cannot happen. As they say in France, *ce n'est pas possible*. While Rolling Stones do sometimes get arrested on a variety of charges, they never go to jail for very long. In this, as so much else, they are different from anyone you might name.

That everyone in the Stones' hierarchy was concerned about what was happening in the south of France would seem to be confirmed by a call made by Prince Rupert Loewenstein to June Shelley during this period. After wanting to know what Shelley had heard about drug parties at Nellcote, Rupert asked if she could do a little private eye investigating on her own as to exactly what had gone on there. Shortly after the shakedown at Nellcote, Cap Ferrat police arrested "ten young people and two Americans" in December 1971 and charge them with bringing hashish and fifty grams of heroin (less than two ounces) to Nellcote on a weekly basis during the summer.

Nearly a year later on November 1, 1972, Bill Wyman and Charlie Watts sit down with Stones' solicitor Paddy Grafton-Green and two French lawyers in Vence. Watts and Wyman then go to Nice where they are each questioned individually for almost an hour by a judge. "It was easier than I expected it to be," Wyman later writes, adding, "We were ready to record in Jamaica, but the spectre of Keith's drug problem in France was very much on our minds. It wasn't just something that affected Keith—it affected our ability to tour, our whole way of life."

A month later on December 1, in Kingston, Jamaica, where the Stones are now staying at the Terra Nova Hotel, the former home of Island Records founder Chris Blackwell, while recording *Goat's Head Soup* at Byron Lee's Dynamic Sounds studio, the band sits down with their lawyers. At this meeting, it is decided that everyone but Keith, who could be arrested as soon he sets foot on French soil, will return to France the following day for a hearing before the judge. Wyman, Watts, and Mick Taylor fly from Jamaica to London where they board an executive jet to Paris that takes them to Nice. After meeting with lawyers in Paris, Mick Jagger joins them the next day.

It is only then that *The Times of London* reports, "Police said that Mick Jagger and three other members of the Rolling Stones have been charged with illegal use of heroin and other narcotics. The charges were made out before they went on a tour of the US this summer but were kept secret. Three young Frenchmen, who police said provided 50 grams of heroin to the Stones and their entourage each week during the summer of last year, were also arrested and present at the hearing."

On Monday, December 4, Mick Jagger, Mick Taylor, Bill Wyman, and Charlie Watts go to the judge's chambers in Nice. Everyone seems nervous save for Bianca, who has accompanied Mick to the hearing and is convinced that he is innocent of all the charges. As the French boys who made the charges are being questioned by the magistrate at the prefecture, the Stones (minus Keith) sit outside the hearing room on a wooden bench like so many naughty English schoolboys summoned to see the headmaster. Chewing her lip and fiddling with her handbag, Bianca opens the hearing room door a crack and listens in as the boys testify.

When an official comes over and asks her to sit on the bench with the others, Bianca says, "This is my husband they are talking about inside this room. I have every intention of listening and don't tell me it is not my affair because where my husband is concerned, everything is my affair." When the Stones themselves are called in to be questioned, Bianca giggles as she reports Charlie Watts' testimony to the others. "Charlie has been asked if he takes drugs. Charlie is telling them he never has, never was, and hardly ever lets a doctor give him a shot." Jagger, Taylor, and Wyman then all go into the room to answer questions and declare their innocence. When the French boys are questioned again, Bianca reports they are now retracting everything they said about the Stones.

As Bill Wyman later writes, "Everything went far better than any of us had hoped. The police witnesses denied everything and insisted that they were made to sign false statements. While this put us in the clear, it still left Keith with a major problem. We returned to Jamaica as the public prosecutor in Nice issued arrest warrants for Keith and Anita on charges of drug trafficking. One rumour had it that they could get the charge reduced to one of straightforward drug usage if they gave themselves up." As the rest of the band flies back to Jamaica, Stones' publicist Les Perrin calls Keith in Kingston to tell him the news.

"At the moment I know they've got a warrant out for questioning," Keith says, "and I don't know if I'm going to go back and be questioned. It's all a bunch of political bullshit . . . I have the feeling the French are trying to show the Americans that they are doing something about the drug problem. But rather than actually doing something about it, they bust a big name. The only thing I resent is that they try and drag my old lady into it. I find that particularly distasteful."

That Mick Jagger, Bill Wyman, Charlie Watts, and Mick Taylor would fly halfway around the world to appear at a hearing in France without knowing in advance what the outcome would be seems unlikely even now. As a Stones insider who was then in a position to know, recalls, "It may have happened that those who swore charges against them were bought off. But it wasn't something that was ever discussed since we had people there handling it. We had a real good French lawyer who said, 'You come back, it's all taken care of.' No one ever spells it out or writes it down. If you pay off a speeding ticket, you don't write it down. No one talks about cash, exactly. But these things don't vanish unless you pay somebody. The only guy who knows it is the one who did it. The bag man. But we would never have flown them into France if we thought there was any danger of them being arrested."

Confirming that this is in fact how the deal went down, another Stones insider will later say, "The band all lost the money they'd saved by moving to France because they had to pay it out when Keith got busted. Huge bribes to the government and lawyers' fees and all that. They each paid an equal share of that, can you imagine? Which seems astounding, if you think about it now."

Nearly nine months later on the morning of October 15, 1973, three days before the end of the Stones' current European tour, Keith's case finally comes before the judge at the correctional tribunal in Nice. Of the twelve people charged in the case, five defendants, including Keith, Anita, Bobby Keys, and Tommy Weber are not present before the court. However, a promoter named Georges Guyot does appear with a medical certificate stating that Keith and his companion Anita have been through detox and that, in April 1972, Anita gave birth to a little girl in perfect health.

As the Stones play before fifteen thousand fans in the Palais de Sport in Antwerp, Keith and Anita are found guilty of the use, supply, and trafficking of cannabis. Both receive one-year suspended sentences and a fine of five thousand francs (a thousand dollars). Bobby Keys is given a four-month suspended sentence and a fine of a thousand francs (two hundred dollars). Two American citizens identified as a student and a house painter are given two months in prison. "Eventually," Tommy Weber recalls, "they all got off and I was the guy who was lumbered with the blame for all this. I've still got all these horrific charges outstanding in France. Which don't die. They don't seem to have a statute of limitations. So I've never dared to go there again. And I've got a house there."

On December 18, 1973, the day Keith turns thirty, the court of appeal in Aix-en-Provence upholds his conviction. He and Bobby Keys are barred from French territory for two years. And so ends the legal process stemming from the nonstop party at the Villa Nellcote during the summer of nineteen seventy-one.

Before any of this happens, Keith and Anita pull a Houdini. No pun intended, they take a powder. Like Bonnie and Clyde, they go on the lam. They skedaddle. They do the cow-cow boogie out the big front door of Nellcote, speed down Avenue de Louise Bourdes, turn left on to the Corniche, and then head as fast as they can for the airport in Nice where they board a plane and fly to safety. Like Elvis, Keith and Anita have now left the building. They have flown the coop.

One moment they are in residence at Nellcote, fearing that at any moment the front door will fly open and the gendarmes will flood into the villa and drag them off to jail, and the next they are gone like a cool breeze. "And we just kind of . . . ran," Anita tells John Perry. From Villa Nellcote, Keith wisely decides to run before they make him do the perp walk with his head down and his hands cuffed behind his back. As always, where Keith goes, the rest of the band must follow.

Just as they did when they boarded a helicopter to escape the chaos at Altamont in 1969, the Rolling Stones move on, leaving it to others to sort out what they have left behind. On November 29, 1971, Mick Jagger, Keith Richards, Anita Pallenberg, Mick and Rose Taylor, Jimmy Miller, and Andy Johns fly to Los Angeles, where they are joined by Charlie and Shirley Watts and Bill Wyman and Astrid Lundstrom. Behind them, Keith and Anita leave the fabulous Villa Nellcote. Neither of them will ever see the house again. They also leave Keith's treasured record collection, most of Anita's extensive wardrobe, and Marlon's toys, not to mention Boots the parrot, Okee the dog, Keith's speedboat, and his Jaguar E-type car.

Though Villa Nellcote now stands empty, Keith continues paying rent on it for another year to maintain the fiction that he is still in residence in France. Over the course of that year, Spanish Tony reports that it costs Keith nearly a quarter of a million dollars in rent and legal fees to keep the authorities from extraditing him back to France for trial. Once a week during this period, June Shelley drops by Nellcote to check on Elizabeth Hiemer whose job it has now become to care for a house in which no one lives. After eight tumultuous months, with their new album not even close to being finished, the Rolling Stones' time of exile in the south of France is over. And so is our first act.

## Charlie Watts, Mick Jagger, and Keith Richards

in the kitchen at Villa Nellcote with cake

# ACT TWO

## 17

**While Los Angeles** may well be, as Neil Young once sang, an uptight city in the smog, it has also always been a Stones town. As far back as the band's first tour of America in 1964, which began with a knockout show at the Swing Auditorium in nearby San Bernardino and then went steadily downhill until the boys blew everyone away at their final gig in New York's Carnegie Hall, the city of falling angels has always welcomed the Rolling Stones as one of their own. What with KMET and KLOS, the two hip underground FM radio stations in town, constantly blasting the Stones, their music has literally become the soundtrack of the city and so it is most definitely here that the Stones belong.

Technically, however, they are still in exile. Although the natives speak a rough approximation of the English language, and cocaine, which soon becomes the drug of choice as the excruciating process of mixing the album begins, is much easier to procure in southern California than it was in the south of

France, LA does not feel like home. But then for those who were born and raised in England, how could it?

Rose Taylor, who has never before been to America, now finds herself living with Mick and baby Chloe in a little ranch house just a stone's throw from Keith and Anita's temporary abode on the very fashionable Stone Canyon Road in Bel-Air. "We moved into this house," Rose Taylor recalls, "and everything was all white and plastic and fake. There was this concrete log in the fireplace and it was just awful. I couldn't stand it. What saved my life that summer or spring or January or whenever it was, because the seasons are so weird there, was the song, 'Oh, Happy Day.' Every morning, Mick and I would wake up and say, 'Oh no, we're still here.' And we'd go back under the bed clothes."

Assuming that such a thing actually exists in Los Angeles, Stone Canyon Road hardly qualifies as a normal neighborhood. Not with the very posh pink stucco Bel-Air Hotel just down the road, record executive Lou Adler and Britt Ekland in residence nearby, and former teen idol Ricky Nelson performing with The Stone Canyon Band. Still, life there on a daily basis does not hold a candle to the decadent madness the Stones have only just left behind in the south of France.

A short drive away, Mick, Bianca, and baby Jade are now ensconced in a thirty-room mansion straight out of Billy Wilder's *Sunset Boulevard*. Featuring an artificial waterfall that has long since gone dry, the house was once owned by Marion Davies, the long-time mistress of William Randolph Hearst, upon whom Orson Welles modeled the central character of *Citizen Kane*. On a regular basis, movie star buses soon begin stopping at the bottom of Mick and Bianca's driveway so tourists can gaze in wonder at the house.

"Still," as Mick himself notes one day shortly before the album is due to be released, "the anonymity here is pretty good. It's not like England, where it's so crowded one has to buy a thousand acres to have any privacy, where they line up outside your house to find out who you fucked the night before. I hate that place. . . . Really, it's such a pathetic little village sometimes." Asked to describe his time in the south of France, Mick just sighs and says, "Do you know there are no more salmon in the rivers of France any more? They've killed them all with pollution. In Nice and Cannes, the French are thieves. I'll never live there again."

Be that as it may, Los Angeles is more than just a change of scene for the Stones. It is where Mick and Keith, much like two heavyweight fighters who have run out of steam at the end of a knockdown drag-out fifteen-round slugfest retreat to their respective corners to await the referee's decision. Setting aside their differences, at least for the time being, they more or less join forces to finish the album so they can begin earning some serious money by touring America during the upcoming summer.

In part, the sea change in their relationship has less to do with their personal feelings for one another than the nature of the work in which they are now engaged. Mixing is to recording as editing is to writing. Where the Stones are concerned, it can also take forever. In the past, whenever the time finally came for Mick and Keith to determine precisely how they wanted their new record to sound, what the levels should be, how much music belonged on each side, and how the songs should be sequenced so as to flow into another like chapters in a novel, they could be like two great millstones grinding against one another, with the end result being a mountain of finely powdered dust. That is not how the process works this time around.

In the south of France, it was always Mick who was waiting for Keith to come up with the music and then give his approval to the way it had been played so recording could proceed. In Los Angeles, Mick steps forward and takes charge. With their services no longer required on a nightly basis now that the basic tracks are done, Charlie Watts and Bill Wyman come and go like sidemen rather than full-time members of the band.

As Mick and Keith continue doing what Andy Johns calls "a bunch of overdubs, nothing absolutely vital, just embellishment stuff, background vocals, et cetera," Johns begins to mix the album, something he could never have done in the mobile outside Nellcote. "It was still a bit tedious," he says, "but we were getting things done and then I started mixing and it was going slowly. And then it got to Christmas and I'd been taking a long time to get mixes. I think we had four or five tunes and Mick thought I was taking too long so I went home for the Christmas holiday and wasn't asked back and they started working with Jimmy Miller's protégé, Joe Zagarino. He tried mixing and I think they may have done one or two tiny overdubs with him but he couldn't make it work."

No longer employed by the Rolling Stones, Johns returns to LA after the holidays to begin another project. "I was working with Jim Price on a solo album out in Malibu," he recalls, "and someone had just given me a hash cookie that had really started to come on strong. And I don't like that kind of stuff anyway which is why I don't do it at all anymore. So I was sitting in my room paranoid as hell with the chair under the door handle so no one could come in and the phone rang and Jimmy [Price] said, 'Oh, it's someone on the phone for you.' And it was Jagger. Who then had to proceed to eat a little bit of humble pie without sounding like it. I said, 'You didn't call to say hello. What is it?' 'Well, you know, those mixes of yours, we can't seem to beat them.'" In typical fashion, Mick then added, "No one seems to be able to mix this because you recorded it so badly." Returning to the fold, Johns spends a day or two with Jagger at Wally Heider's. "It wasn't working," Johns says, "and we went back to Sunset Sound and Mick said, 'Here are the tapes. Just finish the fucking thing. You've got two days.' So I did."

In one marathon forty-eight hour session, Johns mixes thirteen tracks. Jimmy Miller, who was "quite helpful" with Johns' first few mixes, has by now stopped showing up for sessions. Miller does appear in the studio one night as Johns nears the end of his mammoth task only to fall asleep on the couch because, as Johns recalls, "he was so burnt out on the thing, and I didn't blame him."

When Bill Wyman returns to LA at the end of January, he discovers, "Marshall Chess thought the tracks sounded good, but might need remixing (this was a frightening thought). Mick told me 13 tracks were now finished and were all sounding fine. Keith, who seemed to be much better, didn't make the meeting but called me to say that he hoped to finish up within the next two weeks." Wyman then goes back to France. He and Charlie Watts will not return to Los Angeles until late February.

Lest it seem that far more work was done on the album at Nellcote than has so far been indicated, it should be noted that "Sweet Virginia," "Sweet Black Angel," "Loving Cup," "Stop

Breaking Down," and "Shine A Light" were all recorded at earlier sessions for either *Let It Bleed* or *Sticky Fingers*. Of the eighteen tracks on the album, nearly a third predate the Stones' time in the south of France.

An album recorded under the influence of heroin, with songs that end in extended fades that seem to go on and on as though no one could bear the thought of cutting one track short so another could begin, is now being mixed by people snorting high-grade cocaine, a drug that tends to make all decisions just that much more difficult. All the same, there are certain perks to doing this kind of work in Los Angeles. Because it is a showbiz town, the locals are always more than willing to do whatever they can to accommodate their idols.

"We recorded 'All Down The Line' at Nellcote," Andy Johns says. "That was the first one that actually got finished and Mick said, 'This is a single. This is a single!' And I thought, 'He's out of his fucking mind. This is not a single.' And I went out and I said to him, 'You're wrong about this. This is not a single.' And he went, 'Really? Do ya think so?' And that was the first time I realized, 'Jesus, he'll actually listen to me.' "

After trying to mix the track in LA, Johns goes to Jagger and says, "'Jeez, I just can't imagine this on the radio.' And Mick said, 'Do ya want to hear it on the radio?' And I said, 'Yeah. How do you . . . ?' And he said, 'Oh, we can do that.' And he goes, "Stu, call up that radio station. Go round there with the tape. We'll call you from the limo. Have 'em put it on.' "

Johns soon finds himself sitting in the back of a limo with Keith and Mick and Charlie as the song is played. "I was tooling up and down Sunset with the Rolling Stones listening to a mix on the radio. How surreal is that?" Johns says. "And Mick said, 'What do you think?' And I said, 'I don't know, man.' And he said, 'We'll have Stu play it again.' 'Stu, have 'em play that again.' Sure enough. Here it was again. I thought that was pretty cool."

In the end, it is decided that "Tumbling Dice" will be the first single. "I think we may have spent two or three weeks just getting the track on that," Johns says. "That was just a performance thing. And they could play really badly, those guys. Most of the time, they were fucking terrible. There must have been some arrangement of it during that period but what I remember is just looking for a magical performance. But it went on and on and on. I had about thirty or forty or fifty reels of tape on that one song." With each reel of tape half an hour long, Johns is looking at anywhere from fifteen to twenty-five hours of recorded material on just that one song.

Late one night back at Wally Heider's, Mick Jagger walks into the control room and says, "Was this the Beach Boys studio? I mean, I've been here before. You lose all the highs." The regular studio engineer, who is there along with Jimmy Miller and Andy Johns, explains that the studio has been completely rebuilt. "You might think there's too much bottom, but that's because the top is going out over your head." Grimacing, Mick decides to stay. After a rough mix of "Tumbling Dice" is played, Johns asks Mick what he thinks. Looking up at the soundproof ceiling, Mick says, "I want the snares to crack. And the voices to float. It's tricky all right. You think you've got the voices sussed and all of a sudden, the backing track seems. . . ."

As Mick searches for *le mot juste* to describe exactly what he means, everyone in the room waits for what will come out of his famous mouth. " . . . so . . . *ordinaire,*" he says. The tape is reeled and re-reeled. Johns flicks knobs and the bass recedes, the drums become crisp, and the guitars overlap. Doing his best to make Mick Jagger happy, never an easy proposition in any circumstances, especially after he has just heard a take he does not particularly care for, Johns says, "I thought you liked the cymbals like that." Delivering final judgment, Mick says, "They sound like dustbin lids." For a second, Johns pouts. Then he rewinds the tape and begins flicking knobs once more.

While all this is going on, Mick Taylor is having an authentically hard time of it in LA. As Bill Wyman will later write, "Anita and Keith were not the only worry. We all knew that Mick T. had dallied with the hard stuff, but we didn't realise that his situation had left him very depressed." Janie Villiers, who works for Mick and Rose Taylor, has begun finding "little screwed-up notes" in which Mick Taylor has written not only that he no longer wants to be in the Rolling Stones but far worse, as Wyman writes, that "even his life might be at risk."

Occasionally, Mick Taylor will talk to Villiers "about his fears, saying, 'I'm so lonely. I never meet anyone any more.'" At one point in the proceedings, Taylor goes so far as to call Wyman to suggest that along with Charlie Watts, they record some of their own music. Wyman, who is nothing if not loyal, not to mention also very aware of the current state of the band's finances, tells him to forget it.

Six weeks before the album is scheduled to be released on May 7, 1972, Mick and Keith are still listening to alternate mixes. Up on Mulholland Drive in the little pool house where Marshall Chess now lives within spitting distance of both Jack

Nicholson and Warren Beatty, everyone convenes to have yet another go at it. Coming through the door holding album sleeves with Andy Johns by his side, Jimmy Miller says, "Take that shit off and play something good. We've redone five songs."

Getting on the phone, Marshall Chess begins making travel arrangements so he can hand-carry the masters with him to New York on Monday and then deliver them in person to Atlantic Records. On the couch, Mick and Keith sit slumped together, listening yet again to songs that by now they have literally heard a thousand times. With the sun starting to fade behind the hills and the light failing, all anyone can see of them in the gathering gloom is their pale white faces and feathered hair. More than ever, they look like brothers.

As the final chords of "Tumbling Dice" fade away, Mick closes his eyes and says, "They're both good, you know, Jimmy."

"Maybe the old one . . . " Keith mumbles.

Looking around as though hoping someone will come to his aid, Miller says, "I think the new one is more commercial."

In truth, the two mixes are so alike that not even Mick can tell them apart. As though the fate of the free world hinges on this decision, everyone discusses it for a while. The old one, the new one. Which one will sound better in mono? The old one. "Okay," Miller concedes, "the old one. We'll go back and play with it."

"Yeah," Johns agrees. "Just a fraction more on top. It's still a bit dull."

Across the room, Marshall Chess is now talking softly to himself. Considering all the time and the money the Stones have spent on this album, the fact that he has managed to keep the faith for this long is a miracle. As he will admit years later,

"At the beginning, I'm not saying it never entered my mind that they had no idea what they were doing. On nights when Keith would fall asleep or didn't even show up. But overall, I saw that even during *Sticky Fingers,* it would eventually come together. They would just lock. That was what they had. They had this magical ability, the alchemy of elements that combined into one like making steel from iron ore and coke. They wouldn't see each other sometimes for seven months and within two days they would be playing like they were one person, locked together."

As Jimmy Miller and Andy Johns collect the mixes so they can go off to do yet more work on them, Mick Jagger grabs a piece of paper and begins to sketch precisely how he wants the album title to look. "Fanatics," Marshall Chess says to himself as he laughs softly. "Fanatics."

At long last, the new Rolling Stones album is ready to be delivered. As always where the Stones are concerned, there is still one small problem. Keith Richards, the man without whom the band cannot possibly go on tour to support *Exile On Main St.* is in no shape to do much of anything, much less walk out on stage to play for nearly two hours a night for six weeks. And then there is Anita. Now seven months pregnant, she is, in terms often used back then by those around the Stones, also "not doing well." The new album may be finished. But until both of them are on their feet again, the Rolling Stones are not going anywhere to support it.

# 18

**When a reporter** from *Rolling Stone* magazine comes to visit Keith Richards at his home on Stone Canyon Road in Los Angeles on the day the new mixes are to be played for Marshall Chess, Keith is lying on the roof of a vintage two-tone Chevrolet making faces at his son Marlon through the windshield. "Have you heard?" Keith says as he clambers down from the roof. "They're at it again. They decided to re-mix the whole album. Been up for thirty-one hours so far I hear." Laughing at the absurdity of it all, he adds, "Always happens. The more you mix, the better it gets."

Inside the house, chaos reigns because Keith and Anita are packing to fly to Switzerland at four o'clock the next afternoon. Looking hugely pregnant, Anita walks into the kitchen as Keith sits talking to the reporter. "We figured Marlon was lonesome," Keith explains laconically. "So we let it happen." When the reporter asks Anita if she is carrying twins, she sternly replies, "No, it is the dress." She then begins throwing things into what will be the first of nineteen pieces of luggage. Asked if the upcoming Stones' tour will be the last one, Keith says, "I doubt it. We need the money."

Although all sorts of wheels are already turning to get them out of the country, neither Keith nor Anita gives the slightest hint that anything is wrong with either of them. Calling June Shelley in France, Marshall Chess has instructed her to fly to Geneva to meet Keith and Anita after he puts them on a plane the next day in Los Angeles. Chess never tells Shelley why they are going there. Just that he wants her to meet them and that he has already booked rooms for them and her at a hotel in Nyon, a little town outside Geneva. Chess also tells Shelley to have Dave Powell drive Keith's Jaguar to Geneva and that he will have Keith call Powell with a list of which toys and records and books to bring with him in the car from Nellcote.

Arriving in Geneva on Sunday, March 26, Shelley picks up a rental car at the airport and drives to see some friends from whom she borrows a thousand Swiss francs ($500). She checks into the hotel and calls Maitre Nicolai, whom she describes as "a hot shot Swiss lawyer" who represented IOS founder Bernie Cornfeld when he was jailed in Switzerland for a year. Over the phone, Shelley is told that Nicolai and his assistant will also be at the airport to greet Keith and Anita and that they will be arriving with a sixteen-year old girl from California "who was kind of a groupie" but is now serving as Marlon's nanny. Only then does Shelley learn that Keith and Anita are coming to Switzerland to check into a clinic "to get rid of their heroin addiction," news which she finds shocking.

Shelley is also told that Nicolai has found a clinic to accept Keith and Anita that is right across the street from the hotel where they are all meant to stay that night. Although Nicolai himself is on his way to Argentina, he tells Shelley his assistant will be there the next day to handle all the details.

When Shelley asks him why Keith and Anita are doing this, Nicolai tells her that he and people in the Stones' hierarchy have come up with the idea of a voluntary drug cure. If Keith and Anita can get a piece of paper from the clinic certifying that they have gone through detox, they can use this to prove that although they might have been using drugs at Nellcote, they are now clean. Which may do wonders to reduce their sentence or perhaps even persuade the judge to let them off with not much more than a warning and a fine. Since what is really at stake here is the continuing ability of the Rolling Stones to generate vast amounts of cash by touring the world without being denied entry to any country because of a drug bust on the French Riviera,

Keith and Anita would seem to have little choice but to go along with the plan.

Shelley is enjoying a gourmet lunch at the airport when Marshall Chess calls from Los Angeles to say that Keith and Anita have missed their plane. Although this is nothing new, the reason the two of them will not be arriving today is that they both went to the UCLA clinic to obtain enough methadone to keep from withdrawing on the flight. Although Anita did well on the methadone, Chess tells her that Keith got sick at LAX and so did not board the plane. As there is only one direct flight a day from Los Angeles to Geneva, the plan is for them to try again tomorrow.

When Shelley returns to the airport the next day, Keith and Anita come off the plane with Marlon and their new nanny in tow. Dressed outrageously as always, Anita, who is by now quite big with child, looks fine. The same cannot be said for Keith. With them, Keith and Anita have brought so much luggage that Shelley has to make arrangements for a truck to deliver it to the hotel. Throwing three or four suitcases into her rental car, Shelley drives everyone to the hotel for lunch in a lovely little dining room right by the lake. Anita, who seems quite cheerful, keeps saying, "The air is so good here. It must be wonderful for the children." Three or four times, she asks Shelley if she does not think that Switzerland would be a wonderful place to raise a child. As Shelley will later note, Anita seems very bubbly and up and is showing no symptoms of withdrawal whatsoever.

When the food comes, Keith, who has been sitting with his head down, takes one look at it, turns green, and excuses himself to go upstairs. Telling Shelley that Keith has not eaten anything in an awfully long time and that she is concerned for him because he isn't doing very well on the methadone, Anita has Shelley arrange for a bowl of soup to be sent up to his room. After taking another methadone tablet, Keith recovers. By three or four that afternoon, he seems better. Leaving Marlon with the nanny so the two of them can go on playing with the swans by the side of the lake, Shelley gets Keith and Anita into the car and drives them to the clinic for an admittance interview.

From the very start, the doctors seem arrogant, telling Shelley in French that Keith and Anita must come in immediately and cannot have visitors after they are admitted. One of the reasons this clinic has been chosen is that it does not look like a hospital. With bungalows spread out beneath green hills, it seems more like a convalescent home. Based on what Keith has been told, he thinks he will be living here with Anita, Marlon, and the nanny. In French, the doctor informs Shelley that this will not be possible. Here in Switzerland, they do not do that sort of thing. Marlon and the nanny cannot be part of the process. Although Shelley keeps lying through her teeth as she translates to keep Keith from walking out, he gets the message all the same.

An hour and a half after they all leave, Anita calls Shelley and asks her to come to their room. Keith is starting to sweat a little but otherwise seems okay. Anita tells Shelley they will not be going into that clinic and so she has to find them another place. Through a doctor friend who works for the World Health Organization in Switzerland, Shelley learns of a Dr. Denber, an American married to a Swiss woman who runs the Clinic De Nantes in Vevey. Shelley calls him up and says, "I'm here with one of the Rolling Stones. He and his lady are both addicted and they've come up here to drug cure. We were supposed to go to the Clinic de Prangins but that didn't work out . . . " Denber says, "I can handle it. Get them to the Clinique de Cery in Lausanne by twelve-thirty or one o'clock tomorrow and I'll see them."

The next day, Keith just keeps getting sicker. Having thrown up the methadone, he is limp and nauseated. His skin is green and he is going through full-scale withdrawal. Shelley calls Dr. Denber at the clinic in Lausanne and says, "I can't get them there. They're too sick." When Denber tells her he does not make house calls, she begins pleading with him. Hearing the desperation in her voice, he agrees to come to Nyon. When Shelley returns to her room, Anita calls to say, "Keith needs a shot."

Shelley has so little idea of what she is dealing with here that she says, "A shot, how do you mean?" "You know," Anita tells her, "a booster shot." Shelley has no idea how to arrange this until Anita suggests that she go back to the doctors they saw at the clinic the day before. Although Keith and Anita have no intention of admitting themselves there, the doctors do not know this and so Anita believes they will help.

Somehow, Shelley manages to persuade the more arrogant of the two doctors at the clinic that if he does not come to give Keith a shot, she will not be able to get him or Anita there for treatment. As the doctor heads up the stairs to Keith and Anita's room at the hotel, he tells Shelley, "You better have them packed." He then gives Keith the shot. Almost immediately, Keith starts feeling better.

By the time Dr. Denber arrives, Keith is no longer shaking or sweating. His skin is no longer green. When Denber walks into Keith and Anita's room, he finds them both lying on the bed, fully dressed. Pulling a chair up to the side of the bed, Denber says, "Okay. What's the story?" Keith says, "We're on a hundred dollar a day habit." A moment later, Anita adds, "Each." In Los Angeles back then, a gram of very pure and powerful China White heroin could be purchased on the street for a hundred dollars. To use it all in a twenty-four-hour period would mean that Keith and Anita have been fixing every three or four hours, or about five times a day.

Denber asks which one of them is worse off. Anita tells him she is fine. Denber explains that by Swiss law, he cannot permit their son to go with them into his clinic but that Keith can come in tonight to get started. Because Swiss law also states that no one can be admitted to a hospital unless they live in the same canton in which the hospital is located, everyone will have to move to a hotel at the other end of the lake. Keith will be in the clinic for nine or ten days and when he comes out, Anita can go in. "Two separate cures," Denber says, "and how does that strike you?" After Keith agrees to the arrangement, Denber tells Shelley he expects to see Keith there that night. He then charges her five hundred francs ($250) for his visit.

By about six-thirty that night, as the effects of the shot begin wearing off, Shelley realizes Keith is in no shape to make it down the stairs, much less get in a car for a ride to the far end of the lake. Going to the front desk of the hotel, she says, "Monsieur Keith is quite ill and we have to take him to the hospital at the other end of the lake. Is there an ambulance service?" Because the ambulance service is out on a call, they will not be able to come for another hour.

By now, Anita, Marlon, and the nanny have gone into the

dining room to eat dinner while Keith remains upstairs. Unfortunately, the dining room looks out on to the stairs leading from his
room. Concerned that not only Marlon but all the other guests in
the hotel will see Keith Richards of the Rolling Stones being carried down the stairs in a stretcher, Anita asks Shelley to go to the
front desk and ask that the dining room doors be shut. "We
don't want his son to be upset with his daddy sick," Shelley tells
the hotel management, who agree to her request.

When the ambulance finally arrives, Shelley shuts the dining room doors and asks the attendants if there is any way
they can get Keith downstairs without putting him on a stretcher.
The attendants put Keith on a chair, drape something over him,
and carry him down the stairs with his arms around their
necks. Although he looks like a sultan being borne down the
steps of some imperial palace, Keith is by now semiconscious,
green, cold, and pale. As the attendants negotiate their way down
the winding stairway, his head lolls from side to side.

Once they get Keith into the ambulance, the attendants put
him on a stretcher. Shelley, who has never before been in an
ambulance, gets in back with him as Maitre Nicolai's assistant,
Maitre Hariri, follows along in his car. In the darkness, Shelley
is alone with Keith in the back of the ambulance. Holding his
hand, she keeps saying, "Keith, you're going to be fine. I'm going
to be there with you." Although the thought seems childish even
to her, Shelley cannot help but think that if Keith dies, they are
going to blame it all on her. She is going to be the one who lost a
Rolling Stone. Up front, the attendants, who are not paramedics
but simply ambulance drivers, are talking happily and singing
along to music from the radio.

Going ninety miles an hour and speeding through red lights

at crowded intersections so cars are forced to pull over to let them by, the ambulance driver cuts what is normally an hour-and-a-half journey in half. As soon as they reach the clinic, Shelley runs inside only to be confronted by a dragon of a nurse who tells her that Dr. Denber has already left for the night. Shelley tells her she has brought Dr. Denber's patient for admittance, but when the nurse asks who he is and where he lives, Shelley mistakenly gives her the address of the hotel in Nyon.

The nurse informs her that by Swiss law, this patient cannot be admitted here. Fortunately, Shelley has already called the Hotel de Trois Couronnes in Vevey and ordered a large suite with two adjoining rooms at the end of the corridor. "That was where we *were* staying," Shelley tells the nurse. "But we've moved to the Hotel de Trois Couronnes in Vevey. You can call them. They have the reservation."

Really teed off, the nurse demands, "Well, where is this Mr. Keith of yours? Is he in the hotel in Nyon or the Hotel des Trois Couronnes?"

"Don't you have him?" Shelley asks. "Didn't the ambulance drivers bring him in?"

Changing shape, form, and personality right before Shelley's eyes, the nurse suddenly becomes Florence Nightingale. "He's still in the ambulance?" she says.

Running outside, the nurse finds Keith lying in the stretcher. Bringing him inside, she gives Keith a vitamin shot and calls Dr. Denber. When the doctor arrives, he tells Shelley he will be putting Keith on Lucidril, a neuro-energizer and memory and membrane enhancer sometimes used to offset the effects of barbiturate intoxication. The drug can also sometimes help those who do not react well to methadone while withdrawing from heroin. Denber tells Shelley she can come and visit Keith once a day for fifteen minutes but that she cannot bring Anita with her as this might prove to be too upsetting.

Getting into the ambulance, Shelley sits by herself in back as the attendants return to Nyon. When she gets to the hotel, Anita is waiting for her. Shelley tells her that Keith is fine. In her absence, Dave Powell has delivered Keith's Jaguar packed with about a hundred records, Keith and Anita's clothing, a stereo, and Marlon's toys. After he hands Shelley the car keys, Powell leaves, returning to France to rejoin his girlfriend.

Because they are all so excited by the good news that Keith has made it to the clinic, Anita says, "Let's drive into town." Although the hotel staff is shocked that anyone would take such a young child out so late at night, Shelley and Anita drive with Marlon into Geneva along the lake. Feeling kind of crazy from the rush of adrenaline they are experiencing, they shout as they celebrate. Finally, they stop for some ice cream. Then they drive back to the hotel and go to sleep.

Against all odds, Keith has somehow made it from his house on Stone Canyon Road in Los Angeles to a clinic in Vevey, Switzerland. Somehow, he has managed to survive yet another serious bout of heroin use that began at Nellcote but became far worse in LA. Someone made of lesser stuff might have already fallen by the wayside. But not Keith. The good news is that Keith Richards is still alive. The bad news is that when he wakes up tomorrow morning in the clinic, his detox will begin.

## 19

**After moving Anita,** Marlon, and the nanny to their hotel in Vevey the next morning, June Shelley goes to visit Keith in the clinic. With her, she brings chocolates, oranges, and a note from Anita as well as a drawing and a little love letter from Marlon, who, as he hands his gifts to Shelley, says, "Are you going to see my daddy?" When Shelley arrives at the clinic, Keith, who is now being fed glucose and liquid vitamins through an IV, is fast asleep. Although Bill Wyman has already called offering to do anything he can to help, including coming to visit Keith in Switzerland, Shelley has told Wyman not to bother because so far no one has yet realized that "Mr. Keith" is in fact a Rolling Stone. Should anyone see Bill in Switzerland, it might alert the media to the real-life drama in which Keith now finds himself involved.

Day by day, Keith begins regaining his strength. Although Dr. Denber has asked Shelley not to let Keith smoke in his room, this is exactly what he wants to do as soon as he starts feeling better. Out of it one day, Keith lights a cigarette only to drop it on the bed. With their bare hands, he and Shelley beat out the flames. From that point on, Keith has to walk out into the hall-way to smoke like all the other patients. Sitting next to a patient who is catatonic one day, Keith puts a cigarette in his mouth and lights it. As though he is now playing the role of Randle Patrick McMurphy in Ken Kesey's *One Flew Over the Cuckoo's Nest,* he then puts a cigarette in the catatonic's mouth, lights it for him, and says to Shelley, "That guy goes through two packs a day."

Keith's sense of humor may have returned, but he is still so weak that when Shelley shows up with about a thousand dollars' worth of traveler's checks she needs him to sign because Anita is running out of money, he falls asleep before she can give him the pen. Holding his hand, Shelley helps him sign the checks with what she later describes as "the Sanskrit version" of his signature.

By his fifth day in the clinic, Keith is strong enough to walk around a little and go outside. Being Keith, he asks Shelley to bring him one of his acoustic guitars. After strumming it while lying on his bed, Keith goes out in the hallway for a smoke only to be recognized by a sixteen- or seventeen-year-old kid. "*Keith!*" the kid says with delight. "Where's Mick?"

"Ah, he's not here, man," Keith replies. "I'm trying to get my act together. I'm trying to get it straight." Telling Keith he also plays guitar, the kid runs to get his instrument. Soon enough, the two of them are playing together, with Keith doing his best to teach the kid a Stones song.

In the highly unlikely event that anyone has not yet recognized the grave nature of Keith's current situation, the point is underscored when Paddy Grafton-Green, the Stones' solicitor, flies in from London to help June Shelley set up a line of credit in Switzerland. As they sit together in Keith's room at the clinic, Grafton-Green advises Keith, then twenty-nine years old, that this would be a good time for him to make out his will. Grafton-Green takes notes as Keith names Anita as the executor of a will in which Keith makes bequests to his son and his mother, Doris. When Grafton-Green brings up the child Anita is now carrying, Keith says, "Well, let's see what happens. We have time to do that." After Grafton-Green has the will typed, Keith signs it.

At some point during his stay in the clinic, Keith writes Bill Wyman to thank him for offering to help and then goes on to say just how good he thinks Astrid is for him. Keith also says he thinks the two of them should write together more often. Then he adds, "PS: All this is written under heavy sedation, as you can probably tell by the wobble."

Based on a recommendation from Dr. Denber, June Shelley has made an appointment for Anita to see Dr. Merz, the physician who helped actress Sophia Loren give birth to a healthy child in Lausanne after she had suffered two miscarriages. Merz has an office that looks much like the drawing room of a Victorian mansion. When he comes in to see Anita, he begins speaking to her in English with a heavy German accent.

Dressed like a waif, Anita is wearing striped stockings and a very short skirt. One of her teeth is missing and her hair is unkempt. Being Anita, she still looks interesting, not to mention also very pregnant. Quite possibly because of her appearance, Merz says, "I'm sorry to bring this up but is there any problem about money? Because my fee and services are very expensive." When Shelley informs him that there is no problem, the doctor, who is used to eccentric people, accepts this as a fact and moves on to more pressing matters.

"Before we get into the details," he says, "I have a few questions to ask you. Do you smoke?"

"Yeah, sometimes," Anita says.

"Do you drink?"

"A little," Anita answers.

Realizing the doctor has no idea what he is dealing with here, Shelley keeps waiting for Anita to tell him the truth. "Do you drink a lot of coffee?" the doctor asks. On and on with the questions until Merz finally asks, "Are you taking any medication now?"

In a little girl voice, Anita says, "It's a little bit more complicated than that. You see, I'm on heroin."

Merz's mouth falls open as he literally drops his pen. "H-h-h-heroin?" he stammers. "You must stop that. Stop taking that heroin now. You must stop. How long have you been doing this taking of heroin?"

"Since the baby was three months old," she tells him. (In fact, she had been doing so since before the child was conceived.)

"Well," he says, "we have to examine you."

As Merz takes Anita into another room, Shelley says, "Look, you guys, forget about me. Speak German. It's your language." The two of them look at one another and Merz switches immediately to German. When he comes back out, Merz says, "The baby is very small but she's pretty good. I am concerned." He also says that Anita has a vaginal infection and tells Shelley to inform Dr. Denber of this fact so that if she has infected Keith, he will not give it back to her. Although Merz is leaving on vacation, he says he will return in two weeks. This should not be a problem because he has a doctor who covers for him. Besides, he will be back in plenty of time to deliver the baby.

With Keith about to come out of the clinic so Anita can go in, Shelley tells Keith she has a trip to New York that she cannot cancel. Because he and Anita definitely plan on living in Switzerland for a while after the baby is born, Keith asks Shelley to hire someone to help them while she is gone. Shelley finds a very nice Swiss girl in her late twenties who speaks English. She comes to the hotel to meet Anita and they agree on money. Shelley gives the girl all the phone numbers she will need and then she leaves.

Although Anita is very happy at the hotel and Marlon is thriving, riding his little tricycle in and out of the lobby and doing circles around all the tables in the dining room just like a male version of Eloise at The Plaza, the new nanny begins looking for a house to rent. Shelley flies to New York where she sees Jo Bergman and Alan Dunn. When she stops by the Stones' tour office across from Madison Square Garden two days later, someone tells her the shocking news that Anita has just given birth.

Shelley learns that as soon as Keith came out of the clinic, Anita went in and was then put on Lucidril. Within a day and a half she went into labor. Dr. Denber had not delivered a baby in thirty years and Merz was still on vacation. Because it was already too late to get Anita to Lausanne, Denber called the regular clinic in Vevey and said, "Get ready. I'm bringing you a woman in labor who's probably going to give birth to an addicted baby." The doctor to whom he was speaking said, "Hey, I don't know too much about that." To which Denber replied, "You know more than I do."

According to most of the medical literature on the subject, infants born addicted to opiates go through withdrawal as soon as they are separated from their mothers. They shake, twitch, fuss, and sweat. They throw up and cry relentlessly. Some have problems eating. In severe cases, they may suffer seizures. The traditional form of treatment for reducing these symptoms is to administer tincture of opium, a diluted form of morphine, so the newborn child can slowly be weaned off the drug.

Through some miracle that no one can explain, on April 17, 1972, two days after "Tumbling Dice" is released as the first single off the new Rolling Stones album, Anita Pallenberg gives birth to a baby girl who is not addicted and so does not have to suffer through the agony of neonatal abstinence syndrome. However, the child is so small that she is put immediately into an incubator. And although the plan was for Anita to go through her own drug cure, that concept has now also been rendered obsolete.

Instead of flying back to Nice, Shelley changes her ticket and returns to Geneva. As Shelley stands outside the hotel in Vevey talking to the girl she hired to look after Keith and Anita, a big limo rolls up. Looking terrific, out steps Keith. "The *only* way to travel," he says. After lunch, Keith takes Shelley to the hospital to see Anita and the baby. Anita is still on an IV to clear up her infection but otherwise looks just fine. Full of energy, she is talking about having her teeth fixed and all sorts of exciting brand new plans.

"Let's go look at the baby," Keith says.

Keith and Shelley walk down the corridor to a nursery in which there are only three or four babies. The one right in front of them belongs to Keith and Anita. Shelley asks, "What are you going to call her?" Keith says, "We're going to call her Dandelion." At that moment, the most perfect baby Shelley has ever seen opens her eyes. Everybody reacts and Keith says, "This is the first time I've seen her with her eyes open." Just like her mother, the child has very dark eyes that look almost black. "She has Anita's eyes," Shelley says. Insofar as she can tell, Keith is in love.

By all rights, it is here that our second act should end. Our hero Keith, redoubtable as brave Ulysses, has somehow managed to survive his own personal journey through hell. The new Rolling Stones' double album is about to be released all over the world. A slam-bang tour of America will follow. Keith also has a lovely brand new daughter to keep him happy. Having been given a brand new lease on life, no power in the world could ever drag him back to where he was just a few short weeks ago, lying not all that far from death in the back of an ambulance speeding around the lake in Switzerland.

Ah, but if only it were so. If only this were a play, a novel, or a movie in which the ending could be manipulated so as to make everyone feel better not only about ourselves, dear reader, but the human condition as well. Instead, as dark and portentous music thuds heavily in the background, here comes Spanish Tony. As always, he plays the dual role of the bearer of very bad news as well as Keith's evil twin, the dark brother who brings out in him everything he should have already long since learned to leave behind.

According to Tony, Keith calls him in London to tell him about the birth of his baby girl. Before Tony can congratulate him, Keith says, "Look, Anita's coming out of hospital tomorrow, and she's going to be screaming. I want you to fly out here with all the stuff you can get." In an astonishing bit of dialogue that only Tony could have created, he replies that although Keith is his best mate in all the world, for whom he would be happy to do virtually anything, Keith knows Tony would never sell drugs and most certainly never smuggle them, two services that Tony has already most certainly performed for Keith and more than once. Getting "riled," Keith tells Tony to have someone else do it for him then.

Obtaining half an ounce of heroin and half an ounce of cocaine, Tony promises a friend nine hundred dollars if he will carry it on him as he flies with Tony to Montreux where, as Tony writes, Keith and Anita are living in the Montreux Metropole Hotel. Since there is no Metropole Hotel in Montreux, this cannot be right. There is a Metropole in Geneva, but Keith and Anita are most certainly still staying at the Hotel de Trois Couronnes in Vevey, just outside Geneva, which is itself not all that far from Montreux.

While Tony may have gotten his Swiss towns mixed up, he does write that Keith picks him up at the airport in the same big limo that June Shelley remembers. The photographs Tony takes of Keith, Anita, and Marlon in Switzerland which appear in his book confirm that he was there at the time. And so, while we may not like this particular twist in the story, we have no choice but to go along with it and see what develops.

After they arrive at Keith and Anita's hotel, Tony waits until his friend has checked in. Tony then goes to his room, collects the stash, and brings it to Keith and Anita's suite where they "both took deep, grateful snorts, called me their lifesaver, and passed out." By the next morning, when "their euphoria had worn off," neither Keith nor Anita is willing to come up with as much money as Tony has promised his friend for his services. Telling Tony he only has five hundred dollars, Keith says, "He'll have to take it or leave it." As additional compensation for his troubles, Tony gives his friend an extra hundred and fifty dollars from his own pocket.

In five days, according to Tony, Keith and Anita use up all the cocaine and heroin he brought them and ask him to arrange for more drugs to be delivered to them. Keith promises Tony he will pay his friend the full nine hundred plus the four hundred he owes him from the last deal. Accepting the commission, the friend flies over with "a little more heroin and a Baggie of grass." Keith and Anita "devoured it greedily" and arrange for Tony's friend "to bring dope every ten days or so." Becoming "introspective and reclusive," Anita soon begins refusing to leave the suite. "Keith and I would take the children out for walks," Tony writes, while "Anita languished in solitary splendor, smoking joints, jabbing needles into her bottom and musing."

Whenever the hotel maids come to clean, according to Tony, Anita sends them away from behind locked doors. After three weeks, "the place stank of dirty socks and stale cigarette smoke. There were empty bottles everywhere, cigarette burns on most of the mock Louis XIV furniture and the sheets were an uninviting shade of gray." Declaring they can no longer live "in this pigsty," Keith asks to be moved to another floor. Before they clean the abandoned suite, the maids ask that it be defumigated, or so writes Tony.

And now, a question that only someone who has never been through this particular experience would even dare ask. To wit, why would anyone go through the agony of detox only to immediately begin using again? To begin with, there is the physical pain. "It doesn't stop after two or three days," Andy Johns says. "That's total calumny. You are jones-ing for a long time. At least six weeks. It's not throwing-up sick. It's impossible to describe how bad you feel. It's a feeling of absolute discomfort the entire time and it's intense. There's no illness I've ever had that comes close to that. This thing goes to the core of your being and your body is crying out the whole time for some more drugs, relentlessly, the whole time, non-stop, there's not a second's relief. And you know all you've got to do is pick the phone up and not only will you be straight, you'll feel better than normal. That's why it's so tough."

No matter how good someone may have felt while using, they feel far worse going through withdrawal. "Supposing you take it for three years and you want to stop," Johns says, "and you've had a few times when you couldn't score for four or five days and you wanted to kill yourself and all that. Now it goes on for two months. But what happens is that all the mental and physical pain you avoided in those three years comes back but it's compressed into a much shorter amount of time. All the back pain, all the little times you stubbed your toe, all of that, all the stuff you avoided and all the mental shit you avoided, it's there but it's compressed into this two month period as opposed to three years. That's the only way I can put it."

Marshall Chess, who during time of service with the Rolling Stones will have his own problems with the drug, adds, "Heroin is the strongest of all medicines for self-medication. I am not a psychiatrist but there was some part of it that made Keith feel better. Why do you think people in the ghetto get addicted? Because their life is horrible and they have no hope and they feel like shit and don't even know it. It takes years to withdraw, and for that to really wear off. That's why so many junkies become alcoholics afterwards. They have to kill that craving. That gnawing."

In truth, only the addict knows why he or she uses, why he or she continues to use, and why he or she finally stops using. "In the end," Andy Johns says, "you run out of money. That helps. And then if you're not around people who are doing it, then you're okay." Clearly, neither of these conditions apply to Keith or Anita. Although the Rolling Stones have not yet settled their long-running suit with Allen Klein, Keith and Anita still have unlimited financial resources upon which to draw. They also hang out with people who are using and/or willing to supply them with heroin. In terms of how hopeless it is to try to stop someone from becoming a junkie, Marianne Faithfull will later write that it is like trying to stop a train from running down the track.

# 20

**On Friday, May 5,** Mick Jagger phones Bill Wyman to fill him in on the details of legal negotiations with Allen Klein. Although Klein may owe the Rolling Stones as much as seventeen million dollars, Mick tells Wyman that if the band continues to pursue their lawsuit against him, their money could be tied up for two more years. The Stones' lawyers in New York have advised Mick that in order to free themselves of Klein, they should accept a two million dollar settlement, one million for Mick and Keith's song writing and publishing and one million more to be shared equally between the four original Stones and the estate of Brian Jones.

With legal costs split five ways, Bill Wyman and Charlie

Watts will each receive but a hundred and sixty thousand dollars. Wyman talks to Watts about it and then calls Prince Rupert to present another proposal. In order to keep peace within the band, Mick and Keith each come up with another fifty thousand dollars for Charlie and Bill. Feeling "a little more satisfied," Wyman accepts the offer.

In return for permission to release an album that contains songs undoubtedly written and recorded while the band was still under contract to Allen Klein, the Rolling Stones allow him to go on administering the rights to all of their previously recorded material. The actual sum of money they accept in return is, even back then in rock 'n' roll terms, a pittance. To continue enjoying their very expensive lifestyles, the Stones will have to keep recording new albums and touring to support themselves. From their back catalog, they will make only as much as they did when they first signed with Klein. Five days later when the settlement is announced in a press release, Allen Klein says, "Lawsuits are like wars—no one wins."

On Friday, May 12, Bill Wyman flies to Geneva with Astrid, where they are met by Ian Stewart and June Shelley. As Wyman and Astrid check into a hotel in Montreux where rehearsals for the upcoming tour will be held in the Rialto Cinema, they bump into Marshall Chess and, as Wyman later writes, "a Keith Richards who looked so much better. It was a great relief."

On Wednesday, May 24, the Rolling Stones convene as a band at the United States Embassy in London's fashionable Grosvenor Square where Mick Jagger once went to get his fair share of abuse while demonstrating against the Vietnam War.

After, as Wyman will later write, "enduring a lecture like school-boys from an elderly American lady," the Rolling Stones are granted work permits so they can tour America.

A reasonable question to ask at this point in the proceedings might be how it is that during an era when President Richard Nixon is busy sealing America's borders against drugs while doing all he can to destroy the tattered remains of the radical political underground, the Stones manage to gain legal entry to the USA. Ironically, it is not Keith's heroin use but Mick's record that should raise red flags all over the embassy.

On December 19, 1969, nine months after being busted in his flat on Cheyne Walk by Detective Sergeant Robin Constable, Mick pleaded guilty to possession of cannabis. In addition to being ordered to pay a two-hundred-pound fine and fifty-two pounds in court costs, he was given an eighteen-month ban on travel to the United States, thereby making it impossible for the Stones to tour or record in America during this period. Just four months after the ban expired, Mick was back in LA working on *Exile*.

That no one at the American Embassy seems to have any qualms whatsoever about letting Mick Jagger re-enter the United States for what will become to that point in time the highest grossing rock 'n' roll tour in history seems remarkable even now. (As well as the fact that no one administers a blood test to Keith to verify that he is clean.) Can all this just be a stroke of good fortune for the Rolling Stones? A lucky twist of fate for a band who despite all their travails deserve a chance to spread the gospel of rock 'n' roll once more in America? Or, as is so often the case where the Stones are concerned, can it be that some of their friends in high places have interceded for them?

Aside from being the founder of Atlantic Records, Ahmet Ertegun is also the son of the former Turkish Ambassador to the United States. Due in no small part to his great charm, personal charisma, and enormous wealth, there is almost no one Ahmet does not know. To ensure that the Rolling Stones will be allowed to tour America, Ahmet has reached out for a personal favor.

Long before the Stones ever assemble at the embassy, Ahmet puts in a good word for them with Senator Jacob Javits of New York. Sixty-eight years old, Javits is a very liberal Republican who also happens to be the highest-ranking minority member of the Senate Foreign Relations Committee. The senator's connection to Ahmet seems to have come through his considerably younger wife Marian, a friend of the Polish novelist Jerzy Kosinski and a regular in the back room at Max's Kansas City.

In accordance with the rules governing behavior in the social class to which both Jacob Javits and Ahmet Ertegun belong, the senator is only too happy to do what he can to ease the Stones' way into the country. As one Stones' insider recalls, "It was all done correctly but everything is done on technicalities in that world. I don't think they were let in because the money the Stones were going to earn in America was good for everyone. It was good for their record sales. Because *Exile On Main St.* was about to be released. It got smoothed over through personal favors. Because that's the way the system works, isn't it?"

Nor is it just a coincidence that no one at the embassy seems to know the first thing about all the charges pending against the Rolling Stones stemming from arrests made five months earlier in the south of France. Since those charges have not yet been made public, how could they? This too is no accident. Through their extensive political and financial connections in France, including their relationship with a well-known viscount as well as the Rothschilds, the first family of merchant banking and fine wine in France since the time of Napoleon, those in the Stones' hierarchy have made certain that the case is proceeding with all due deliberation. Which is why the charges will remain secret for another six months, only to suddenly emerge once the Stones' American tour is over.

As the Stones are granted official permission to enter the United States, the band is told there have already been so many advance orders for *Exile On Main St.*, released in America just two days earlier, that they have already been awarded a gold record for the album. On Thursday, May 25, they all fly to Los Angeles to continue rehearsing for a tour that kicks off in Vancouver, Canada, on June 3, ending six weeks later in Madison Square Garden on July 26, Mick Jagger's twenty-ninth birthday.

Before the tour begins, the Stones agree that with the exception of Bill Wyman, who steadfastly refuses to abide by the rules, none of them will bring their female companions with them on the road, thereby making it easier for them all to concentrate on playing kick ass rock 'n' roll night after night in smoky, crowded hockey arenas from coast to coast. While Bianca makes a guest appearance in Madison Square Garden, walking out on stage at the end of the last show of the tour to present Mick with a giant panda and a birthday kiss, Anita is nowhere to be seen. In no shape to travel, she remains in exile with her newborn daughter in Switzerland.

For those interested in reading about the Rolling Stones' journey through America in the summer of 1972, just one short year after they all convened at Villa Nellcote in the south of France to record their only double album, a book about that tour is still in print. To be sure, it reads nothing like this one. In part, that is because it was written thirty-three years ago, back when the Rolling Stones and everyone around them was not only still relatively young but also much better looking than they are today. At the time, no one would have believed how many of those people would, in the immortal words of Pete Townshend, die before they got old.

**Keith, Bianca, Mick, and Anita,** through a glass darkly,
Villa Nellcote, July 1971

# AFTERMATH

## 21

**And what of** the album itself? Funny you should ask. Considering the human toll exacted while *Exile On Main St.* was being recorded, it would be lovely to report that the end result is a work of art so astonishing that all the suffering was worthwhile. If only life and art, insofar as the Rolling Stones are concerned, have ever been quite that simple.

(**Note to Reader:** Those seeking a track-by-track analysis of *Exile On Main St.* detailing how each song was recorded, overdubbed, and mixed, along with a complete list of every musician involved and what they played, are hereby advised to consult the works mentioned at the end of this book, this sort of travail having always been the bailiwick of rock critics as opposed to rock writers, assuming there are in fact any of them still left alive.)

Having said this, let us now dispel the myth that *Exile On Main St.* came into this world like a lead balloon, landing with a deadly thud at the feet of an audience not yet ready to comprehend what their boys, the Rolling Stones, were putting down. Witness the unsigned entry in Wikipedia, which notes, "Initially greeted with lukewarm reviews, the double LP has since been critically reappraised and is now commonly considered one of the best albums in The Rolling Stones' entire catalogue. . . . Although its initial critics considered *Exile On Main St.* to be a ragged record, its legend grew steadily over time and has since been considered by many as The Rolling Stones' finest hour."

In other words, like some legendary Bordeaux that absolutely reeked of vinegar when it was first put in the bottle, the songs on *Exile On Main St.* have mellowed and ripened with age, becoming an elixir so powerful that it is best sampled only on memorable occasions. Like so much of what passes as the truth about the Rolling Stones and their collective *oeuvre*, this is not quite true.

In a review in *Melody Maker* entitled "The Stones: quite simply the best," which appeared when the album was released, Richard Williams wrote, "*Exile on Main Street* is definitely going to take its place in history. It is, I think, the best album they've made, which is pretty remarkable because it's a double album and consistency has never been the Stones' forte. . . . Once and for all, it answers any questions about their ability as rock 'n' rollers."

In the June 4, 1972, issue of *Record Mirror,* Norm Jopling wrote, "'Exile On Main Street' is a great record packed with energy, excitement, and repetition. . . . Lots of styles and influences, but unlike the Beatles' pristine white double album, it works much more on the physical level. . . . Many of the tracks are absolutely tremendous. . . . The Stones have gone on and on churning out the same music, and they've reached a definite peak here."

In the *New York Times* on the same day, Don Heckman noted, "The recordings are the best cross-section yet of the unique elements that make up the Stones' music. . . . 'Exile On Main Street' has enough rock music, of all shades and styles, to make anyone happy. . . . The Stones are looking inward now, and if they help you to understand something about yourself, that just might be the most revolutionary act of all."

While none of these reviews can be categorized as luke-warm, there were those who had their doubts about *Exile*. In the July 6, 1972, issue of *Rolling Stone,* Lenny Kaye, who went on to have a pretty fair career as the lead guitarist in the Patti Smith Group, wrote, "There are songs that are better, there are songs that are worse, there are songs that will become your favorites and others you'll probably lift the needle for when their time is due." (See, kids, back then, people listened to music on Victrolas with . . . ah, never mind.)

Kaye also noted that the album "spends its four sides shading the same song in as many variations as there are Rolling Stone readymades to fill them, and if on the one hand they prove the group's eternal constancy and appeal, it's on the other that you can leave the album and still feel vaguely unsatisfied, not quite brought to the peaks that this band of bands has always held out as a special prize in the past."

*Exile,* Kaye added, is "the Rolling Stones at their most dense and impenetrable. In the tradition of Phil Spector, they've constructed a wash of sound in which to frame their songs, yet where Spector always aimed to create an impression of space and airiness, the Stones group everything together in one solid mass, providing a tangled jungle through which you have to move toward the meat of the material."

Two years later, Paul Williams, who founded *Crawdaddy* magazine and bears the awful responsibility of having first brought serious thought to the business of reviewing rock records, expressed a somewhat similar (albeit far more personal) opinion by writing, ". . . the album, a big double-set with arty cover and blues pretensions, just never grabbed me, the music seems garbled and doesn't seduce me, doesn't speak to my secret reality. This time there aren't even perfect songs, just perfect moments inside the songs, and it's not enough."

Bear in mind that when *Exile* first appeared and for a good while thereafter, no one knew a thing about the drug-induced chaos of that summer at Nellcote. Whereas *Beggars Banquet, Let It Bleed,* and *Sticky Fingers* had mirrored the lives of those who loved the band, this was not the case with *Exile.* For most Stones fans back then, heroin was not the drug of choice. Nor had they ever spent a summer living in the south of France. The state of metaphysical exile about which the Stones were now writing and singing had not yet found its way to the street.

Like some great two-headed monster no one could understand or control, *Exile On Main St.* simply confused many of those who had always looked to the Stones for the soundtrack of their lives. Sure it was rock 'n' roll and blues and country, but taken as a whole, what the hell was it really? A mess or a masterpiece? Back then, no one could say for sure.

When the Stones toured America in 1972 shortly after *Exile* was released, they regularly played six songs from the album on stage (out of a total of sixteen). In the order performed, they were "Rocks Off," "Happy," "Tumbling Dice," "Sweet Virginia," "All Down The Line," and "Rip This Joint." "Sweet Black Angel" also made its way into the set on at least one occasion, but "Loving Cup," "Torn and Frayed," and "Ventilator

Blues" were only performed during the long and fairly disorganized opening show at the Pacific Coliseum in Vancouver and then dropped from the set, never to reappear.

Wisely, the Stones chose to give fans who had not seen them since 1969 a comprehensive overview of their entire catalog, opening with the double sledgehammer blow of "Brown Sugar" and "Bitch" from *Sticky Fingers* followed by "Gimme Shelter," Robert Johnson's "Love In Vain," "You Can't Always Get What You Want," and "Midnight Rambler" from *Let It Bleed* before concluding with "Jumpin' Jack Flash." The encore consisted of "Street Fighting Man" from *Beggars Banquet* and then "Satisfaction" from *Out of Our Heads,* released in 1965. "Satisfaction" was sometimes supplanted by "Honky Tonk Women," which was released as a single before *Let It Bleed* but appears on the album as "Country Honk."

Night after night on that tour, the single best song the Stones performed from *Exile* was "Sweet Virginia," which Mick would sing in a blue spotlight with Keith and Mick Taylor sitting on either side of him on high wooden stools playing acoustic guitars. "Happy" was always moving, if only because Keith was still singing in a voice that had not yet been shattered beyond recognition. Perhaps because of all the work they had done on the track in the studio as well as the multitude of mixes that followed, "Tumbling Dice" always seemed dead on arrival when the Stones played it live. While "Rocks Off," "All Down The Line," and "Rip This Joint" rocked hard on stage, they served primarily as filler, allowing the crowd to regain its collective breath before the Stones hit them with yet another masterpiece. Or so it seemed back then.

Nine years later, *Village Voice* rock critic Robert Christgau wrote of *Exile,* "More than anything this fagged-out masterpiece is difficult—how else to describe music that takes weeks to understand? Weary and complicated, barely afloat in its own drudgery, it rocks with extra power and concentration as a result. More indecipherable than ever, submerging Mick's voice under layers of studio murk, it piles all the old themes—sex as power, sex as love, sex as pleasure, distance, craziness, release—on top of an obsession with time more appropriate in over-thirties committed to what was once considered youth music. Honking around sweet Virginia country and hipping through Slim Harpo, singing their ambiguous praises of Angela Davis, Jesus Christ, and the Butter Queen, they're just war babies with the bell bottom blues." Christgau gave the album an A+.

In 1977, a panel of fifty English and American deejays and rock critics polled by rock writer and BBC deejay Paul Gambaccini named *Exile* as the seventh best rock album of all time. Ten years later, it sank to number eleven on the list. (Which only goes to show you what a decade can do.)

The most frequently quoted review of *Exile* was delivered in 1995 by Mick Jagger (who should have been in a position to know) when he told Jann Wenner in *Rolling Stone,* "It's a bit overrated, to be honest. It doesn't contain as many outstanding songs as the previous two records. I think the playing's quite good. It's got a raw quality, but I don't think all around it's as good. . . . I don't think it's our best stuff. I don't think it has good lyrics. We flew off all edges." Twenty-three years earlier when the album was first released, Mick Taylor confirmed this by saying, "I think *Exile On Main Street* is more forceful than *Sticky Fin-*

*gers* but it's not as imaginary or as adventurous. That's purely a personal opinion."

As varying accounts of the making of *Exile* began to emerge over the years, it became a canon of rock criticism that the album was a masterpiece. As Barney Hoskyns wrote in *The Observer* in June 2004, "All rock records should be made in dank basements of old Nazi strongholds on the Cote d'Azur, with reliable heroin connections in Marseille and Gram Parsons hovering in the paneled hallways. That way they might sound half as good as *Exile On Main St.*"

Not surprisingly, those who were actually there at the time also offer wildly differing views of *Exile*. "It had such a hard birth, didn't it?" says Rose Taylor. "It was a lousy place to record an album. Absolutely awful. I never listen to the music. I have not heard *Exile* in thirty years. I don't even know what's on it. 'Sweet Virginia?' Oh, yeah. I thought the cover was grotesque and Mick Taylor was always complaining about how he had been mixed out or cut off or he'd be in the middle of some wonderful solo and that had gotten taken out in the mix. On what grounds is it their masterpiece? Absolutely, I would say *Let It Bleed* is amazing."

"I think *Exile* is by far the best of the albums I worked on with them," says Marshall Chess, who was with the band through *Sticky Fingers, Exile On Main St., Black and Blue,* and *It's Only Rock 'n' Roll.* "I like *Exile* better than *Sticky Fingers* because it's more spontaneous. A kind of spontaneous creativity happened there that was really unique. It was like, 'No rules.' You woke up at three in the morning, you could have whatever you wanted. It was living the album."

"To this day, Mick has never acknowledged the enormous importance of that work," says Tommy Weber. "It was seminal. We were already into the seventies. That's absolutely crucial for the whole timing and the bearing of everybody there and the attitude in *Exile* which is a genesis of the second half of the century and the darkness that was coming. We were all just privileged to be there as instigators and their supporting band."

Of course, no discussion of *Exile On Main St.* would be complete without mentioning Liz Phair, who in 1993 helped bring the original work to the attention of an entirely new generation by releasing *Exile In Guyville,* which many rock critics considered the number one album of the year. Described by Barney Hoskyns in *Mojo* in 1994 as a "track-by-track response to a foundational rock 'text'—The Rolling Stones' masterpiece *Exile On Main Street*," *Guyville* is in fact nothing of the kind.

As CD Times rock critic Eamonn McCusker noted, "Phair talked up *Exile In Guyville* as a song-by-song response to The Rolling Stones' *Exile On Main Street*. As much as the music press adored the idea, it utterly fails to hang together, not only from the first song where Phair's strutting 'feeling better now I'm rid of you' song, '6'1' bears little connection to the Stones' chronicling of the high life, 'Rocks Off,' but also to the very end. Being honest, anyone seeking an indie reworking of *Exile On Main Street* would be better served by tracking down a copy of Pussy Galore's cassette-only reworking of the Stones' classic than *Exile In Guyville* but all credit to Phair for publicising her debut album with such a canny statement, which was sure to prick the interest of music journalists who wistfully recall their attendance at Altamont."

According to the entry about the original album in Wikipedia, *Exile* "is currently certified triple platinum in the US alone. In 1998 *Q* magazine readers voted *Exile On Main St.* the 42nd greatest album of all time while in 2002, it was listed as number 7 on the *Rolling Stone*'s list of the '500 Greatest Albums of All Time.' Furthermore, in 2003, the TV network VH1 placed it at number 12 on their best albums survey, and Pitchfork Media ranked it number eleven on their Top 100 Albums of The 1970s."

For those who do not peruse *Billboard* and *Cashbox* on a daily basis, *Exile On Main St.* going triple platinum in America means that more than three million copies of it have been sold in the United States alone. By comparison, *Exile In Guyville* has sold about two hundred thousand copies in America. In this particular case, the "call" has outsold the "response" by a margin of fifteen to one. In a business where the number of units moved has always been the barometer of success, the original would still seem to be the greatest.

As always, the final word on what is his album belongs to Keith. Asked by Barney Hoskyns in an interview in *Mojo* in November 1997 whether he recalled being "miffed by any of the negative reviews of *Exile* when it first came out," Keith replied, "Oh, I look back on those as a wonderful portfolio of mistakes! Any guy who interviewed me who'd written one of those, I'd say, Oh, you know *everything*, right? But it was quite understandable being that double albums have a lot going against them. You know, there's gonna be a certain amount of confusion, with so much material. At the same time, what *Exile* did was it just kept growing until it made its mark over a period of time. It slowly seeped in."

Much like blood from a shallow wound, this is precisely what happened. Over the course of the past thirty-five years, the music from *Exile On Main St.* has oozed, drained, dripped, and percolated into our culture. Although the album is now older than Mick and Keith were when they made it, people still seem fascinated by its provenance. What better proof can there be of its enviable longevity than the plethora of books that have been written about *Exile On Main St.*? And so without further ado, our rock criticism section has come to an end.

# 22

**Of all the great** rock artists of the early sixties, only Bob Dylan (primarily through his back pages) and the Rolling Stones continue to update and enlarge their own myth. While the full-page ads paid for by Fidelity Investments, the sponsor of Paul McCartney's latest tour, celebrating him as "Quarryman, Beatle, Wing, Poet, Painter, Father, Frontman, Producer, Business Mogul," before concluding "The Key Is, Never Stop Doing What You Love" may provoke vague nausea in those who remember the cheeky but adorable lad who bragged about getting high in the loo at Buckingham Palace before shaking hands with the Queen, he now bears little real resemblance to who he used to be. Even when he does let rip with a few golden oldies between halves of the Super Bowl, the truth is that Paul lost his band years ago and must now tread that long and winding road on his own.

Not so the Rolling Stones. Although Mick has been knighted for reasons that no one, Keith most of all, seems to understand, the saga of the Stones is the never-ending story of rock. And because it is still Mick and Keith and Charlie up there performing in front of people who are more than willing to pay exorbitant prices to see them, time has in some way stood still for them all. There is no better example of this than the story told by Marshall Chess, who during the Stones' *Bridges to Babylon* tour in 1998 decided the time had finally come for him to reestablish contact with the band after having walked away from them twenty-one years earlier to save his own life.

Uncertain as to how he would be received by the Stones, Chess arrived at Madison Square Garden long before the concert only to find that all the backstage passes and laminates he needed to gain entrance to the inner sanctum were waiting for him. After a guard escorted Chess backstage, he found himself in a room with Stephen Tyler of Aerosmith and Ahmet Ertegun (who actually attended Chess' bar mitzvah) as well as various assorted media stars. Catching sight of Chess as he stepped into the room, Charlie Watts hugged him and said, "Marshall! Marshall! So good to fucking see you. C'mon. Keith wants to see you."

Charlie then led Chess past another security barrier into a huge dressing room with a fireplace, two couches, a giant make-up table, and a bathroom with mirrors and big lights. Although there were no drugs in sight, Keith and Ronnie Wood, who had long since replaced Mick Taylor in the band, were guzzling vodka straight from the bottle. Delighted to see Chess, Keith and Ronnie hugged him. They then introduced him to their new wives—the former Patti Hansen, a fashion model born on Staten Island whom Keith married in 1983, and the former Jo Howard, a convent girl from Essex, England who had also been a model and whom Ronnie Wood married in 1980.

Although security guards kept coming up to Keith to tell him that all those assembled in the outside room were waiting to see him, Keith said, "Well, let them wait. They can't come in." Getting to the business at hand, Chess told Keith, "You know, man, I had to come. All these years, I felt I had a bad closure when I left. And it's been bothering me. And I thought it would be good for me to come and clean that up."

Keith looked at Chess as though he was speaking in a foreign tongue. "Mah-shall," he said. "What the fuck are you tah-kin' about? You were there. Now you're here." Insofar as Keith was concerned, it was not twenty-six years since Chess had flown from Los Angeles to New York to deliver the masters of *Exile On Main St.* but only yesterday. Now that the two of them were together in another dressing room before another show during yet another stop along the road, everything was just as it had always been. Which in essence is the world according to Keith Richards.

When someone suddenly announced, "We go on in an hour," Keith ordered everyone but Chess to leave the room. When Keith stripped down to his shorts to get dressed to go on stage, Chess saw he was still carrying a big curved Moroccan dagger under his pants. "Marshall," Keith said as he dressed, "you gotta see this! You're gonna love it! You're gonna fuckin' love it!"

"Love what?" Chess asked.

"We always wanted to make money from these fuckin' star fuckers and we can do it now! I want you to see it!"

"What do you mean?" Chess asked, still not getting it.

"The first part," Keith explained, "is that other backstage.

Those people pay thousands of dollars to go back there. And all we have to do is come by and circulate for two minutes with them." It was then Chess realized that unlike him (and no doubt Ahmet and Stephen Tyler as well), the lesser luminaries in the outer green room had paid for their backstage passes.

Coming up to Keith, a guard said, "Time for the meet-and-greet."

"Keith," Chess said, "what the fuck is a meet-and-greet?"

Gleefully, Keith answered, "You're gonna see. You're gonna fuckin' love it."

Trooping out into the corridor, they were met by Charlie and Darryl Jones, the gifted bass player who had replaced Bill Wyman in the band but was most definitely not a Rolling Stone. Suddenly, Mick appeared. "When Mick saw me," Chess recalled, "he got real uptight. I put my arm around him and he turned into a rock. But you know what? I know that before he goes on, he has stage fright. He's in a weird state. I knew that. Plus, I'm a face from twenty years ago. I'm sure he was shocked. I know Keith must have loved doing that to him."

As a group, they all then began walking down a curving concrete corridor to a big canvas tent. Someone pulled open the drape and in they went. "I walked in last," Chess recalled, "and there was a table with a couple of big bottles of Chianti, cheese, and funky fruit." The tent itself was jammed with executives from Sprint, the phone company. For a brief moment, the Stones posed with the executives. A photographer took two pictures and the band walked out.

As they did, Keith turned to Chess and said, "Ha-ha! That was a quarter of a million dollars!" In return for the privilege of posing for photographs taken with the Rolling Stones, Sprint had paid the band more money than they had grossed from any one show on the 1972 tour. "It said everything about how it had changed," Chess recalled. "Because we would always laugh about those people. Starting with Truman Capote on the 1972 tour. Now they had found a way to make money from them."

Let us now do a slow dissolve through to 2005, when the Stones announced that not only were they about to tour America again but would also be releasing *A Bigger Bang,* their first new album since 1997. If nothing else, Mick seemed to have learned a lesson from all that had gone down at Nellcote thirty-five years earlier. When asked by David Fricke of *Rolling Stone* magazine to describe the concept behind the new album, Mick replied, "Concentrate on what you're doing. No fucking about or jamming for days. I thought, 'We can't do this album the way we've been doing them, spending months in a studio with hundreds of people. It's difficult, expensive, and not much fun."

Save for not having much fun, the same could be said about Mick's life since his days at Nellcote. After both he and Bianca had engaged in a series of highly publicized extramarital affairs, the two parted company in 1977. On November 5, 1980, their divorce was finalized in England for what was thought to be one of the largest financial settlements in history to that point in time.

During this period, Bianca was a regular of the Studio 54 scene in New York and could often be seen at parties, restaurants, and discos with Liza Minelli, Calvin Klein, and her close friend Andy Warhol, who once called Bianca "the greatest movie star who never made a movie." Turning her back on café society, she then became a full-time human rights activist, working with

Amnesty International, Human Rights Watch, and the Washington Office for Latin America. In 1994, she received the United Nations Earth Day Award. Three years later, the Rain Forest Alliance gave her the Green Globe Award for her work to save tropical rain forests and protect indigenous peoples. A staunch opponent of the death penalty, she was also named "Abolitionist of the Year" by the National Coalition to Abolish the Death Penalty.

On November 22, 2005, as Mick was performing before a sold-out crowd at the Delta Center in Salt Lake City, Utah, Bianca and Reverend Jessie Jackson visited Crips founder Stanley "Tookie" Williams on death row in San Quentin. Although Bianca made a tearful public plea asking California Governor Arnold Schwarzenegger to grant Williams clemency, he was put to death for murder on December 13, 2005.

Mick and Bianca's daughter, Jade Sheena Jezebel Jagger, born in Paris as *Exile On Main St.* was being recorded in the south of France, grew up in Manhattan where she was often baby-sat at the Factory by Andy Warhol. At the age of sixteen, Jade ran away from an all-girls boarding school in England to live with her boyfriend Josh Astor, the son of a lord. While attending art college, she met Piers Jackson with whom she had two daughters, Assisi, born in 1992, and Amber, born in 1995. She then lived for many years on the island of Ibiza where she designed jewelry for Asprey of London. Recently, Jade moved her base of operations to New York City where she has lent both her name and design skills to JADE, a building of "laid-back luxury condominiums" at 16 West 19th Street in Manhattan.

Hair streaked blonde, looking lovely in a white dress and

matching pumps with a tasteful necklace she must have designed, Jade can be seen staring into the camera on a very orange bed in magazine ads designed to entice prospective buyers to purchase condos ranging in price from $550,000 to $1,425,000. As the ad copy duly notes, the building is "within easy reach of every buzz-worthy spot in Manhattan." Which is more than anyone could have said of Nellcote.

Before parting company with Bianca in 1977, Mick had already begun an affair with Jerry Hall, perpetually described in print as "a leggy blonde super model from Mesquite, Texas" to whom he was first introduced by Bryan Ferry, the lead singer of Roxy Music, who was then her boyfriend. After Hall gave birth to Mick's daughter Elizabeth and his son James, Mick married her in a Hindu ceremony in Bali in 1990. Nine years later, after giving birth to Mick's daughter Georgia and his son Gabriel, Hall filed for divorce on the grounds of adultery and asked for a fifty-million-dollar settlement. Although Mick's lawyers contended that the wedding in Bali was merely ceremonial and not legally binding, the case was settled out of court. The two remain friends.

Now sixty-two years old, Mick's continuing well-publicized sexual exploits have transformed him from the dashing Casanova he often seemed to be at Nellcote into an aging Lothario. For the past four years, he has kept company with L'Wren Scott, a thirty-eight-year-old, six-foot-four-inch former model and fashion stylist born Luann Bambrough in Roy, Utah, where she grew up with a Mormon family who adopted her. Scott not only made Mick's stage outfit for the *Bigger Bang* American tour, but was also reportedly trying to get Keith and Ronnie Wood to give up smoking (good luck on that one, honey) while urging the band to undergo a fashion makeover. Someone even went so far as to call her the "Yoko Ono of the Stones." As though any woman, no matter how tall, beautiful, or talented, could ever come between Mick and Keith, The Glimmer Twins until the day they die.

While Mick himself has never been the sort of chap to dwell on the past and most likely never gives a passing thought to all those with whom he once sojourned back at Nellcote, we need, if only to gain some closure on all this *sturm und drang,* to take one last look back at some of those who played supporting roles in the drama enacted that summer at Keith and Anita's villa in the south of France.

Bill Wyman, who left the band in 1993, two years after getting divorced from Mandy Smith, whom he had first begun dating when she was thirteen and he was forty-seven, is now seventy years old. During their marriage, Bill's son Stephen, then thirty-three, became engaged to Mandy's mother, Patsy. Had the two of them married, Bill would have become his own wife's grandfather-in-law, clearly a difficult situation for all concerned.

Happily married for the past thirteen years to the former Suzanne Accosta, Bill is the father of three young daughters. He owns a restaurant in London called (what else?) Sticky Fingers, has written two books about the Stones and one about his friend, the artist Marc Chagall, and continues to play bass with his R&B combo, the Rhythm Kings. Because he hated the drug-induced chaos at Nellcote, the events of that summer seem to have had little or no bearing on his life. For others, Nellcote was the place where they were first introduced to a lifestyle which in time proved impossible for them to sustain.

Mick Taylor left the Rolling Stones in December 1974 to become a member of the Jack Bruce Band, which recorded just one album before breaking up. He has since toured with former Ten Years After front man Alvin Lee, a re-formed version of John Mayall and The Bluesbreakers, and Bob Dylan. Although his health of late has not been all that good, Mick Taylor continues to play the blues, albeit to far smaller audiences than those who saw him perform with the Stones. Whether he has ever been adequately compensated for the work he did with the Rolling Stones during that period remains a bone of contention.

"Mick Jagger promised him credit on 'Moonlight Mile' and a couple of other things but never gave it to him," a Stones insider recalls. "He saw Keith a couple of years ago and Keith was crying and saying, 'Oh, we really owe you, man. We really owe you.' But nothing came of it. I think Ronnie Wood said, 'Well, Mick Taylor was never really a Rolling Stone.' And he was right. He wasn't. I think Mick always felt he had sold his soul for rock 'n' roll. And didn't get paid nearly enough in exchange. But then you never do, do you?"

Rose Taylor, who went through her own personal hell after she and Mick Taylor parted in 1977, has remarried and now considers herself a born-again Christian. Her daughter Chloe, who was a babe in arms at Nellcote, is thirty-five years old. Looking back on Nellcote, Rose Taylor says, "Unlimited access is not good for anyone, is it? I'm sure people didn't know what they were getting into back then. And there was this awful arrogance of being somehow immortal. I suppose it had to do with being young. And the fact that you were protected and very privileged and not on the street."

In 1987, Keith's good friend Stash Klossowski produced the first album by The Dirty Strangers, a band featuring Keith and Ronnie Wood. Five years later, Stash wrote, directed, and produced a film entitled *Shining Blood* based in part on the Arthurian legend. He is the author of two books, *Alchemy: The Secret Art* and *The Golden Game: Alchemical Engravings of the Seventeenth Century.* Involved in the movie business, he lives in Malibu with his son.

After his work on *Exile,* Andy Johns went on to produce Joe Satriani, Van Halen, Ozzy Ozbourne, Eddie Money, Jack Bruce, Free, Television, Derek & The Dominos, Eric Clapton, Ginger Baker, Delaney & Bonnie, Traffic, Blind Faith, and Jethro Tull. His latest venture, Godsmack's *IV,* entered the charts in May 2006 at number one. Happily married and the father of two sons, he is alive and well in Los Angeles.

Sadly, the same cannot be said for the redoubtable Ian Stewart, whose drugs of choice were always single malt whiskey and beef. On December 12, 1985, Stu died of a massive heart attack at the age of forty-seven while sitting in the waiting room of a clinic in London. Olivier Boelen is presumed dead as are Spanish Tony and Rene D'Amico, who was apparently one of the cowboys. No one seems to have a clue as to what happened to Jacques the cook.

After leaving France with his sons, Tommy Weber met a woman named Joanna Harcourt-Smith on Marbella. Together, they traveled to Switzerland, where they spent some time with Keith and Anita, then living not all that far from Timothy Leary, a fugitive from justice who had only recently escaped from prison in America. When Tommy went off to Amsterdam to buy a boat from which yet another Radio Caroline–like pirate radio station was to be launched, Leary and Harcourt-Smith began a long-term relationship. On Christmas Day, Tommy was waiting for them in Cairo at the pyramids when Leary and Harcourt-Smith were arrested in Kabul and returned in custody to the United States. Tommy then spent a year in Denmark so his sons could learn his native language. Returning to England, where he still lives, Tommy enrolled Jake and Charlie in Summerhill, the progressive school founded in 1921 by A.S. Neill. Charlie Weber, who has a son named Beau, is now a musician and video editor.

A graduate of the Juilliard School of Drama in New York City, Jake Weber has had an extensive career as a stage and film actor and currently plays the role of Patricia Arquette's husband on the NBC series, *Medium*. Thirty-three years after leaving Nellcote, Jake ran into Mick Jagger one night at the always fashionable outdoor dining terrace at the Chateau Marmont in LA. Walking over to Mick, who had always been the soul of kindness to him in the south of France, he introduced himself as "Jakey, from Nellcote."

As is his wont when confronted by someone from his past, Mick said, "Oh, right . . . . That was a long time ago, wasn't it?" After a pause, Mick asked if Jake had seen Dominique Tarlé's book. Jake said he had and that the photos were beautiful. "Are you having a good time tonight?" Mick asked. Aware he was being brushed off, Jake excused himself and went back to his table. At some point later in the evening, Mick and his party moved out to the garden. Although Mick found himself sitting beside Jake, the two never exchanged another word, not even when someone with Mick began talking to Jake. About an hour later, Mick left without acknowledging him.

Keith would never have reacted in this manner, but then as Bill Wyman recently noted, "Keith used to say Mick's a lovely bunch of guys. . . . I can go in a room and he will be, 'Hi, Bill, lovely to see you, man!", give me a hug and all that. Then I can go in a room three days later when there's some celebs there and he don't even come over to talk because whoever's in the room. It's bizarre."

Which brings us once more to the never-ending dichotomy between Mick, the middle class lad who adopted the persona of a bounder and a cad, and Keith, the product of sturdy working class stock, who chose instead to become a member in good standing of the league of gentlemen. As Tommy Weber says, "The guy is a real gent. His idea of behaving well is what we would call forgiveness. It's absolutely amazing the understanding that he carries about in his whole demeanor. Really, popes should be like that. The one thing Keith cannot stand is bullshitters who hurt others. If you're real, you can make many mistakes with him and be forgiven. I should know. But if he thinks you're going to hurt someone, he'll pull his gun on you."

In terms of the continuing dynamic between Mick and Keith, there seemed to be no doubt who was in charge of everything on the *Bigger Bang* tour. No one but Mick would have accepted Ameriquest as the sponsor of the tour. Based in Orange County, California, the company that calls itself the "Proud Sponsor of the American Dream" is the number one mortgage lender to homeowners with bad credit. On the same day Ameriquest disclosed that it had decided to pay $325 million to settle a thirty-state investigation into complaints about what the *Los Angeles Times* called "overcharges, hidden fees, puffed-up appraisals, and fabricated borrower income statements," President

George W. Bush nominated Ameriquest's chairman and sole owner, billionaire Roland E. Arnall, to be ambassador to the Netherlands.

Arnall and his wife Dawn had by then already each raised at least $200,000 for Bush's re-election campaign while Ameriquest employees and the Arnall family had donated another $242,500. In addition, Dawn Arnall had donated $5 million to the Progress for America Voter Fund, an independent political group that spent $35 million in a media blitz to attack Democratic presidential candidate John Kerry. The Arnalls had also cochaired the Bush inaugural committee and contributed more than $1 million to help elect Arnold Schwarzenegger as the Governor of California.

Ameriquest then gave "The Governator" a block of coveted center-stage seats and a luxury box for the Stones' opening show at Fenway Park in Boston so he could offer them to wealthy contributors to his re-election campaign. In return for a donation of $10,000, Arnold's supporters got to sit in front of the stage and attend a private preconcert reception with the former bodybuilder turned movie star turned politician. For a cool $100,000, donors got to sit right beside him in his luxury box.

But then on a TV ad that played over and over as the tour began, a very straight middle-aged spokesman in a suit and tie could be seen in the midst of a crowd at a Stones concert. As Mick performed on stage, the spokesman explained just how proud Ameriquest was to be sponsoring the tour.

All things considered, it only made perfect sense. With the top ticket for a Stones' show going for around four hundred and fifty dollars, and those who had the money paying twenty-five hundred bucks to stand inside the windows of the huge faux office building that framed the stage, and the tour t-shirt retailing for thirty-eight dollars (plus shipping if ordered from the website), the aging fans who followed the band from town to town and called themselves the "Shidoobees" (after the refrain in "Shattered") were probably refinancing their homes with Ameriquest so they could afford to see more than a single show. On the *Bigger Bang* American tour, the Stones played ninety-two dates in twenty-seven venues, selling 1.2 million tickets at an average price of $133.98 per ducat, for a total gross of $162 million.

None of which stopped Mick from recording "Sweet Neocon" on the new album, a song in which he plaintively asked where the money had gone in the Pentagon and how his sweet neocon could be so wrong. If Secretary of State Condoleezza Rice had now replaced Angela Davis of "Sweet Black Angel" as the unattainable object of Mick's affection, what of it? As Mick himself told *USA Today*, referring to the *New York Times* columnist who had relentlessly pilloried the Bush administration, "Maureen Dowd is no more qualified to have opinions than I am."

When it came to having his cake and eating it too, there has never been anyone in the history of rock like Mick Jagger. The man is the unchallenged master of the form. In itself, this is nothing new. It is the way he was born and the way he was at Nellcote. The only difference now was the number of zeros on the checks he was collecting.

When Eric Gillin of *Maxim* magazine asked Mick why the Stones' tour, once sponsored by Budweiser, was now being put on by Ameriquest, Mick replied, "Well, they offered us the most money, that's how it happened. What you really need sponsors for is advertising money and visibility; you don't get a lot of cash for yourself. It's fine as long as they're people you can deal with, whether it's a phone company or a mortgage company or a beer company. I don't equate rock 'n' roll with beer any more than I equate it with bottle tops—it doesn't make much of a difference to me." When Gillin asked Mick to name the Stones' greatest accomplishment, he answered, "Surviving with most of our fingers intact."

No other band would have allowed "Streets of Love," the latest video from their new album, to have its premiere on the NBC soap opera *Days of Our Lives* and then be used as background music for four weeks to "celebrate the show's fortieth anniversary and the emergence of the Stones in the mid-sixties." (If there is a real connection between these two events, someone else will have to make it.) Randy Miller, the executive vice president of marketing at Virgin Records, noted that the soap opera was "the perfect vehicle for promoting the Rolling Stones and their latest single." Uh, say what?

Who else but the Stones would have agreed to work once more for their good friends at the phone company by consenting to perform during the Sprint halftime show at the fortieth Super Bowl in Detroit? As Sprint proudly announced on the official Super Bowl website, the previous year's show, which featured none other than Beatle Paul, had been watched by a hundred and thirty-three million viewers in the United States, thereby making it "annually the nation's highest-rated TV program." During their formative years, the Stones had always been accused of copying the Beatles. Where Paul McCartney had so boldly gone before, the Stones were now more than willing to follow. For what had to be an astronomical fee, to be sure.

Putting all this into proper perspective, the National Football League then announced that because of the physical demands of having to stand for so long in a crowd, no one over the age of forty-five would be allowed to join the two thousand fans on the field for the show. As the *New York Times* reported on January 9, 2006, "But after hearing that many fans over 45 wanted to attend, the NFL has lifted the age limit."

Good thing they did, since the ban would have meant that neither Mick nor Keith nor Ronnie Wood nor Charlie Watts would have been allowed to attend the show as a spectator. Instead, the league decided that audience members would be allowed to wait in a tunnel for much of the first half and then enter and exit the field quickly. (Feel free to insert tired joke about aging rockers on walkers playing to aging fans in wheelchairs here.)

Three days before the game, Charlie, resplendent in a suede jacket and matching turtleneck, Woodie, looking much like a wealthy British shipping magnate in a blazer with brass buttons, Mick, casual yet elegant in a white shirt and a dark jacket, and Keith, clearly making the definitive fashion statement by sporting a black headband, killer shades, and a tight-fitting crushed black taffeta garment that zipped up the front and had a pointy collar but defied all further description (in which he would also perform on Super Sunday), walked out on a stage in the Motor City to take questions from seven hundred reporters. Speaking into hand-held microphones, the boys did their best to entertain the assembled horde without the benefit of musical accompaniment.

In the *New York Times* the next day, Joe Lapointe wrote that when the Super Bowl first began in 1967, it stood for "marching bands, crew cuts, and cold beer." Noting that the Rolling Stones had "represented a different kind of music, a different sort of hairstyle, and different types of refreshment,"

Lapointe asked, "So what does the intersection of these two entertainment juggernauts say about American popular culture? Have the Stones moved closer to the mainstream, or has the mainstream moved closer to the values of the Stones?"

All things considered, it was a damn fine question, which Mick answered at the press conference by saying, "I think both, to be perfectly honest. America's obviously changed since we first came here. It's almost unrecognizable and it's very hard to imagine what the United States was like 40 years ago. We've definitely grown with the American culture changes." But then as Lapointe also wrote of the press conference, "For audience members of a certain age, it was a little like watching one of those old Rat Pack shows, with Jagger in the role of Frank Sinatra and Richards as Dean Martin."

With Janet Jackson having shocked the world by baring her right breast at the end of a less than memorable duet with Justin Timberlake during the Super Bowl halftime show just two years earlier, it seemed only natural for one and all to wonder how the Rolling Stones might choose to upset the proverbial apple cart when they took the stage at Ford Field on Sunday. At the press conference, Mick assured the ABC television network that they had no reason to be concerned about what the Stones might sing on game day. "They needn't worry about it," Mick said. "Calm down and take life as it comes." Being Mick, he then "underscored his remark with a blunt obscenity, to humorous effect." Mick also joked that Aretha Franklin would disrobe while singing the national anthem on Sunday, thereby putting network executives in "a bit of a crisis."

Aside from being a media feeding frenzy of the first order, the press conference was just good fun in the classic Rolling

Stones manner. For those who cared, there was also some actual pop history thrown into the mix. On January 15, 1967, the day that the first Super Bowl (then called the world championship game) was played in Los Angeles, the Stones appeared on the Ed Sullivan Show on CBS to sing their current hit single, "Let's Spend The Night Together." The notoriously straight-laced Sullivan (so stiff a presence on the small screen that some believe he had actually died years before he ever introduced the band) insisted they change the lyrics to "Let's spend some *time* together." In what became one of the defining moments of his career, Mick held up his end of the bargain but also "rolled his eyes while he sang," thereby letting everyone under the age of twenty watching the show at home that night with their parents know just how lame he thought Ed Sullivan and all he stood for really were. Forty years on, history was not about to repeat itself at the Super Bowl. Or, was it?

Beyond all doubt, the massive midweek press conference also served to prove that the Stones had now reached a level of fame and notoriety so legendary that even sports reporters, traditionally the most jaded of all media types when it came to viewing those they covered on a regular basis with any degree of real respect, much less actual hero worship, could be reduced to jelly just by being within shouting distance of the band. Giddy as an English schoolgirl at her first Bay City Rollers (alternately, read: Arctic Monkeys) concert, one television correspondent (apparently a grown man) filed an entire report consisting of the breathless news that he had actually gotten to ask his idol Mick Jagger a single question at a press conference attended by six hundred and ninety-nine other fully credentialed Super Bowl press representatives.

The question he asked Mick was whether he had a favorite professional football team. Always a sports fan, Mick recalled that while living in New York City during the seventies and eighties, he would sometimes watch the Pittsburgh Steelers who by a stroke of good fortune also happened to be playing in this Super Bowl as well. Mick remembered their very graceful Hall of Fame wide receiver Lynn Swann as well as his "levitation leap." When Swann, who had just forsaken his lucrative career as a television personality to become the Republican candidate for Governor of Pennsylvania (only in America, baby) was informed of this, he admitted with a shy smile just how pleased he was to know that he had fans from another walk of life whom he had never met.

And so it went on and on throughout an apparently endless week of hype for the single greatest corporate event in sports, the commingling of commercial merchandising and crass materialism that is the Super Bowl. Although relief efforts were still underway in the city of New Orleans, devastated by Hurricane Katrina at the end of August (to their credit, the Stones had donated a million dollars to aid the victims) and the body count in the war in Iraq kept mounting at an alarming rate, most Americans seemed far more interested in the super halftime show at the Super Bowl by the super Rolling Stones on Super Sunday. While it all might have been just a tale told by an idiot, filled with sound and fury but signifying nothing, the media commotion seemed to speak volumes about the current state of the culture without offering a single clue as to where it might be headed.

And then there was the show itself. At halftime, with the Steelers leading the Seattle Seahawks by a score of seven to three in a game that had been nothing to write home about, Mick, dressed all in black in a tuxedo jacket replete with tails (the preacher look, no doubt), which he then doffed to reveal a tight black sleeveless t-shirt cropped just above the midriff to reveal just the barest flash of pale white flesh, strutted out on a curving stage built around a huge red tongue. What had by now become the ultimate corporate logo in rock then rolled back to reveal a highly enthused crowd, a concept directly ripped off from the heart-shaped area around which U2 regularly performs.

While there had been a good deal of discussion among Stones aficionados beforehand as to which three songs the band might play, the running order was completely predictable— "Start Me Up" followed by "Rough Justice" and then "Satisfaction," which Mick introduced by saying, "We could have done this one at Super Bowl One. All things come to he who waits."

Mick's shocking use of the nominative pronoun rather than the objective one ("he" as opposed to "him") then became the subject of a lengthy discourse by William Safire in his "On Language" column in the *New York Times Magazine,* with no less an authority than Jacques Barzun, the ninety-eight year old cultural historian and professor emeritus from Columbia University, who had "manned the ramparts of proper usage and accurate etymology since Hector was a pup," weighing in with the opinion that Mick's grammar was in fact quite all right with him. (As opposed to he, it goes without saying.) Suffice to say, forty years on, Mick's public utterances, both on-stage and off, were still being deconstructed by others in terms of both form and content.

What Mick did not also bother to add was that the song had come to Keith late one night as he lay in bed in yet another hotel room along the road and that he had sung it into his ever-present pocket tape recorder only to then fall back asleep without realizing he had just come up with "a snarling 10-note figure" that *Blender* magazine would call "the most famous guitar riff in history." Considering how the mini-set had gone up till then, there would have been no point.

As is so often the case when a band plays live through the public address system in a huge stadium (there were more than sixty-five thousand people at Ford Field that day), the sound on television was atrocious. Charlie Watts, Ron Wood, and bassist Darryl Jones seemed not to have been miked at all and Mick's vocals were muddy at best. As always where the Rolling Stones were concerned, it was not the quality of what they sang but rather the lyrics that no one could hear that soon became a topic of national debate.

As rock critic Jon Pareles wrote in the *New York Times* the next day, "The Rolling Stones sang three songs for the Super Bowl XL show last night and were censored in two of them— not a bad average for a band of sexagenarians who still ride a reputation as provocateurs." To wit, the word "cum" could not be heard in "Start Me Up," and the word "cocks" could not be heard in "Rough Justice." Although Mick actually sang the lyrics on stage, they were not audible in either the stadium or on the broadcast. A day later, NFL spokesman Brian McCarthy said, "As planned and agreed upon with the Stones, we turned down Mick's mike for two specific seconds. The Stones were fine with it. They didn't have an issue. Mick knew that's what our plan was."

The Stones quickly issued a statement of their own in which they termed censorship of their lyrics as "absolutely ridiculous and completely unnecessary." Their spokeswoman, Fran Curtis, a publicist at Rogers & Cowan, said that although band members might have known about the NFL's plan (no doubt designed to preserve the virgin ears of more than a hundred and forty-one million viewers who had never before heard these particular lyrics despite all the records the band had sold), this did not also mean that they liked it. She added, "The band did the songs they were supposed to do and they sang all the words. There were many, many conversations back and forth and the band clearly was not happy about it."

Forty years on, it was the Ed Sullivan Show all over again. Like a character from *The Tales of Hoffmann*, Michael Philip Jagger seemed doomed to keep repeating himself. Despite being a man of overwhelming wealth and fame, Mick still wanted to act like a naughty schoolboy on national television, thereby demonstrating that neither he nor his band of rough and ready working class lads from London would ever knuckle under to the onerous demands of the man (whoever that man might now actually be). At the age of sixty-two, it was a position not only difficult to maintain but also an issue perhaps better suited for personal therapy sessions. However, being Mick, he also knew the publicity could only be good for the Stones.

This time around, however, both the Rolling Stones and the culture were far different than they had been forty years ago. The Stones were not just undeniably old, but also rich and famous beyond even their wildest dreams. The super hype about their super halftime show at the Super Bowl as well as the media dust-up about the missing lyrics that followed served to expose the band to scathing criticism from an entirely new segment of the media—the rapidly burgeoning sports establishment in America.

And so it was that one sportswriter noted that the only comment his daughters had when he returned home from the

Super Bowl XL was, "What's up with that flabby old-man skin hanging down from Mick Jagger's arms?" On *Pardon The Interruption,* a daily sports talk show on ESPN cohosted by Tony Kornheiser and Michael Wilbon, two fast-talking *Washington Post* sportswriters, Wilbon said of Mick, "What is he, a hundred and sixty-two years old?" Wilbon, who counted Stones' bassist Darryl Jones as one of his homeboys from Chicago, then went on to suggest that the band should next perform in Depends, the brand name of a line of adult diapers.

Commenting some months later on the living arrangements demanded by Vice President Dick Cheney whenever he went on the road, Jon Stewart, the host of Comedy Central's *The Daily Show,* noted that Cheney's rider was much like that of a rock star, only with "less condoms and more defibrillators." With an impish grin, Stewart then added, "Although with the Rolling Stones . . . ." Back when the Stones had first started out, the press had mocked them for being dirty long-haired louts. Now, people were laughing at them for being old and rich and famous.

As always, none of it seemed to bother the boys. Twelve days after the Super Bowl, they were on stage at a free concert (not their first one since Altamont) on Copacabana Beach in Rio de Janeiro during Carnival Week performing for the biggest crowd of their career—more than 1.2 million people. The five-hour show, which also featured two popular Brazilian bands and was broadcast live throughout the nation on television and radio as well as around the world via satellite radio and the Internet, cost around four and a half million dollars and was sponsored by two large telecommunication companies as well as the city of Rio. Reportedly, the Stones were paid $750,000 to perform.

"Depending on the quality of the performance," Larry Rohter wrote the next day in the *New York Times,* "a DVD may be issued later this year." Considering that the show was filmed by more than 50 cameras, "including some mounted in helicopters or aboard boats just offshore, where numerous yachts with partying fans were anchored," it seemed a fairly safe bet to assume that some record of the event would soon be made available to the general public at a price.

One of those who watched the Stones from a special VIP area at the side of the stage was former swimsuit model and Brazilian television hostess Luciana Gimenez-Morad who had sued Mick for thirty-five thousand dollars a month in child support for their son Lucas, now six years old, born out of wedlock after a brief assignation. Ever the dutiful father, Mick "incited a mob scene among paparazzi and fans when he tried to pick up" the boy from school before the concert.

During the show itself, many girls in the massive crowd sported a t-shirt reading "MICK JAGGER—FACA UM FILHO EM MIM." As Diego Perri reported in *Rolling Stone* magazine, the Portuguese phrase means, "Mick Jagger—put a baby in me." Considering how much child support Mick was paying the mother of his Brazilian love child, the long-term financial benefits of such a request seemed obvious. Once the show was over, Mick did not fly off with the rest of the Stones to their next gig at the River Plate Stadium in Buenos Aires, followed by shows in Mexico City and Monterrey, Mexico, but rather "stuck around for two days to spend time with his son. . . ."

In March, a full-page photo of Mick with arms crossed in an open shirt from the summer of 1971 in the south of France was featured in the Spring 2006 issue of *Men's Fashions of the Times*. The accompanying article identified him as "a pop Byron" who during the sixties had not only been "dirty" but also "exuded an air of supernatural menace." "As he ages," the article went on, "his physicality, too, reflects his perversity. At 62, he is at once Dorian Gray and the portrait in the attic, the lined face of a debauched satyr set upon a body that remains as lithe and lean as any of today's freakishly skinny man-child models." To put it another way, at an age when most men were wondering whether their monthly Social Security check would arrive on time, Mick was still a fashion icon of legendary proportions.

As always, the Stones themselves were still on the road and much too busy to care what anyone wrote about them. On April 8, 2006, they made their debut in China at the relatively small (at least for them these days) eight-thousand-seat Grand Stage in Shanghai before an audience comprised in large part, in the words of Kathleen E. McLaughlin of the *San Francisco Chronicle* Foreign Service, of "foreign expatriates, the fans most willing in China to pay up to $375 to see the rock band." McLaughlin went on to note that although unlike Madonna, U2, and Gwen Stefani, the Stones did not "command must-see status for locals," their "stock might rise after the concert" when state-run China Central Television would begin broadcasting taped footage of the show nationwide during the coming year.

The Stones had originally been scheduled to perform in Shanghai and Beijing in 2003 but were forced to cancel the shows because of the outbreak of SARS, also known as severe acute respiratory syndrome. Back then, the Chinese government had ordered the band not to perform "Brown Sugar," "Honky

Tonk Women," "Beast of Burden," and "Let's Spend The Night Together"—"presumably," as the Associated Press reported, "because of their racy content." Although the band was permitted to play the first two songs during their Hong Kong shows in 2003, the Ministry of Culture, which has a "regimented approval process for acts that want to play in China" not only continued the ban this time around, but also added "Rough Justice" to the list.

"Fortunately," Mick told reporters at a press conference the night before the show in Shanghai, "we have 400 more songs that we can play, so it's not really an issue." With what the Associated Press called his "trademark sarcasm," he then added, "I'm pleased the Ministry of Culture is protecting the morals of the expatriate bankers and their girlfriends that are going to be coming." As Howard W. French noted in the *New York Times,* the price of a single ticket was more than what most people in China earned in a month. A twenty-three-year-old Chinese man who did attend the show was quoted by French as saying, "It's actually tragic if you think about it: a foreign performance borrowing Chinese land, but Chinese people cannot come because of price or other issues."

On the night in question, Mick did his best to connect with the few locals in attendance by greeting the crowd in Chinese and then urging them to join in on the chorus of their favorite songs by shouting out, "*Zai yiqi!*" or "All together!" When the Stones did "Wild Horses," the song Keith wrote for Anita so long ago, they brought out singer-songwriter Cui Jian, who is sometimes referred to as "the father of Chinese rock," to join them on rhythm guitar. In 1989, Jian's song "Nothing To My Name" was an anthem for students involved in the mass protest in Tiananmen Square that resulted in the death of what may have been as many as five thousand people. "This is the 20th-year anniversary of Chinese rock 'n' roll," Jian told the crowd after the song was done. "We have an appointment. In the near future, they will be back, and we'll rock again in Beijing."

After their show in China, the Stones did four shows in Australia and New Zealand. On April 27, 2006, nine days after leaving New Zealand, Keith Richards literally and figuratively fell out of his tree. Being Keith, he chose to do so while on holiday with wife Patti and band mate Ronnie Wood at Fiji's very exclusive Wakaya Club, located on a tiny dot of a private island in the middle of the South Pacific, where the cheapest room cost nineteen hundred dollars a night and the top tier accommodations went for a cool seventy-six hundred per night. (Prospective Guests, Please Note: A five-day minimum stay is recommended.)

Keith, who freely admitted he had been knocking back a few tropical coolers (containing God only knows how much 151 rum) with Ronnie (who in six weeks' time would enter an alcohol rehab clinic in London) before they both decided to shinny up a palm tree to pick some coconuts, reportedly wound up falling more than sixteen feet to the ground. Although Keith suffered what was initially described as a "mild concussion," he then seems to have also fallen off a Jet Ski. All in all, a rough afternoon for having fun. At some point, it was determined that Keith had a significant head injury and he was flown to Ascot Hospital in Auckland, New Zealand, where local fans began a vigil outside the hospital.

On May 9, 2006, Keith underwent surgery which was described by the *New Zealand Herald* as intended "to relieve a blood clot on the brain, an operation that normally involves drilling a hole through the skull to drain the clot." Because Keith would need a few weeks to recuperate, the first fifteen dates of the Stones *Bigger Bang* European tour, including those scheduled for June 3 and July 2 at the Stade de France stadium in Paris, had to be canceled.

In terms of Keith's own very colorful medical history, it was just another in a series of never-ending mishaps beginning in 1971 when he crashed his Bentley with Michael Cooper in England and then overturned his go-kart while racing Tommy Weber in the south of France. During a European tour in 1990, he punctured his finger on a guitar string. When it became infected, the Stones had to cancel some shows. In 1998, just before the start of the Stones' European *Bridges to Babylon* tour, Keith broke three ribs and punctured a lung when he plummeted from a ladder while trying to retrieve a book in the library of his Connecticut home.

This time around, however, Keith was sixty-two years old and it was his brain and not his finger that had been punctured. Although it would be ludicrous to suggest that the whole world waited with bated breath to see whether he would recover, it was most definitely an intimation of mortality for the world's most wrinkled rocker. Although the jokes came thick and fast ("Did Keith suffer brain damage? How can you tell?"), the undeniable truth was that anyone who ever loved the Stones had to reflect for a brief moment just how much worse the world would be without Keith Richards playing his guitar in it.

On May 11, Keith was discharged from the hospital but told to remain in New Zealand for outpatient care. In a photograph taken on the day he was released, Keith looks small and old and frail. Wearing shades, his damaged head covered with a thick wool stocking cap on top of which he has placed a Chairman Mao cap, he raises his left hand to his forehead in a forlorn salute. For the first time, he seems completely mortal. A defanged Dracula, he is Superman without his cape, the Lone Ranger without a mask.

Twelve days later, he was back home in Connecticut and "feeling great." On June 3, it was announced that the Stones' European tour would begin on July 11 at the San Siro Stadium in Milan. The rescheduled tour included twenty-one stadium shows in eleven countries. In a statement only he could have made, Keith said, "Excuse me, I fell off my perch! Sorry to disrupt everyone's plans but now—it's FULL STEAM AHEAD! Ouch!"

At one point during the opening show in Milan, Mick Jagger congratulated Italy on its World Cup victory and then brought Italian national soccer heroes Alessandro Del Piero and Marco Materazzi out on stage. Referring to the vicious head butt Materazzi had taken from Zinedine Zidane of France in the World Cup final game, Mick said in Italian, "Materazzi and Richards have something in common tonight: they both recently had head-related problems." But, hey, if you can't laugh at your closest mate after brain surgery, who *can* you laugh at? And in September, the Stones began the second American leg of what Billboard magazine predicted would become the biggest-grossing rock tour in history with a show in Gillette Stadium outside Boston.

Since both Mick and Keith already had more than enough money to live in luxury for the rest of their lives (some estimated Mick to be worth as much as half a billion dollars, but then who was counting?), one might be tempted to ask why the band would choose to keep up such a killing pace. To be sure, playing live on stage was not only what the Stones did but also what they were best at. Still, the real reason they kept doing it was more elemental.

As Marshall Chess noted, "There are so many layers now that the only way they can get the buzz is to go on stage. It's like a drug. And the only way they can get it is to go on tour. The old blues guys worked all their lives because they needed money and let me tell you, it's the same shit. The blues guys not only needed money, they needed the applause of fifty people even if it was only in a small bar. The Stones love that shit. Because the feeling on stage is like being held in your mother's arms. It's the power. That's why these guys still do it. The only time they feel alive is when they're on stage."

In terms of the direction in which Mick, a brilliant business-man who if he had been born in any other era would never have dropped out of the London School of Economics, had taken the Stones and all those who loved them, it was just as Jefferson Air-plane once sang. One generation got old, and one generation got sold. Only now they were one and the same. When it came to the bottom line, not to mention having his cake and eating it too, Michael Philip Jagger was the greatest genius in rock. (Lest it be seen as piling on, there will be no mention here of the Tuesday night ABC sitcom "The Knights of Prosperity," which was ini-tially entitled "Let's Rob Mick Jagger," featuring, yes, you guessed it, who else but Mick.)

But then, injuries aside, what of our boy Keith? Although Buckingham Palace had yet to release an official statement on the matter, it did not seem likely that the Queen would ever offer him a knighthood. But then only Keith would admit to, as Nigel Williamson wrote in *The Guardian* on December 5, 2003, going "fucking berserk" when he heard the news that "Mick Jagger accepted a knighthood on the eve of the singer's 60th birthday last year—an honour bestowed by 'the same establishment that did their very best to throw us in jail and kill us.'"

As Keith also told Mick at the time, "It's a paltry honor . . . hold out for the lordship, mate." Too right, my son. But then for himself, Keith no doubt had something a bit more grand in mind. Lord Richards of Redlands, as Williamson suggested, would never do. Thane of Cawdor perhaps. Better yet, the Duke of Earl.

Although Keith and Anita parted in 1979, Anita has also somehow managed to survive and now lives in London. A close confidante and bosom buddy of impossibly beautiful super model Kate Moss, Anita can on occasion be seen pedaling her bicycle down the King's Road in Chelsea. Currently working as a fashion designer, Anita can be seen playing the Devil in an episode of *Absolutely Fabulous* in which Marianne Faithfull appears as God.

Unlike Mick, Keith's domestic situation these days seems both rock solid and utterly tranquil. He and Patti Hansen have been married for twenty-two years. Their daughters, Theodora, twenty-one, and Alexandra, twenty, both regulars on the high-fashion scene, have been described as "the anti-Hilton sisters because of their rejection of the party lifestyle." But then as Keith himself recently said, "I occasionally borrow pot from my kids. They do a little weed occasionally. 'Here, Dad,'—or more likely, 'Dad, have you got any?'"

Keith's son Marlon, the blond cherub who wandered like a blithe spirit through the chaos at Nellcote, is now thirty-seven years old and looks much like a younger version of his father. He is married to the model Lucie de la Falaise, daughter of Yves St.

Laurent fashion muse and designer Loulou de la Falaise, whose second husband is Thadee Klossowski, the son of Balthus the painter and younger brother of Stash, Keith's great pal from the days at Nellcote. A recent article in *The Guardian* described Marlon as being "of an artistic bent (he's art director of the hip anti-fashion mag *Cheap Date* and has shown work at London's Zolar the Magnificent) . . . ." Despite the manner in which he grew up or perhaps because of it, Marlon is, as *The Guardian* also noted, "now a pretty settled sort of guy."

Once called Dandelion, Keith and Anita's daughter Angela, who was raised by Keith's mother Doris, is a teetotaler who is married to a carpenter and works as a stable girl in Dartford. Although Keith never married Anita, he still maintains a friendly relationship with her and, in the words of the Wikipedia, "often refers to having two wives, in the traditional sense of Rastafarian polygamy . . . ."

On stage night after night with the Stones, Keith is still playing his ass off. Physically, there is no one in the world who resembles him. His hair in Hasidic dreads, an earring dangling from his left ear, that silver skull ring on the fourth finger of his right hand, a silver bracelet bearing tiny handcuffs on his left wrist (a replica of which can be bought on eBay, among other places) to remind him never to get arrested again, he peers out at the world through eyes rimmed with kohl like an aging but wary raccoon. In publicity photos for the new album, he can be seen wearing a hat that would not be out of place in Brooklyn's Crown Heights neighborhood on Friday night.

Keith's face is now so deeply lined and creased and worn and wrinkled that he seems to have been preserved in formaldehyde or perhaps pickled in his own brine. The man looks not only ravaged and wasted but also somewhat mad in a manner that he finds endlessly amusing. Like Yoda in a headband or some ancient turtle basking on a rock in the sun, Keith seems entirely content, having not only accepted his lot in life but also his role in the current configuration of Les Rolling Stones.

If Michael Philip Jagger has now somehow become the Bing Crosby of rock (while being a far better father than Der Bingle ever was to his seven children—his daughter Karis from his relationship with Marsha Hunt; his daughter Jade from his marriage to Bianca; Elizabeth, James, Georgia, and Gabriel from his marriage to Jerry Hall; and his son Lucas from his brief liaison with Luciana Morad), Keith more closely resembles Bing's boon companion, the bandleader Phil Harris, who lived to be ninety-one and until the very end of his days remained both raucous and ribald, saying, "I'm going to be around until the Atomic Energy Commission finds a safe place to bury my liver."

When *Spin* magazine compiled a list of the "most incredible body parts" of rock stars, with Madonna's navel at number one, it was Keith's liver that came in second, having proved so durable that, as Marc Spitz wrote, ". . . when Richards finally passes, they'll line the exterior of the space shuttle with his liver tissue."

Unlike Mick, Keith makes no bones about what he has done and where he has been and all that he has seen. He does not try to hide his sins under the cover of the night. Simply, it is not the way he is made. He was like that at Nellcote and he is like that now. After all is said and done, Keith is our hero. He is also our antihero. But then if you have made it this far in the story, you already know that.

Asked by John H. Richardson in *Esquire* magazine to list some of the things he learned over the years, Keith said, "To me, smack is the big deal. That is such a cheeky, cheeky, cheeky little drug. That one can get you right by the tail before you know it, man. It's a real leveler. I'm a fucking superstar but when I want the stuff, baby, I'm down on the ground with the rest of them. Your whole lifestyle becomes just waiting for the man and talking to junkies about whether the shit's good or not—'It's not as good as the last lot, is it? I'm not going to pay him then.' And guys pulling shooters on you, 'Give me your stuff!' and all that. You just become a wreck. Which is kind of disgusting in a way, but at the same time, I can't say I regret going there."

Mick and Keith and Keith and Mick. Forty years on, still the longest-running soap opera in the history of rock. But then any old way you choose it, it's gotta be rock-roll music. If you wanna dance with me. If you wanna dance with me.

# THE END

**Keith,** a knife, and the forbidden fruit, lunch at Nellcote, July 1971

## ACKNOWLEDGMENTS

**First and foremost,** I would like to thank Ben Schafer of Da Capo Press for giving me the gift of this book. Without his urging, I would never have embarked on my own private journey through the past to reconsider what really happened at Villa Nellcote thirty-five years ago. I would also like to thank Will Nash, who encouraged me to go ahead with this project by saying that as long as the Stones kept touring, I could go on writing about them.

I would like to thank Georgia Bergman, Bruce Byall, Marshall Chess, Elizabeth Hiemer, Andy Johns, Jerry Pompili, Rose Taylor, and Tommy Weber for sharing their recollections of that time with me. Throughout this book, I have used the term "Stones insider" to refer to sources who did not want to be identified by name in the text. For their cooperation, I thank them as well. My thanks to Adam Cooper for the information about his parents and for his father's photographs. Thanks to Jake Weber for lunch at the Chateau. Astrid Lundstrom and Peter Rudge were also of great assistance to me. My gratitude to David Tillier, who really tried. A tip of the chapeau to Janet Saines for doing all she could.

Thanks to Sam McAbee at fiveminutestolive.com for providing me with a videocassette of *Performance* and a DVD of *Donald Cammell: The Ultimate Performance*. Thanks to Yoga Greg, the king of Sunday morning, for finding Keith's final quote. Thanks to Rick Rosen for getting me that number. Thanks also to Barney Hoskyns and Tony Keys for the incredible rock archive they have created at rocksbackpages.com.

For those who want to know more about the making of the music on *Exile On Main St.*, I heartily recommend John Perry's *Exile On Main St.: The Rolling Stones* and Steve Appleford's *The Rolling Stones—It's Only Rock And Roll: Song by Song*, both published by Schirmer Books. I'd also like to thank Donna, Sandy, and Anna for putting up with me as I spent my days once more at Villa Nellcote.

While it is sometimes easy to forget the living, the dead are always with us. I would like to remember all those who were at Nellcote that summer but have since departed for other realms. Most of all, this book belongs to them. May they rest in peace.

Robert Greenfield
July 14, 2006

# SOURCES

## INTERVIEWS

Georgia Bergman, February 10, 2005

Bruce Byall, May 9, 2005

Marshall Chess, March 29, 2005

Elizabeth Hiemer, May 27, 2005

Andy Johns, April 5, April 26, 2005

Jerry Pompili, February 11, 2005

Rose Taylor, March 21, 2005

Tommy Weber, March 22, 2006

## BOOKS

Anderson, Christopher, *Jagger Unauthorized,* New York: Delacorte Press, 1993

Appleford, Steve, *The Rolling Stones—It's Only Rock And Roll: Song by Song,* New York: Schirmer Books, 1997

Blume, Mary, *Cote d'Azur: Inventing the French Riviera,* New York: Thames and Hudson, 1992

Bockris, Victor, *Keith Richards: The Biography,* New York: Poseidon Press, 1992

Booth, Stanley, *Keith: Standing in the Shadows,* New York: St. Martin's Press, 1995

Bowie, Angela, with Patrick Carr, *Backstage Passes,* New York: G.P. Putnam's Sons, 1993

Brando, Marlon, and Cammell, Donald, *Fan Tan,* Edited with an afterword by David Thomson, New York: Alfred A. Knopf, 2005

Brown, Mick, *Mick Brown on Performance,* Bloomsbury Movie Guide No. 6, New York: Bloomsbury Press, 1999

Cohen, Rich, *Machers and Rockers: Chess Records and the Business of Rock & Roll,* New York: Atlas Books, W.W. Norton & Company, 2004

Cohodas, Nadine, *Spinning Blues Into Gold,* New York: St. Martin's Press, 2000

Davis, Stephen, *Old Gods Almost Dead: The 40 Year Odyssey of the Rolling Stones,* New York: Broadway Books, 2001

Faithfull, Marianne, with David Dalton, *Faithfull,* Boston: Little, Brown & Co., 1994

Fong-Torres, Ben, *Hickory Wind: The Life and Times of Gram Parsons,* New York: St. Martin's Press, 1991

Greenfield, Robert, *STP: A Journey Through America with the Rolling Stones,* New York: Saturday Review Press/E.P. Dutton & Co., Inc., 1974

Hemingway, Ernest, *A Moveable Feast,* New York: Charles Scribner's Sons, 1964

Hotchner, A. E, *Blown Away: The Rolling Stones and the Death of the Sixties,* New York: Simon & Schuster, 1990

Janovitz, Bill, *Exile On Main St. (33⅓),* New York: Continuum Books, 2005

Leitch, Donovan, *The Autobiography of Donovan: The Hurdy Gurdy Man*, New York: St. Martin's Press, 2005

Leonard, Thomas, Crippen, Cynthia, and Aronsen, Marc, *Day By Day: The Seventies, Volume One*, New York: Facts on File Publications, 1988

*Our American Century: Time of Transition—The 70s*, Alexandria, Virginia: Time-Life Books, 1999

Paytress, Mark, *The Rolling Stones: Off the Record*, London: Omnibus Press, 2003

Perry, John, *Exile On Main St.: The Rolling Stones*, New York: Schirmer Books, 1999

Phillips, John, with Jim Jerome, *Papa John*, New York: Doubleday & Company, Inc., 1986

Salecwicz, Chris, *Mick and Keith*, London: Orion, 2002

Sanchez, Tony, *Up and Down with the Rolling Stones*, New York: William Morrow and Company, Inc., 1979

Schulman, Bruce J., *The Seventies: The Great Shift in American Culture, Society, and Politics*, New York: The Free Press, 2001

Shelley, June, *Even When It Was Bad . . . It Was Good*, Xlibris Corporation, 2000

Tarlé, Dominique, *Exile: The Making of Exile On Main St.*, London: Genesis Publishing, Ltd., 2001 (limited edition: 2000 copies)

Walker, Jason, *God's Own Singer: A Life of Gram Parsons*, London: Helter Skelter Publishing, 2002

Wyman, Bill, with Ray Coleman, *Stone Alone*, New York: Viking Press, 1990

Wyman, Bill, with Richard Havers, *Rolling With The Stones*, New York: DK Publishing, 2002

## NEWSPAPERS & MAGAZINES

"ABC Cleans Up the Sexagenarian Stones' Lyric Malfunction," Jon Pareles, *New York Times,* February 6, 2006

"A Foundling of the Louvre: Balthus: 1909–2001," Robert Hughes, *Time,* March 5, 2001

"Ameriquest Prepares to Settle States' Probe," E. Scott Reckard and Kathy M. Kristof, *Los Angeles Times,* July 29, 2005

"Balthus, Painter Whose Suggestive Figures Cause a Stir, Is Dead at 92," John Russell, *New York Times,* February 19, 2001

"Bianca's Retribution," "Talk of the Town," *The New Yorker,* August 16, 1993

"Big Bang," Phillip Matier and Andrew Ross, *San Francisco Chronicle,* August 24, 2005

"China Debut for Stones," Lawrence Van Gelder, *New York Times,* March 1, 2006

"The Detective, the Star, and the White Powder," Thomas Vinciguerra, *New York Times,* August 7, 2005

"Gimme Tax Shelter," *New York Times Magazine,* "Men's Fashions of the Times," Part 2, Spring, 2002, pp. 33–45

"Hot Tickets In 2005," Shelly Freierman, *New York Times,* January 2, 2006

"In a First, the Stones Rock China, but Hold the Brown Sugar," Howard W. French, *New York Times,* April 9, 2006

"It's Halftime and They Like It, They Like It, Yes They Do," Joe Lapointe, *New York Times,* February 3, 2006

"JADE," Real Estate, *New York Times,* June 29, 2006

"Jagger Shines In Stones' SBC Park Concert," Brad Kava, *San Jose Mercury News,* (reprinted in the *Monterey County Herald*), November 15, 2005

"Jagger's Edge," Horacio Silva and Zarah Crawford, *Men's Fashions of the Times,* Spring, 2006

"Jagger Takes Censorship in Stride," Associated Press, *San Francisco Chronicle*, April 8, 2006

"Keepin Up With The Stones," Steven Kurutz, *New York Times*, October 21, 2006

"Keith Richards: The Rolling Stone Interview," Robert Greenfield, *Rolling Stone*, Issue 89, August 19, 1971

"Keith Richards Back Home," Lawrence Van Gelder, *New York Times*, May 24, 2006

"Keith Richards Leaves Hospital," Lawrence Van Gelder, *New York Times*, May 12, 2006

"Keith Richards Turns Pirate," Lawrence Van Gelder, *New York Times*, July 6, 2006

"The Last Days of Jim Morrison/A rare look into the rock god's journals," Stephen Davis, *Rolling Stone*, July 8, 2004

"Le Proces de Keith Richard," *Extra*, December, 1973

"Magazine's navel-gazing," Entertainment Report, *San Francisco Chronicle*, August 24, 2005

"Mick Jagger: Big Banger," David Fricke, *Rolling Stone*, December 29, 2005–January 12, 2006

"Mick Jagger Digs Deep Into His Vocals, and the Stones Find Another Way To Be The Greatest Rock 'n' Roll Band," Joel Selvin, *San Francisco Chronicle*, November 15, 2005

"Mick Jagger: We Want Answers!" Eric Gillin, *Maxim*, October, 2005

"Muscling Up Stones' Tickets," Carol Beggy and Mark Shanahan, *Boston Globe*, August 12, 2005

"'No F#@*ing About,'" David Fricke, *Rolling Stone*, August 25, 2005

"No Satisfaction," *New York Times*, February 8, 2006

"Not Only Rock 'n' Roll: Mick Jagger Joins a New Sitcom," Bill Carter, *New York Times*, April 26, 2006

"Not Too Old to Rock," Ben Sisario, *New York Times,* January 9, 2006

"Paul McCartney Tour Ad," *New York Times,* October 2, 2005

"Penalize the Super Bowl for Ugliness," Reggie Hayes, *The News-Sentinel* (Fort Wayne, Ind.), reprinted in the *Monterey County Herald,* February 7, 2006

"Personality Parade," Walter Scott, *Parade,* August 21, 2005

"Pop Notes," Ben Sisario, *New York Times,* June 17, 2006

"Richards Back, Stones Roll," Ben Sisario, *New York Times,* June 3, 2006

"Rio Readies for the Stones," Lawrence Van Gelder, *New York Times,* February 14, 2006

"The Rolling Stones Enter Political Fray," Lawrence Van Gelder, *New York Times,* August 11, 2005

"The Rolling Stones—Part I: The 1960's and 70's," *Blender,* March, 2006

"Rolling Stones Rock China with Censored Song List," Christopher Bodeen, Associated Press, *Monterey County Herald,* April 9, 2006

"Rolling Stones Try Topping Carnival in Rio," Larry Rohter, *New York Times,* February 19, 2006

"Standing Corrected," William Safire, *New York Times,* March 19, 2006

"The Stones Blast Through the Land," Thomas Thompson, *Life,* July 14, 1972, pp. 30–36

"Stones Call Super Bowl Censorship 'Absolutely Ridiculous,'" David Bauder, *San Francisco Chronicle,* February 8, 2006

"Stones Don't Roll," Lawrence Van Gelder, *New York Times,* May 25, 2006

"Stones on Soap Opera," Entertainment Report, *San Francisco Chronicle,* October 14, 2005

"Stones on the Beach in Rio," Lawrence Van Gelder, *New York Times,* December 14, 2005

"Stones Rock Rio," Diego Perri, *Rolling Stone,* March 23, 2006

"Stones Roll in Milan," Lawrence Van Gelder, *New York Times,* July 13, 2006

"Stones Roll Out Their Hits for Mainland China," Associated Press, *San Francisco Chronicle,* April 10, 2006

"Stones Speak Out," *Rolling Stone,* September 8, 2005

"Stones, U2, McCartney Top Tours of '05," Associated Press, December 31, 2005

"The Stones Will Play Shanghai, but China Hasn't Rolled Out the Red Carpet," Kathleen E. McLaughlin, *San Francisco Chronicle,* April 6, 2006

"Surgery for Keith Richards," Lawrence Van Gelder, *New York Times,* May 9, 2006

"To Stand Out in a Crowd: Don't Shout (Mick Excepted)," Cathy Horyn, *New York Times,* September 15, 2005

"What I've Learned: Keith Richards," John H. Richardson, *Esquire,* November, 2005

"Who's Your Daddy?" Robert Christgau, *Blender,* November, 2005

**E-MAIL**

Adam Cooper, July 12, 2005

**WEBSITES**

*a-ggroup.com*

   "Asprey London," A&G UK Ltd, 2005

*angelfire.com*

   "Lama Anagarika Govinda," with some editing adapted from: *The Western Quest for Secret Tibet,* by Harrow Oldmeadow *bartleby.com*

"Minnesinger," The Columbia Encyclopedia, Sixth Edition, 2001–05

"Tannhauser," Ibid.

*bbc.co.uk*

"Jagger and Hall: Rock's golden couple," July 19, 1999

"Jerry Hall: Graduate role model," Chris Jones, June 20, 2000

"Keith Richards 'tree fall' injury," April 29, 2006

*breitbart.com*

"Rolling Stones Agreed to Censor Super Bowl Show: NFL," February 6, 2006

*cdtimes.co.uk*

"Liz Phair—Exile in Guyville—2-10-2003," Eamonn McCusker

*contactmusic.com*

"Jagger's Drug Bust Detective Regrets Arrest," July 8, 2005

*divorceuk.com*

"Case Studies/Jagger vs Hall"

*eonline.com*

"It's a Boy (Anybody Seen My Mick?)," Daniel Frankel, December 8, 1997

"Keith Richards Falls on His Coconut," Joal Ryan, May 1, 2006

"Richards Down, Stones Too," Daniel Frankel, May 19, 1998

*en.wikipedia.org*

"Bobbie Clarke," March 24, 2006

"Cui Jian," April 15, 2006

"Exile in Guyville," February 18, 2006

"Exile On Main Street," February 20, 2006

"Haileybury and Imperial Service College," March 4, 2006

"Loulou de la Falaise," October 9, 2005

"Keith Richards," January 10, 2006

"Mary Celeste," July 10, 2006

"Tannhauser," February 17, 2006

"Tiananmen Square protests of 1989," April 17, 2006

"Vince Taylor," March 31, 2006

*faithfull.marianne-the-lyrics.com*

"Lady Madeleine," January, 1977

*guardian.co.uk*

"Alive and Kicking," Nigel Williamson, December 5, 2003

"Father's Little Helper," John Robinson, August 23, 2003

"I made a complete mess of everything," Simon Hattenstone, March 10, 2006

*imdb.com*

"Biography for Bill Wyman," Richard Baker

"Shining Blood, 1992"

*iorr.org*

"The Rolling Stones—A Bigger Bang, Spring 2006"

"The Rolling Stones—A Bigger Bang World Tour—European Tour 2006"

*levity.com*

"An Interview with Stanislas Klossowski de Rola," Joseph Caezza and Dan Kenney, September 6, 1998

*lintency.com*

"Thomas Coryate (1577(?)–1617), Katharine Craik, October, 20, 2001 *logosjournal.com*

> "A Conversation with Bianca Jagger, Human Rights Advocate," Kurt Jacobsen, September, 2003

*music.monstersandcritics.com*

> "L'Wren Scott reportedly causing problems within the Rolling Stones," October 3, 2005, Bang Media International

*mirror.co.uk*

> "Mick's Found a Loin Tamer," Barbara Davies, July 26, 2003

*nyrock.com*

> "Sex, Drugs, and Slimeballs: Jerry Files For Divorce," Otto Luck, January 16, 1999

*nzgirl.co.nz*

> "Next Big Thing: Alexandra Richards," 2004

*oceanstar.com*

> "Lenny Kaye," contributed by Jimmie Purvis, with additions by Bruce Hanson and Fiona W.

*officialsolicitor.gov.uk*

> "Court of Protection Financial Cases—Official Solicitor"

*people.aol.com*

> "Stones' Keith Richards Injured in Fiji," Stephen M. Silverman, May 1, 2006

*phinnweb.com*

> "The Acid House," Rebekah Wood, *Neon,* March, 1998

*rocksbackpages.com:*

> "An Outlaw At The Ritz: Keith Richards," Chris Welch, *Melody Maker,* January 13, 1979

> "Gram Parsons: The Good Old Boy," Barney Hoskyns, *Mojo,* July, 1998

"Keith Richards: How Do You Stop?" Barney Hoskyns, *Mojo*, November, 1997

"Keith Richards: The Pusher Behind the Stones," Barbara Charone, *Creem*, October, 1976

"Liz Phair: Fresh outta Guyville," Barney Hoskyns, *Mojo*, November, 1994

"Out of the Cage: An Interview with Keith Richards" Ira Robbins, unpublished, September 19, 1988

"The Rolling Stones: Exile On Main St." Lenny Kaye, *Rolling Stone*, July 6, 1972

"The Rolling Stones: Sticky Fingers and Exile on Main St." Barney Hoskyns, *The Observer*, June, 2004

"The Stones: It Wasn't Only Rock 'n' Roll (And I Liked It)," Paul Williams, *Crawdaddy*, November, 1974

*salon.com*

"Bringing Up Mick Jagger's Baby," Carina Chocano, August 4, 2000

*smh.com.au*

"Bianca's Plea for Tookie," AFP, November 22, 2005

*superbowl.com*

"The Rolling Stones to Perform During Sprint Super Bowl XL Halftime Show on ABC," November 29, 2005

*superseventies.com*

"*Exile on Main St.* Bonus Reviews!—Robert Christgau, *Christgau's Record Guide*, 1981"

*talkleft.com*

"Mick Jagger Claimed Frame-Up in 1969 Drug Raid," *The Guardian*, February 23, 2004

*telegraph.co.uk*

"Mrs. Ronnie Wood: the rock chick with rock chic," Hilary Alexander, May 8, 2005

*toru.com*
> "The Rolling Stones 1972 North American Tour"

*travelinfo.gr*
> "Patmos Island"

*vh1.com*
> "Keith Richards," Steve Huey, All Music Guide, 2005

*xs4all.nl*
> "Top 100, Paul Gambaccini 1978"
> "Top 100, Paul Gambaccini 1987"

## FILMS

*Donald Cammell: The Ultimate Performance,* IFC Films,
    directed by Chris Rodley and Kevin MacDonald

*Performance,* directed by Nic Roeg and Donald Cammell